CIVIL RELIGION AND MORAL ORDER

Recent Titles in Contributions in Sociology
Series Editor: Don Martindale

CIVIL RELIGION AND MORAL ORDER
Theoretical and Historical Dimensions

Michael W. Hughey

Contributions in Sociology, Number 43

Greenwood Press
Westport, Connecticut • London, England

Library of Congress Cataloging in Publication Data

Hughey, Michael W.
  Civil religion and moral order.

  (Contributions in sociology, ISSN 0084-9278 ; no. 43)
  Bibliography: p.
  Includes index.
  1. Religion and sociology. 2. Civil religion.
3. Civil religion—United States. I. Title. II. Series.
BL60.H83 1983   306'.6   82-15429
ISBN 0-313-23522-8 (lib. bdg.)

Library of Congress Catalog Card Number: 82-15429
ISBN: 0-313-23522-8
ISSN: 0084-9278

First published in 1983

Greenwood Press
A division of Congressional Information Service, Inc.
88 Post Road West
Westport, Connecticut 06881

Printed in the United States of America

10 9 8 7 6 5 4 3 2 1

To JAN ATCHISON
with love and appreciation

and

To ARTHUR J. VIDICH
whose ideas and example have
made this work possible

CONTENTS

ACKNOWLEDGMENTS

A number of people contributed to this project. Arthur J. Vidich was especially generous with his ideas, many of which found their way into the present work. My debt to him extends far beyond the specific ideas, suggestions, and criticisms he contributed to these pages. In him I have been fortunate to witness at firsthand the insightful power of a true sociological imagination, and I am most grateful for the opportunity.

I have also made free use of the comments and suggestions made by Stanford M. Lyman and Jeffrey Goldfarb to an earlier conception of this project. Lyman particularly offered some rather relentless criticisms that ultimately made an important contribution to the direction and tone of this work.

From several others I have profited in a more general way, including especially Joseph Bensman and the late Benjamin Nelson. Although they made no specific contribution to this project, the ideas and leads they provided immeasurably affected its outcome.

I should also like to express my gratitude to the Graduate Faculty of the New School for Social Research, which honored me with its Fellowship for Democratic Studies and thus contributed financially to the completion of this project. My deepest appreciation is reserved for Jan Atchison, without whose financial and emotional support this work would never have been completed. Finally, I wish to thank Linda Kalland for her diligence and patience in typing the manuscript.

INTRODUCTION

The present work focuses on perhaps the original and certainly still one of the most fundamental sociological inquiries: How is society possible? More specifically, it is concerned with the relationship between what are held to be common values and the production and maintenance of social order. And more specifically still, it constitutes an effort to critically examine the empirical validity of a theoretical tradition that has given sustained attention to this relationship.

The theoretical tradition examined is that outlined originally by Emile Durkheim and modified and empirically applied by his intellectual descendants in sociology and anthropology. Generally, it holds that every relatively stable society will possess a set of shared beliefs and symbols that express the highest values of the society and that are considered sacred. Against the many conflicts present in everyday life, the collective sharing of these values serves to remind members of society of what they hold in common, thereby providing for the order, stability, and integration of the society as a whole. Periodic collective rites, during which the shared values are celebrated and reaffirmed, constitute the specific mechanisms through which these states are attained and sustained. These themes, which constitute the central components of Durkheim's related sociologies of religion and morality, are elaborated in Chapter 1.

Critical examination of any interpretation of social reality presupposes an alternative viewpoint from which the criticism can be leveled and, presumably, from which the reality in question can be better viewed. In the present case, the "better view" is offered through the work of Max Weber and, more narrowly, through that of anthropologist Paul Radin.

The decision to juxtapose Weber's sociology of religion to that of Durkheim should surprise no one. Despite Talcott Parsons's (1968) attempted grand synthesis, it has since been generally recognized that Durkheim and Weber are not the most compatible intellectual bedfellows. Actually, as Bendix (1971) and others (for example, Collins, 1968; Pope, et al., 1975; Giddens, 1971a) have made abundantly clear, they represent two very different theoretical traditions, each of which has its own distinctive epistemology, aims, and methods for investigating the social world. Nowhere, perhaps, are these differences more apparent than in their respective contributions to the sociology of religion.

The decision to consider Paul Radin's work with Weber's deserves some explanation. First, some of Radin's arguments are directly relevant to Radcliffe-Brown's descriptions of certain Andaman rites, with which we shall deal briefly. Second, Radin is a neglected thinker whose work deserves far more recognition than it has received. The opportunity to call attention to it is simply too great to be disregarded. Finally, and most important, Weber's and Radin's views concerning the nature of religion and the proper means of studying it are very much in agreement. This congruence is apparently not the result of direct influence, for nowhere does Radin, the younger of the two, cite Weber's work or even indicate an awareness of its existence. Instead, like Weber, he appears to have been strongly influenced by Marx, though his work displays none of Marx's ideological passion. Of course, despite similarities, the perspectives and arguments offered by Weber and Radin are by no means identical. Each was an original and compelling thinker in his own right. Nonetheless, the extent of their intellectual kinship warrants their combined treatment, which is undertaken in Chapter 2.

In setting out the central ideas of Durkheimian and Weberian (including Radin) perspectives, these initial chapters center on their divergent interpretations of the origins, development, and operation of religion with respect to the establishment and maintenance of social order. If this section appears theoretically self-conscious to some readers, as I suspect it will, I can only beg indulgence on the grounds that the effort behind it was at least partly pedagogical, the very act of setting ideas to paper being at once a way of coming to terms with them. In any case, this section is intended to provide the theoretical framework for the remaining and more important portion of the book, which concentrates on empirical applications of Durkheim's ideas by some of his intellectual heirs.

Durkheim's intellectual descendants have applied his ideas in both "primitive" and "modern industrial" contexts, thus adding specific substance to his general theoretical framework. In doing so, they have, of course, borrowed selectively from his work. Often, for instance, they have tended to concentrate on value consensus and social order to the relative neglect of his original emphasis on both moral and institutional change. Of perhaps greater importance than such modifications, however, is that Durkheim's heirs have on the whole accepted major elements of his theory and approach. Generally, they have tended to accept beforehand the idea that every relatively stable society will possess a set of shared beliefs and symbols that express the highest values of the society and whose general integrative functions transcend the particular social structure of the society. Accordingly, in their own empirical studies, their essential problem tends to be one of identifying the particular shared values they already "know" to exist. In other words, they have tended to treat what is primarily a theoretical position as a resource in dealing with empirical materials rather than as a heuristic device, a topic in its own right to be evaluated against the empirical realities examined. As a result, their treatments of the specific values and symbols identified tend to be empirically limited and questionable both as description and explanation of the materials examined.

In Part II of this work, the same sets of values and symbols treated somewhat systematically by Durkheim's heirs are reexamined in the manner of Weber and Radin, that is, in terms of the historical and sociostructural context to which they refer. Two related goals indicate my reasons for doing so.

First, in line with Weber's contention that the object of the social and cultural sciences should be empirical rather than theoretical understanding, the chapters in Part II constitute an effort to offer alternative and more empirically complete and accurate accounts of the same phenomena examined by Durkheim's heirs. Special attention is given to a more empirically and historically grounded account of what these values and symbols are in each case and to identifying their relationship to social order. Thus Chapter 3 considers A. R. Radcliffe-Brown's treatment of Andaman food rituals and suggests the framework of an alternative interpretation of those rites. Given the inadequacies of our historical knowledge of Andaman society, our consideration of it is necessarily brief. The remainder of the book examines three Durkheimian accounts—by W. Lloyd Warner, Talcott Parsons, and Robert Bellah, respectively—of the "common faith" of Americans, or American civil religion as it has come to be known. These chapters, constituting the heart of the book, are intended as a contribution to our empirical understanding of America's "ancient faith"—its origins, underpinnings, social history, and current status.

Second, these empirical reexaminations allow the Durkheimian theory of religion and social order to be treated as a topic for critical consideration. In particular, they offer us a way of judging its empirical validity as an explanation and description of the foundations of social order. As these accounts should make clear, the theory is quite limited in that its focus neglects a range of empirical materials important to the subject. This is not to suggest, of course, that Durkheim and his followers are simply wrong, either in their theoretical contributions or in their empirical accounts of particular values and symbols. The social world may be approached from many perspectives, each with its own questions, interpretations, and insights. All perspectives are not, however, equal in explanatory, analytic, and descriptive capacity. It is with the limits of the conclusions reached, and not their falsity, that the present study is concerned.

PART I

RELIGION, IDEOLOGY, AND SOCIAL ORDER: THE THEORIES OF DURKHEIM, WEBER, AND RADIN

DURKHEIM, RELIGION, AND SOCIAL ORDER

The Origins of Moral and Religious Phenomena

Morality and religion, Durkheim observed, have been inextricably connected in a wide variety of historical circumstances.
At the dawn of human society, religion was the primordial
fount from which emerged morality as well as virtually all subsequent "manifestations of the collective life."[1] For centuries
thereafter, these "two systems of beliefs and practices" have
been "interlaced," moral authority being sustained and more
easily expressed by the transcendental power and imagery of
its primogenitor. Indeed, Durkheim noted, "only yesterday
they were supported on the same keystone: God, the center
of religious life, was also the supreme guarantor of moral order"
(1961, p. 8). While today their historical association has been
eroded to some degree by the infusion of secular reason, morality and religion have not yet and probably never will drift completely apart.[2]

The historical propinquity of morality and religion can hardly
be considered surprising. To the contrary, Durkheim suggests,
it is altogether natural and indicative of the more essential characteristics they share. It is the nature of these shared characteristics which, within the general context of his sociological
approach, betrays the social essence and origin of moral and
religious phenomena.

Morality and religion are invested with aspects of the sacred, the difference between them in this regard being one of degree rather than substance.[3] This common endowment strictly separates both from all that is profane. To the profane sphere, as Durkheim defines it, belong all activities, thoughts, and objects that are routine, vulgar, commonplace, and drab, including especially all economic activity. It is the order of the ordinary, the world of everyday life, and, as such, it has no special meaning for the individual. The sacred, on the other hand, is experienced as not merely different from but also opposed and slightly hostile to all that is profane. So complete and absolute is the separation between these two spheres that "in all the history of human thought there exists no other example of two categories of things so profoundly differentiated or so radically opposed to one another . . . . [T]he sacred and profane have always and everywhere been conceived by the human mind as two distinct classes, as two worlds between which there is nothing in common" (1965, pp. 53-54). They are in fact "two distinct sorts of reality" (1965, p. 243). While human beings are able to pass from one reality to the other, they can do so only by ritually exposing themselves to a "veritable metamorphosis," as in initiation rites.

If the sacred is set apart from the individual in everyday life, it is also set above him. The individual experiences the sacred (that is, social) properties of all moral and religious phenomena as both authoritatively and qualitatively superior to himself.

In the former sense, Durkheim observes, there is in all moral rules, including those of religion, an inherent authority "which bends our wills" and which "kicks back with such force when we fail to abide by their injunctions" (1961, pp. 29, 90). We perceive them as commands, obey them as duties, and, in general, defer to their superior force. Like "so many molds with limiting boundaries into which we must pour our behavior," moral rules "determine" our conduct, constrain our appetites, limit our horizons. In short, Durkheim argues, "the idea of authority plays an absolutely preponderant role" in all moral and religious systems.

The inherently authoritative character of moral rules is not, however, a sufficient explanation of their compelling force. "If we yield to its orders," Durkheim observes, "it is not merely because it is strong enough to triumph over our resistance" (1965, p. 237). In addition, the individual regards moral rules and religious beliefs as deserving of "venerable respect," or even awe, owing to the greater richness, dignity, and vitality with which they, like all sacred phenomena, are endowed. In addition to its superior power, then, morality is also regarded in some respect as good and loved.[4] Thus, if obedience to moral and religious injunctions is demanded of us, we also desire it.[5]

Having identified what he regards as the essential and permanent components of all religious and moral phenomena, Durkheim is led to consider the source that underlies the dichotomization of experience and from which their compelling power is derived. Clearly, he argues, the experience of the sacred cannot be composed merely of a "tissue of illusions." It is, after all, "an essential postulate of sociology that a human institution cannot rest upon an error and a lie, without which it could not exist" (1965, p. 14). The central importance of this postulate for Durkheim's work should not be overlooked.[6] Its authority is invoked, first of all, to dismiss Durkheim's theoretical competition. Animism and naturalism, he states, are based upon the erroneous contention "that men have superimposed upon reality . . . an unreal world, constructed entirely out of the fantastic images which agitate his mind during a dream, or else out of the frequently monstrous aberrations produced by the mythological imagination under the bewitching but deceiving influence of language" (1965, pp. 256-57). Moreover, Durkheim admitted that his own "entire study [of religion] rests upon this postulate" and upon the incomprehensibility that such errors and illusions could have been long sustained against the more convincing authority of actual social and historical experience.

If one grants Durkheim's assumption that any illusory foundations of religion would be revealed and eliminated in an inevitable confrontation with empirical experience, it follows that religion must have as its basis some more durable reality. It is in this sense that Durkheim claims no religions to be false, even though "the reasons with which the faithful justify them may be and generally are erroneous" (1965, p. 14).

According to Durkheim's famous argument, the reality that underlies religion and all other moral powers is, of course, society itself. In so flatly stating his argument, however, care must be taken to avoid the misinterpretation so frequently voiced that Durkheim adhered to an extreme and vulgarized doctrine of social realism. That society constitutes a reality *sui generis*, existing independently of any single individual, Durkheim took for granted. He insisted, however, that society and social facts do not exist independently of the individual in the same way that the physical environment does. On the contrary, as he stated frequently, "society exists and lives only in and through individuals . . . it is real only in so far as it has a place in human consciousnesses" (1965, p. 389). Thus, only individuals can be the "active forces" of society and to hold otherwise Durkheim justly recognizes as an "obvious absurdity."

According to Durkheim, society is an emergent reality created by the association of its individual components. "The system which they form by uniting together, and which varies according to their geographical disposition and the nature and number of their channels of communication, is the base from which social life is raised" (1974, p. 24). Although Durkheim admitted some confusion over its precise working,[7] he was nonetheless convinced that the very fact of association creates new elements and conditions that individuals are unable to supply on their own. It is, in particular, the *sui generis* synthesis of so many interacting, individual minds that creates the *conscience collective* and collective representations.[8] Both realities (for Durkheim did not regard them as merely conceptual) constitute "a psychic individuality of a new sort" whose characteristics are irreducible to those of its constituent parts. Whether focused or generalized, "the group thinks, feels, and acts quite differently from the way in which its individual members would act were they isolated" (1938, p. 104).

Sacred representations, like all others, are born of association. Since, however, the sacred is everywhere experienced as qualitatively different from and superior to ordinary life, it follows that the interaction from which it is derived cannot be ordinary. The experience of the sacred could not emerge from routine, everyday interaction. Collective ceremonies, Durkheim suggests, provide the occasions during which interaction is most intense and social forces are most creative and keenly felt. During such periods, the group attains an emotional effervescence inaccessible to purely private or routine states of consciousness. The "general exaltation" lifts the individual out of his mundane existence and endows him with "more confidence, courage and boldness in action." He experiences within him "an abnormal over-supply of force which overflows and tries to burst out from him." This force, which dominates and carries him away, "makes him think and act differently than in normal times." Given such extraordinary circumstances, primitive people could hardly have avoided postulating a reality separate from and incomparable to their profane existence. Hence, it is in the collective effervescence produced by intense social interaction that religious ideas are forged.

The complex religious representations and the sentiments they inspire during these states of shared excitement are finally transferred to some object or symbol about which the collective sentiments can be more easily expressed. When a "certain number" of sacred objects and symbols are brought together and manage to "sustain relations of co-ordination or subordination with each other in such a way as to form a system having a certain unity, but which is not comprised within any other system of the same sort" (1965, p. 56), the resulting product is a religion. But whatever the varied objects and symbols through which the sacred is expressed, all are founded on the social forces of which people have been made collectively aware. Religious beliefs, then, are those ideas through which the individuals "represent to themselves the society of which they are members, and the obscure but intimate relations they have with it" (1965, p. 257); religious rites "organize and regulate" these relations. Religion, in other words, is the symbolic manifestation of social self-consciousness, and religious symbols express nothing more than the moral *conscience* of society itself.[9]

In concluding that society is the reality on which all moral and religious systems are founded, Durkheim characteristically dismissed other proposed determinants of the sacred. His rejection of illusion, for instance, has already been considered.

Neither is the underlying reality to be found, Durkheim contends, among the objects in which the sacred is thought to inhere. Animals, plants, and rocks as well as various man-made artifacts have all, at some time or other, served as repositories of the sacred. Since, therefore, virtually any object may be regarded as sacred, it follows that the source of the sacred may not be attributable to properties inherent in the objects themselves.

Of far greater importance, drawing upon a postulate central to his own sociological framework, Durkheim further contends that the reality underlying religious imagery and sacred objects cannot be the individual himself, nor are they the products of his conscious or unconscious efforts. Rather, moral and religious beliefs and practices, as well as the sacredness with which they are invested, all come to the individual from some external source. "The church-member finds the beliefs and practices of his religious life ready made at birth; their existence prior to his own implies their existence outside himself" (1938, pp. 1-2). Thus, the individual himself cannot be the source of the sacred.

The same conclusion is suggested by the constraining, authoritative character of moral and religious rules of conduct. The wants and appetites of biological (presocial) man, as Durkheim conceives him, are inherently insatiable, his goals chronically expansive. Unless somehow regulated, "our capacity for feeling is itself an insatiable and bottomless abyss" (1951, p. 247), and each ambition achieved serves only to inspire another. Everyman is Tantalus, each seeking to quench his own personal and unquenchable thirst. Under such circumstances, the individual could never attain satisfaction, much less happiness, and ultimately social life itself would be impossible. At the very least, all sorts of individual and social pathologies would emerge. Thus, Durkheim suggests, the continued existence of social life requires that human passions be morally regulated. Since, however, individuals are themselves inherently incapable of self-restraint, it follows that the regulating force comes from outside the individual consciousness. And since, finally, moral and religious rules are constraining, logically they cannot originate with the individual; again, he is not their "underlying reality."

Given the general framework of Durkheim's sociology, it is

inconceivable that he could have allowed the individual to play a determining role in the emergence of religion or any other social phenomena. To have done so would have undermined the very foundation on which he sought to establish sociology as an objective science independent of psychology and whose validity approached that of the natural sciences. This is not to say that Durkheim found psychological and subjective factors to be completely irrelevant. They may well explain, for instance, why within the same moral environment some people are driven to suicide and others are not. However, because collective representations express collective realities, no analysis that begins with the individual can hope to understand social phenomena. Indeed, Durkheim argues, "every time that a social phenomenon is directly explained by a psychological phenomenon, we may be sure that the explanation is false" (1938, p. 104).[10] It is on this basis that Durkheim advances his famous principle that "the determining cause of a social fact should be sought among the social facts preceding it and not among the states of the individual consciousness" (1938, p. 110).

Quite far from playing a determining role in the emergence of religion, the individual is only a medium through which the religious representations are expressed. As Poggi (1971, p. 233) has argued in reference to Durkheim's theory of the origins, not just of religion, but of all institutions:

> [S]ociety not so much *makes* as itself *is* the universe of such (collective) representations. They are the property of the society as a distinctive realm of being, of that "consciousness of consciousnesses," as Durkheim calls it at one point. At the same time, *qua* representations (i.e., purely "mental" entities) they must find their vehicle in the consciousness of individuals; they, as it were, think themselves *through* and *within* those consciousnesses, but are not "thought up" by them. In *statu nascendi* institutions are complexes of representations, of images which the individuals entertain not in their capacity as members of the society; not severally (as discrete,

self-activating entities), but jointly (as subservient, "acted-on" organs of a greater entity). [Poggi's emphases]

Thus, in Durkheim's view, the individual is not an active participant in the genesis of religion, but merely the prism in which and through which the collective light is refracted. Subjective, emotional, intellectual, and purely private motivations, to the extent that Durkheim considers them at all, are usually regarded only as the *products* of collective forces, not as their causes.[11]

One of the more obvious results of this approach is its neglect of any creative efforts made by particular individuals, such as magicians, shamans, prophets, and priests. Moreover, since all members of a society share the *conscience collective*, Durkheim is at something of a loss to account for history's great innovators (for example, Jesus, Mohammed, Calvin) who led religious revolutions, often successfully, against the reigning representations of their time. Durkheim's own response to precisely this objection, put to him directly, can only be considered evasive. "The problem of great religious personalities and their role," he said, "is certainly important. The study that I undertook (1965) did not consider it. I do not have to advance a hypothesis concerning such a complex problem, which has never been studied methodically" (quoted, from an exchange with Marc Boegner, in Lukes, 1973, p. 520). Perhaps the closest Durkheim came to dealing with the role of individual creativity in religious development was his discussion of the orator at a collective rite. Here too, however, the speaker's command of the crowd, his grandiloquence and force, all "come to him from the very group he addresses" (1965, p. 241).

Apart from purely methodological constraints, Durkheim's neglect of individual factors may also be attributed to his conception of primitive peoples, with whom, he assumed, religion was born. Specifically, Durkheim ruled out of order the possibility that primitive people could be impressed, exalted, and dominated by anything other than collective forces. W. E. H. Stanner, one of the more perceptive critics of Durkheim's anthropology, has justly pointed out in this connection that Durkheim's view of primitives was "very depreciatory." While he stopped short of Levi-Bruhl's "pre-logical mentality" or Frazier's "thoroughgoing idiocy" (which he criticized), Durkheim failed to credit the primitive "with any capacity to form judgments of experience, to objectify in symbols determinants of social life more ultimate than any which arises from human association as such, or from an idealization of it" (Stanner, 1967, p. 236). So complete, that is, was Durkheim's "sociocentric fixation" that he could not admit even the possibility that religious symbols could have as their referent any aspects of human life other than social life.

"When the individual has been eliminated," Durkheim argued, "society alone remains" (1938, p. 102). It therefore seems unlikely, short of resorting to theological assumptions (which he justly dismissed as unscientific), that he could have located the origins of moral and religious force anywhere other than in society. The problematic feature of this argument is that the individual did not have to be eliminated in the first place. This consideration is addressed in Chapter 2, which discusses the views of Weber and Radin.

Religion, Moral Solidarity, and Social Structure

The significance of Durkheim's formulations of the nature and origins of moral and religious phenomena cannot be fully understood apart from their position in his broader theoretical framework of historical and institutional change. With many other thinkers of his generation, Durkheim shared the conviction that society had undergone a crucial, structural transformation in the course of its development from a "lower" primitive type to the emergent modern form. While the nature of this transformation is given explicit attention only in Durkheim's first major work, *The Division of Labor in Society* (1933), each of his subsequent works must be read as an attempt to deal with some aspect of it, especially as concerns the modern type; all have an historical dimension even if it is only implicit.

While Durkheim shared with his contemporaries a recognition of the importance of the social transformation that had taken place, he took issue with their efforts to analyze it, especially with their conceptions of its emergent outcome. For them—

Tönnies, Spencer, and the utilitarian economists were his special targets at one time or another—the society of today is completely unlike that of yesterday. The "natural," internally spontaneous and moral life of "lower" societies *(Gemeinschaft)* had given way to a "modern" type *(Gesellschaft)* produced by "the wholly external stimulus of the state" and based upon the egoistic, and hence nonmoral, pursuit of individual self-interest. In short, social order in the first type is produced naturally, and in the second artificially.

Durkheim largely accepted the *Gemeinschaft* conception of primitive society. Against his rivals, however, Durkheim insisted that its transformation had not changed society fundamentally. Its "internal anatomy" had certainly been altered, thereby affecting the relations sustained between itself and its members, but the essential nature of society was unaffected.

> I believe that the life of large social agglomerations is just as natural as that of smaller groupings. It is no less internal. Outside of these purely individual actions (egoistic activity) there is a collective activity in our contemporary societies which is just as natural as that of smaller societies of previous ages. It is certainly different; it constitutes a distinct type, but however different they may be, there is no difference in nature between these two varieties of the same genus. . . . We have to choose: if society is originally a natural phenomenon, it stays such until the end of its life. [Written in review of F. Tönnies, *Gemeinschaft und Gesellschaft;* quoted from Durkheim, 1972, pp. 146-47]

Society cannot, therefore, change its nature. Indeed, to put the matter in the language Durkheim adopted soon after the above passage was written, society was, is, and forever remains a moral reality *sui generis.* Since it is in fact *the* moral reality that underlies all others, it follows for Durkheim that as society changes, so must the moral and religious representations through which it is manifested. It and they do not cease to be moral, but the morality assumes a different expression; it becomes a different type. Somewhat more specifically, Durkheim suggested that the moral and religious representations of a society are intimately related to its social structure.

To be sure, Durkheim's own appreciation of the relationship between morality and religion and social structure hardly remained constant. In his early work, best represented by the *Division of Labor*, he clearly assumes the *conscience collective* to be a product of society's morphological base. It is a passive reflection of the social structure and must therefore vary directly with any changes in society. History has "irrefutably demonstrated," he writes in a characteristic passage,

> that the morality of each people is directly related
> to the social structure of the people practicing it.
> The connection is so intimate that, given the general
> character of the morality observed in a given society
> and barring abnormal and pathological cases, one
> can infer the nature of that society, the elements of
> its structure and the way it is organized. Tell me the
> marriage patterns, the morals dominating family life,
> and I will tell you the principal characteristics of its
> organization. . . . In a word, each social type has the
> morality necessary to it, just as each biological type
> has a nervous system that enables it to sustain itself.
> A moral system is built up by the same society whose
> structure is thus faithfully reflected in it. [Durkheim,
> 1961, p. 87]

Toward the end of his career, Durkheim began increasingly to move beyond this strictly materialistic point of view to a recognition of the relative autonomy that collective representations (that is, ideas) may attain. Thus, in *The Elementary Forms*, he asserts that the *conscience collective*

> is something more than a mere epiphenomena of its
> morphological basis, just as individual consciousness

is something more than a simple efflorescence of the
nervous system. In order that the former may appear,
a synthesis *sui generis* of particular consciousnesses
is required. Now this synthesis has the effect of dis-
engaging a whole world of sentiments, ideas and
images which, once born, obey laws all their own.
They attract each other, repel each other, unite,
divide themselves, and multiply, though these combinations are not commanded and necessitated by
the condition of the underlying reality. The life thus
brought into being even enjoys so great an independence that it sometimes indulges in manifestations
with no purpose or utility of any sort, for the mere
pleasure of affirming itself. [Durkheim, 1965, p.
471]

Unfortunately, this passage is as extreme as the first. Although
he clearly did come to grant a greater independence to collective
representations, Durkheim never fully embraced idealism just
as he had never truly been a materialist. Throughout his many
works, Durkheim pointedly asserts that he wishes to be associated with neither of these positions. Making use, perhaps, of
his talent for synthesizing diverse points of view, Durkheim
fully accepted or rejected neither materialist nor idealist claims.
Despite some movement toward the idealist position, he seems
to have accepted the fact that the relationship between the
social structure and the *conscience collective* is characterized
by constant interaction and mutual influence, even though he
never analyzed the specific means by which this interaction
occurs. At any rate, at least one aspect of this relationship is
made exceedingly clear in Durkheim's works: the enormous
structural changes in society produced by the expanding division of labor have engendered equally significant changes in its
moral and religious representations.

"Lower," primitive societies, Durkheim suggests, are characterized by what he termed "segmental" social structures, each
segment being a clan formed of homogeneous units. The division
of labor and, indeed, any kind of specialization, if it exists at
all, is only slightly developed at best. Such societies are "almost

entirely amorphous or without structure." Moreover, because "all the members . . . are on the same level," life is roughly the same for each. They perform the same or roughly similar tasks, share the same body of knowledge and belief and in an all but literal sense are themselves identical. In short, segmental societies are characterized by a similarity of parts.

Corresponding to this type of social structure, Durkheim suggests, is a characteristic form of moral solidarity that is also based upon likeness. As indexed by the existence of penal law and repressive sanctions, under such circumstances the *conscience collective* attains its most pervasive state, endowing the society with a strong moral consensus and completely dominating the individual. So strong and all-encompassing is the *conscience collective* that no individual particularities and idiosyncrasies are allowed to develop. Personality is denied by conformity and conformity is ensured by commonality. In fact, the individual *conscience* is nothing more than the *conscience collective* writ small: all members of society share the same mental contents and thus, in any consequential sense, each member is like every other. To the degree that this is the case, the constituent parts of the collectivity respond to social directives mechanically and automatically, and moral solidarity based upon likeness reaches its maximum effectiveness.

Under these circumstances, it becomes readily apparent why, for Durkheim, the primitive individual failed to contribute to the genesis of religion: for all intents and purposes, he did not then exist (Durkheim, 1933, p. 194). As a social product, on the other hand, religion very much did exist in primitive societies. "It is . . . a constant fact," Durkheim observed, "that, when a slightly strong conviction is held by the same community of men, it inevitably takes on a religious character" (1933, p. 169). Since, therefore, all convictions were held in common, all were religious as well. "Morality, law, the principles of political organization, and even science" were embraced and regulated by a set of religious conceptions that "comprises all, extends to all." As Durkheim argues, the *conscience collective* was composed almost wholly of religious contents. If, then, in segmental societies, all persons are pressed from the same mold, that mold is fundamentally religious.

As the division of labor advances, segmental social structures and the clan solidarity on which they are based are displaced by a more "organized" type. Society is no longer composed of an amorphous mass, but of associations of persons who engage in similar work and activities. Each association is different and relatively autonomous, and each performs a different function based upon its specialized occupational role. Moreover, because work becomes more personal, individuals begin to differ and the personality can finally be developed. Unlike primitive social structures, in short, organized types are composed of widely divergent constituent parts.

According to Durkheim, the type of moral solidarity that corresponds to organized societies is based precisely on the differences between its parts. Since individuals and groups become specialized producers, they can no longer be self-sufficient, relying instead on products and services contributed by others. Each plays a specialized role on which all other groups depend. The relationship between groups is thus one of reciprocity and functional interdependence, and the characteristic morality of this relationship, as indexed by civil law and restitutive sanctions, is based on cooperation. Differentiation channels activities along divergent avenues, allowing them to meet in a cooperative rather than conflictual manner. The division of labor, then, is itself a moral phenomenon in that it is the means by which potential conflicts between so many identical producers are either eliminated or moderated.

In general, Durkheim holds that as the moral division of labor advances, it displaces the moral *conscience collective*, which grows "weaker and vaguer." The latter is progressively enfeebled, diminished in intensity and consisting of more diffuse, abstract, and less determined sentiments. Accordingly, it is increasingly unable to constrain and integrate members of the society. As the hold exercised by the *conscience collective* over individuals is weakened, they come to hold increasingly less in common:

> To the extent that societies become more volumi-
> nous and expand over vaster territories, traditions
> and practices, in order to accommodate themselves

to the diversity of situations and to the mobility
of circumstances, are obliged to maintain themselves
in a state of plasticity and inconstancy which no
longer offers enough resistance to individual variations. These variations, being less well restrained,
are produced more freely and multiply; that is to
say, everyone goes off in his own direction. At the
same time, as a result of a more developed division
of labor, each mind finds itself oriented to a different point on the horizon, reflecting a different
aspect of the world, and consequently *the contents
of consciousness (conscience) differs from one
person to another.* [Durkheim, 1973, p. 51, my
emphasis]

Moral consensus, so strong in primitive societies, is dissipated,
and "collective sentiments no longer have the same force to
keep the individual attached to the group under any circumstances" (1933, p. 380). Despite more recent interpretations,
then, it is clear from Durkheim's statements that he did not
assume a strong moral consensus to be essential to the solidarity of modern societies.

Perhaps the most important effects on the *conscience collective* resulting from specialization are those relating to its
religious content. As the *conscience collective* shrinks and
fewer convictions are shared by all members of society, religion also begins to embrace less of the world and is gradually
set apart from more worldly institutions. "If there is one truth
that history teaches us beyond doubt," Durkheim says,

it is that religion tends to embrace a smaller and
smaller portion of social life. Originally, it pervades
everything; everything social is religious. . . . Then,
little by little, political, economic, scientific functions free themselves from the religious function,
constitute themselves apart and take on a more and
more acknowledged temporal character. God, who

> was at first present in all human relations, progres-
> sively withdraws from them; he abandons the world
> to men and their disputes. . . . The individual really
> feels himself less *acted upon;* he becomes more a
> source of spontaneous activity. [1938, p. 169]

But although religion becomes less pervasive in influence,
Durkheim is convinced that it can never disappear entirely, for
it is clear to him that religion is an essential and permanent aspect of all human societies. Yet, "if it is true that religion is, in
a sense, indispensable, it is no less certain that religions change,
that yesterday's religion could not be that of tomorrow" (1973,
p. 51). The problem for Durkheim is to identify the type and
form of religious representations in a world structurally revolu-
tionized by specialization.

As individual differences are amplified, Durkheim argues,
the only common conviction that remains, and hence the only
possible object of religious reverence, is the respect accorded
the individual as such and those aspects of humanity that he
shares with all other people. With reference to this value the
conscience collective is even strengthened, although Durkheim
fails to suggest how or why, save that no other common focus
for its attention exists. The human person at any rate becomes
the object of a modern cult and is considered sacred in a ritual
sense. The same divine and mysterious sentiments formerly
reserved for the gods are now the exclusive property of the
individual person, who is himself both god and worshipper.
"Since each of us incarnates something of humanity," Durkheim
argues, "each individual consciousness contains something
divine and thus finds itself marked with a character which ren-
ders it sacred and inviolable to all others. Therein lies all individualism" (1973, p. 52).

Despite this last contention, the individualism of the modern
cult (that is, moral individualism) is clearly unlike the nonmoral,
egoistic individualism to which Durkheim also often refers. The
latter type, in fact, is defined precisely by the absence of social
restraint; it is the condition that emerges when the *conscience
collective* is very weak or nonexistent, its integrative and regulative strength undermined. No longer properly constrained, the

individual directs his efforts toward no "higher" principles than the satisfaction of his own personal desires and interests which, without moral constraint, are insatiable. Egoism thus refers to a *detachment* from society, which for Durkheim can only be considered amoral and often results in a pathological increase in suicides. Moral individualism, on the other hand, is the expression of a *conscience collective* whose integrative and regulative capacities are retained. Moral individualism, therefore, implies not the progressive elimination of the *conscience collective*, but its transformation in such a way as to join the individual to society in a new manner.[12] He is still dominated by the *conscience collective*, but that domination is now the very condition of his liberation as an individual.

Durkheim's effort to account for both types of individualism, as well as his analysis of the relationship of each to the *conscience collective*, is fraught with inconsistencies and ambiguities. Specifically, although they are obviously derived from opposite conditions of the *conscience collective*, he clearly considers both to be intrinsically connected to the emergence of the differentiated, modern social type. He cannot, however, have it both ways. At only one point in his work, in *Suicide*, does Durkheim apparently recognize and address directly the contradiction between these positions. Instead of choosing one over the other, however, he attempts to reconcile the two by suggesting a sort of kinship between them. Where the cult of the individual inspires, as it must, "a very high idea of one's self, certain combinations of circumstances readily suffice to make man unable to perceive anything above himself. Individualism is not of course necessarily egoism, but it comes close to it; the one cannot be stimulated without the other being enlarged" (1951, p. 364).

The effort inevitably fails. Durkheim's suggestion that a relationship of covariation exists between the two individualisms can produce only absurd contradictions. On the one hand, if the cult of the individual (assuming it is a current social fact) stimulates a rise in egoism, then it undermines its own content and actually contributes to weakened social integration and, by definition, to a weakened *conscience collective*. If taken seriously, this circumstance implies that a state of morality

(the cult) fosters its own breakdown, that a religion inspires
its own sacrilege. Proper social integration would, in this case,
give rise to pathological, egoistic suicide, which is defined as
resulting from a state of inadequate integration. Yet, a society
cannot be simultaneously normal and pathological, well and
poorly integrated. On the other hand, it appears even less likely
that so many individual hedonists, devoted to nothing but self-
fulfillment, could respect the dignity and worth of any individual
person but their own. It is at least implausible that self-devoted
people could generate moral interests superior to those of the
individual and which necessarily begin with disinterest. For
this to occur, immorality would have to beget its opposite;
weak social integration would have to generate its own strength;
and pathology would have to inspire normality. Such conceptions are logically inconsistent at the very least.

These inconsistencies are not resolved in Durkheim's work,
nor are they resolvable. Durkheim managed to go beyond them
only by ignoring the contradiction and making his choice by
reasserting in his subsequent work the importance of moral
individualism in differentiated societies. That he made this
choice is hardly surprising. Having declared that all societies
possess a moral and religious foundation, and having already
recognized the moral inadequacies of the present transitional
and abnormal forms of the division of labor, he could not very
well give up moral individualism without conceding to the
utilitarians. Hence, in his final conception, moral individualism
remains as the moral and religious expression of the common
conscience.

The Functions of Religion in Primitive
and Modern Societies

Durkheim's interest in religion was not, of course, restricted
to its origins and forms. In addition, he sought to point out
its functional utility in ensuring social order, "its relation to
some social end" (1938, pp. 110-11). Durkheim's famous analysis was concerned with religion not simply as an expression
of social solidarity, but as the fundamental condition of its

continued existence. Its own functional indispensability, more-over, ensures that the presence of religion be universal.

According to Durkheim, everyday life and its activities are characterized by constant conflict. For the most part, routine conduct is egoistic, directed toward "utilitarian and individual avocations." In the profane world, as Durkheim conceives it, "every one attends to his own personal business; for most men this primarily consists in satisfying the exigencies of material life, and the principal incentive to economic activity has always been private interest" (1965, p. 390). While social (moral) sentiments are forever present to some degree, "they are constantly combatted and held in check by the antagonistic tendencies aroused and supported by the necessities of the daily struggle" (1965, p. 390). Without some means of renewal and revitalization, Durkheim suggests, moral constraint would certainly dissipate and individuals would revert to their biological (presocial) natures. Once the boundaries were lifted from their insatiable desires, individuals would begin ruthlessly destroying themselves and others and social life itself would degenerate into a Hobbesian nightmare.

The only way in which social forces can be revitalized, Durkheim insists, is to retemper them occasionally in the very periods of intense association in which the sacred was originally born and forever inheres. Moreover, because the functional core of all religion is precisely this effervescent association, its role is largely unaffected by the innumerable historical variations in religious beliefs, symbols, and practices, some of which are suggested by Durkheim himself. All rituals—representative, imitative, piacular, and even negative rites—serve the same social end.

In allowing individuals to relive the rich, emotional experience of the sacred, religious rituals "strengthen the bonds" between the individual and his god, and hence, "at the same time really strengthen the bonds attaching the individual to the society of which he is a member, since the god is only a figurative expression of the society" (1965, pp. 257-58). The participants remember the attachments forged in these collective rites even after the effervescence has passed, for it cannot last long, and the memory sustains them until the next sacred reunion. Sacred rites are, therefore, the means by which the social group itself is periodically reaffirmed, its members integrated and reminded of their unity, and the *conscience collective* revived. Through them, society and its members are together reborn and reunited, enabling the individual to "lead a life superior to that which he would lead, if he followed only his own individual whims," that is, ensuring his subjection to moral (social) forces.[13] Since for Durkheim social life is possible only on this basis, the crucial importance of religion is obvious.

Since the specific character of solidarity differs in segmental and differentiated societies, and since in differentiated societies the individual is joined to society "in a new manner," logically it should follow that the ritualistic mechanisms that ensure moral integration will be somewhat different in each. Durkheim, however, does not agree. There is, he suggests,

> something eternal in religion which is destined to
> endure all the particular symbols in which religious
> thought has successively enveloped itself. There can
> be no society which does not feel the need of up-
> holding and reaffirming at regular intervals the
> collective ideas which make its unity and its person-
> ality. Now this moral remaking cannot be achieved
> except by the means of reunions, assemblies and
> meetings where the individuals, being closely united
> to one another, reaffirm in common their common
> sentiments; hence come ceremonies which do not
> differ from regular religious ceremonies, either in
> their object, the results which they produce, or the
> processes employed to attain these results. What
> essential difference is there between an assembly of
> Christians celebrating the principal dates in the life
> of Christ, or Jews remembering their exodus from
> Egypt or the promulgation of a new moral or legal
> system or some great event in the national life?
> [1965, pp. 474-75]

Whatever the society, religious rituals always function in the same way to attain and maintain social and moral order.

Durkheim's theory of ritual integration is significantly less problematic with regard to primitive societies, where individual similarities are greatest. Collective effervescence, by definition, subjects the individual to intense social forces that lead and dominate him, thereby replacing personal with common ends. His own will, and thus his own individuality, are submerged in an identification with the group and he is reborn, so to speak, in the image of society. Hence, collective rites reaffirm what is held in common, that is, the *conscience collective.* Since in segmental societies likenesses extend to all aspects of the individual *conscience*, rites reaffirm the very conditions on which mechanical solidarity rests. Logically, then, where individual similarities are greatest, the integrative function of religious ritual will be most efficacious.

Although his functional theory of religion was assumed to have universal applicability, Durkheim's own studies of it were restricted by a somewhat questionable methodological premise to the primitive or "simplest" societies. More specifically, while assuming that collective effervescence appeared in various historical periods and in both primitive and modern societies,[14] he devoted attention to its integrative function only in regard to the totemic tribes of Australian aborigines in *The Elementary Forms.* Nowhere does he specifically analyze it as serving to integrate a differentiated society. His failure to do so may be taken as a sign of his own inability to work out the inherent contradiction between increasing specialization and his conception of ritual integration.

In segmental societies, collective rites served to sustain social solidarity and moral integration by reinforcing those characteristics that made each member of society like every other, that is, by reaffirming the *conscience collective.* However, with the breakdown of mechanical solidarity, the mental contents of individuals are dissimilated and personalized. Modern societies emphasize not the likenesses of individuals but their inherent differences. How, then, do collective rites function to integrate the members of modern differentiated societies, as Durkheim insists they must?

One assumes that rites function in modern societies by reaffirming moral individualism, the remaining expression of the *conscience collective* and thus the final commonality. It too, however, accepts the now fundamental distinctions between people and stresses their similarities only abstractly, as members of humanity or as men in general. In fact, Durkheim claims, the end of moral individualism "is not (even) social . . . It is still from society that it takes all its force, but *it is not to society that it attaches us;* it is to ourselves. Hence it does not constitute a true social bond . . . All social links which result from likeness progressively slacken" (1972, p. 145, my emphasis). Since rites function only by reaffirming commonality, their efficacy under conditions of moral individualism must be regarded as uncertain. At the very least, since religion now touches a much smaller portion of their minds and emotions—a lowest common denominator, so to speak—its hold over individuals must have weakened considerably. As a result, the same sacred symbols, beliefs, and rites should no longer be able to mobilize identical emotions with a similar intensity in each individual. Thus, the integrative power of religious rites would appear to have been significantly undermined by individuation. It seems apparent, in any case, that some contradictions do exist between Durkheim's theories of ritual integration and specialization in modern societies, and that these are not resolved by locating the sacred in moral individualism.

Neither are these inconsistencies entirely resolved by the postulation of an organic solidarity of "mechanical" parts, each periodically reintegrated through its own religious rituals. In modern societies, Durkheim contends in the Preface to the *Division of Labor*, the only type of organization that could conceivably play such a role is the corporation or professional association. However, as he observes in the same book, the corporation of today can hardly be expected to attain an internal solidarity which even approaches the mechanical type. The same division of labor from which the corporation emerges in the first place also restricts its influence to the occupational life. In all other respects, again, the individual is free to follow his own lead. This is not to say, of course, that corporations cannot attain internal solidarity, but that the corporate *conscience* envelops but a portion of the individual *conscience* and that, therefore, the "mechanical solidarity" of the corporation is somewhat limited. The functional efficacy of group rites should vary accordingly.

Even if an ideal moral integration could be achieved within each professional association, a more general social solidarity does not necessarily result. Organic solidarity depends upon a spontaneous consensus of parts, a condition produced only by the *normal* development of the division of labor. Only to the degree, he argued, that occupational specializations correspond to the natural talents of individuals, that the functional inter-relationships between organs are uncoerced, and that external inequalities are eliminated can the division of labor produce social solidarity. In each respect, he realized, the current state of the division of labor must be regarded as deficient and thus "abnormal" (both anomic and forced). This recognition is very likely what led Durkheim to turn increasingly to moral individualism, the inconsistencies of which have already been noted, as the solidarity-inducing agent in modern societies.

For Durkheim, moral individualism was much more than a matter of theoretical concern. Writing at a time when his own nation was divided by partisan conflicts, Durkheim clearly sought not only to intellectually comprehend the foundations of social order, but also to forge a new moral framework for the integration of France particularly and modern society generally. This could not be accomplished, he recognized, on traditional religious grounds, for, indeed, conflicts among religious groups (as epitomized in the Dreyfus affair) were a significant part of the problem. Rather, he argued, "we must discover those moral forces that men, down to the present time, have conceived of only under the form of religious allegories. We must disengage them from their symbols, present them in their rational nakedness . . . " (1961, p. 11). And yet, if society is to survive its own secularization, a new, overarching moral *conscience* must be constructed. Thus, "not only must we see to it that morality, as it becomes rationalized, loses none of its basic elements, but it must, through the very fact of secularization, become enriched with the new elements" (1961, p. 11). Those elements recommended by Durkheim include reason,

a concern for human dignity, and "a greater thirst for justice"—
in short, moral individualism. This new religion, expressed as
a secular civic morality transcending internal social divisions,
would be embodied in the state, instilled through the public
schools, sustained by collective rituals, and capable of engen-
dering the moral integration of the whole society. At least at
one level, Durkheim's work constitutes an intellectual construction and ideological endorsement of social ecumenism
and points to some of the means for achieving it.

Durkheim is certainly not alone in dealing with rationalization, secularization, and their consequences for individualism
and for the modern world. These issues are, of course, also
central to the work of Max Weber. Weber's analysis of these
themes, however, points in a very different direction—not to
the reconstruction of an overall vision but to the emergence
of numerous competing "gods," of which Durkheim's moral
individualism is but one. From this perspective, it appears at
least partly due to Durkheim's commitment to this "god" and
to his efforts to build a new moral framework around it that
he was largely unable to see the ideological implications of his
own intellectual efforts, or for that matter, to recognize the
significance of intellectuals, prophets, and individuals generally
in the formulation and rationalization of religious and moral
ideas. Such issues are given prominent treatment, however, in
the more detached perspective of Weber and Paul Radin, next
to whose works the limitations of the Durkheimian approach
become more easily discernible.

IDEOLOGY AND ORTHODOXY: WEBER AND RADIN ON THE PRODUCTION AND DISTRIBUTION OF VALUES

The Production of Religious Ideas

Radin and especially Weber were far less concerned than Durkheim with the origins and essence of religious phenomena. Instead, they preferred to investigate particular religious behaviors and their empirical consequences. In the references they did make to this topic, however, they were agreed—as against Durkheim—that understanding must begin with a recognition of specific and concrete rather than generalized individuals. Once this was done, they contended, one could not fail to recognize that all societies encompass a wide variability of human temperaments, inclinations, and abilities relevant to their capacities for religious experience and expression.

In Radin's anthropological studies, these variations are categorized into two distinct psychological types: the man of action and the truly religious formulator. While the particular role of each is conditioned by the socioeconomic structures within which they exist, Radin insists that the two types are not themselves socially derived but universal "basic and inherent attributes of the human psyche." Overwhelmingly the predominant type, as Radin conceives him, the man of action is sensitive to the "religious thrill" only intermittently, as during crises or important tribal rituals. Too involved in the actual day-to-day living of life to give much thought to its meaning, his interests are confined largely to "practical results" and rarely extend beyond. Intellectual probings into the ways of the world are for him unnecessary inasmuch as he is "satisfied that the world exists and that things happen." A preference for the repetition of events characterizes his "mental rhythm," and the monotony of everyday life is experienced as comforting. Generally, he is "not articulate" in religious matters.

The religious formulator, on the other hand, always few in number, is able to call up religious feelings easily and spontaneously in order to experience and contemplate them. Although he, too, is interested in practical results, the formulator is "impelled by his whole nature" to come to terms with his own subjective states, be they artistic, emotional, neurotic-epileptoid, or simply an awareness of "the limitations of man and the importance of what lies beyond human power." The mental rhythm of this type finds unacceptable the man of action's simple postulation of a mechanical relation between events. Adequate explanation for him is often abstract and always requires some type of coordination and consistency. He requires, in short, wholeness and meaning. (See Radin, 1957a, pp. 231-33; 1971, pp. 37-39, 94.)

Radin's arguments strongly suggest a similar and equally important division in Weber's work between religious virtuosos and the mass of religiously "unmusical." "That men are *differently qualified* in a religious way," he suggests, "stands at the beginning of the history of religion . . . The sacred values that have been most cherished, the ecstatic and visionary capacities of shamans, sorcerers, ascetics, and pneumatics of all sorts, could not be attained by everyone" (1946, p. 287). Like Radin, Weber observed that the formulations of the virtuoso may be at least partly based on his own subjective states or "inner needs," the most dramatic example of which is the pathological ecstasy or even schizophrenia of the Judaic prophets. For the most part, however, Weber simply took for granted that people possess markedly different capacities for religious experience and developed his analyses accordingly. It is clear, in any case, that such distinctions are fundamental to his conception of the genesis of religion.

For Weber and Radin, as these comments suggest, religion is not the product of some mystical social consciousness, but of specific individuals with specific characteristics that are not necessarily shared by the rest of the group. In formulating their religious conceptions, these individuals respond to certain fundamental and universal conditions of human existence, including physical, social, economic and material, intellectual, psychological, and cosmological concerns. More specific among these are a profound awareness of the finiteness of life, the certainty of death, physical insecurity and pain, various material and environmental conditions, scarcity and type of food, and psychological tensions.

For Radin, at least in regard to the root of religion, most of the fundamental conditions of human existence are reducible to fear, and more particularly to economic insecurity and its correlate "psychical insecurity and disorientation with all its attendant fears, with its full feeling of helplessness, of powerlessness, and of insignificance. It is but natural for the psyche, under such circumstances, to take refuge in compensation fantasies" (1957, p. 8) and, in striving to validate those fantasies, to turn to religious conceptions. Radin insists, however, that such religious conceptions cannot be assigned a "sacred" sphere of their own, separate from the "profane." Rather, they are "merged and interpenetrated" with the harsh necessities of living and surviving under not always congenial conditions. Religion, then, "is the emotional correlate of the struggle for existence in an insecure physical and social environment" (1957, p. 5).

According to Weber's well-known argument, on the other hand, religious conceptions are generated by a confrontation between the virtuoso and a fundamental "problem of meaning," the first perception of which was the apparently senseless and arbitrary distribution of suffering and fortune. Every religion, he suggests, originates in a metaphysical need to somehow make sense of the cosmos, to experience the world as being rationally organized and meaningful, and, in doing so, to provide a theodicy of suffering or good fortune, as the case may be. Religion thus represents the first human efforts to intellectually rationalize the world, a quest characteristically borne by intellectuals.

Although Radin and Weber appear to offer very different interpretations of the conditions of human existence to which

religious formulators respond, their accounts are not all that
dissimilar, and what differences do exist are largely attributable
to differences in the levels of sublimation of the respective
religions they studied. Since the religions studied by Radin
were relatively unsublimated, he did not focus on the more
complex issues of theodicy which Weber made central, such
as inequalities of status and wealth, suffering and fortune.
Primitives tend to be somewhat more equal in these respects,
the rounds of life being much the same for each. It is quite
possible, in this sense, to view fear as an unsublimated version
of the more general problem of meaning. Certainly fear may
itself be regarded as a form of suffering, and its existence cannot fail to suggest a certain senselessness to the world. And
even if religious theodicies do not alleviate fears, at least they
justify or validate them, thereby explaining why people fear,
and why they must. That the problems of fear and meaning are
closely related is stated eloquently in the following passage,
which relates an Eskimo angakoq's efforts to explain why his
people believe as they do.

> Aua pointed out over the ice, where the snow
> swept this way or that in whirling clouds. "Look,"
> he said impressively, "snow and storm; ill weather
> for hunting. And yet we must hunt for our daily
> food; *why?* Why must there be storms to hinder us
> when we are seeking meat for ourselves and those
> we love?"
> *Why?* . . .
> Aua led me again, this time to the house of
> Kuvdlo, next to our own. The lamp burned with the
> tiniest glow, giving out no heat at all; a couple of
> children cowered shivering in a corner, huddled to-
> gether under a skin rug. And Aua renewed his
> merciless interrogations: "Why should all be chill
> and comfortless in this little home? Kuvdlo has
> been out hunting since early morning; if he had
> caught a seal, as he surely deserved, for his pains,
> the lamp would be burning bright and warm, his
> wife would be sitting smiling beside it, without fear

of scarcity for the morrow; the children would be
playing merrily in the warmth and light, glad to be
alive. Why should it not be so?"
Why?
Again I could make no answer and Aua took me
to a little hut apart, where his aged sister, Natseq,
who was ill, lay all alone. . . .

And for the third time Aua looked me in the face
and said: "Why should it be so? Why should we
human beings suffer pain and sickness? All fear it,
all would avoid it if they could. Here is this old sister
of mine, she has done no wrong that we can see, but
lived her many years and given birth to good strong
children, yet now she must suffer pain at the ending
of her days?"
Why? Why? . . .
"You see," observed Aua, "even you cannot answer when we ask you why life is as it is. And so it
must be. Our customs come from life and are directed towards life; we cannot explain, we do not believe
in this or that; but the answer lies in what I have
just shown you.
"We fear!
"We fear the elements with which we have to
fight in their fury to wrest out food from land and
sea.
"We fear cold and famine in our snow huts.
"We fear the sickness that is daily to be seen
amongst us. Not death, but the suffering.
"We fear the souls of the dead, of human and
animal alike.
"We fear the spirits of earth and air.
"And therefore our fathers, taught by their fathers
before them, guarded themselves about with these
old rules and customs, which are built upon the experience and knowledge of generations. We know
not how nor why, but we obey them that we may be
suffered to live in peace. And for all our angakoqs
and their knowledge of hidden things, we yet know

so little that we fear everything else. We fear the
things we see about us, and the things we know from
the stories and myths of our forefathers. Therefore
we hold by our customs and observe all the rules of
tabu." [Rasmussen, 1969, pp. 129-31]

As this passage suggests, in any particular case the related
problems of fear and meaning are more than matters of abstract concern. Rather, they are defined and given content and
direction by specific conditions under which the formulator
lives and to which he responds. These conditions, which may
be both empirical and ideal, shape the formulator's perception
of the world and, consequently, his religious requirements in
the face of it.

The empirical determinants of world images will obviously
vary greatly from case to case. Perhaps because primitive societies are more directly dependent upon their physical sur-
roundings, Radin generally emphasized the material and economic conditions that shape the world images of formulators.
Clearly, for instance, in Aua's explanation above—one of Radin's
favorite examples—the world image of the Eskimo is conditioned
more than anything else by the harsh, imposing physical environment against which he struggles daily to survive. Beyond such
basic environmental factors, the type, availability, procurement,
and distribution of food assume greatest importance.

Weber, on the other hand, who studied the written histories
of more economically complex civilizations, does not restrict
the empirical foundations of world images to material and
economic conditions, but extends them to include the particular historical and sociostructural situation in which the
virtuoso finds himself. Thus, for instance, he observed that the
international political situation was decisive in shaping the
world images of pre-exilic Judaic prophets and, consequently,
of the contents of their prophecies (1952, pp. 267-69).

However important such empirical conditions may be, Weber
and Radin agree that they are never alone in shaping the presuppositions of religious formulators. Established preconcep-
tions as to the meaning of the world—prior intellectual rationalizations—are equally important as baselines for subsequent
intellectual rationalizations. Radin, for instance, observes that

the "life values" and "magico-folklore background" of the formulator contribute immeasurably to his image of the world and, hence, to the ideas he produces. Weber makes much the same point. To continue with the example of the Judaic prophets, for example, if their world images were influenced by international politics, the whole matter was framed by their prior conception of a covenant *(berith)* relationship between Israelites and a single, omnipotent god.

While Weber and Radin recognize that the religious formulator's ideas are influenced by both empirical and ideal aspects of his background, they differ to some extent regarding his approach to that background. One possibility, since particular individuals are involved, is that purely personal interests play a role in generating religious formulations and especially in shaping their contents. For Radin, this is almost certain to be the case. After all, he suggests, primitive formulators share with all other men the same fears of suffering, starvation, and death. It is therefore understandable that they compose their doctrines with an eye for their own welfare, especially in providing justifications for themselves to be released from daily work and to be provided with food. Beyond these minimum securities, their ideas "are dictated by the formulator's economic status and political power" (1957, p. 20). Thus, to Radin, the very act of formulation involves an attempt to gain or sustain access to certain goods and privileges.

Although Weber also recognized that personal, social, political, and economic interests might influence religious formulations, he insisted that religious or any other ideas may be produced relatively autonomously and are not necessarily derived either from the psychological needs or the social and class interests of the thinker. They may be inspired instead by the demands of "intellectualism as such [and] more particularly the metaphysical needs of the human mind as it is driven to reflect on ethical and religious questions, driven . . . by an inner compulsion to understand the world as a meaningful cosmos and to take up a position toward it" (1968, p. 499). Against Nietzsche, for instance, Weber argued that, even though the repressed masses have been most in need of a prophet or redeemer, "the prophet has not regularly been a descendant or representative of depressed classes," nor have his formulations "been derived preponderantly from the intellectual horizons of the depressed classes" (1946, p. 274).[1] The Judaic prophets of doom, for instance, whose ideas generally favored the poor and underprivileged against the rich and powerful, constituted a group of marginal intellectuals who generally existed on the fringes of society and who were drawn originally from diverse social backgrounds.

Finally, as is implicitly suggested in Weber's work, the production of religious ideas may be not only autonomous, but even unintentional or accidental. Thus, Weber suggests, the very important notion of the "calling" as a "God-given, worldly life-task whose fulfillment was the highest moral duty of the individual" did not exist before the Reformation. The idea, its meaning, and subsequent importance to Protestantism (and to rational capitalism) may well have been the result of Luther's own independent intellectual activity and, more specifically, of his error of translation (Weber, 1958, pp. 79-92).

Weber further contends that the very existence of prior systematic conceptions of the world inevitably inspires further innovations and rational formulations, in both religious and secular terms. The more systematic religious intellectuals were able to make their religion and the fewer magical and mystical elements it contained, and thus the more it was codified and doctrinally expressed, the greater was its exposure to demands of consistency. No such rational constructions, however, have ever succeeded in integrating the universe and its meaning into a single totality. In every case, the universe has proven incapable of total rationalization, never systematized "with nothing left over." Especially when religion becomes book religion, the "gaps" in every rational system give rise to the requirement that either the doctrine or the world be made more rational and consistent. Efforts of the first sort result in priestly apologetics and casuistry. In the second case, lay prophets emerged to systematize and rationalize the way of life around the pursuit of some sacred value. Ultimately, the "gaps" allowed intellectual rationalization to find secular expression in the form of skepticism, philosophy, and, later, science. Thus, intellectualism was wrested from priestly control.

These comments should not be taken to mean that Weber eschewed any concern with the influence of ideal and material

interests[2] on the production of ideas, religious or otherwise.
To do so, as he recognized, would be to correct Marx's excess
by means of another, equally excessive position. The point,
rather, is that intellectual activity of any sort is not *necessarily*
bound up with the thinker's interest situation. But although
Weber does not discount the influence of ideal and material
interests as factors in the production of religious ideas, he
generally anticipates their influence only in the next phase of a
religion's development: its adoption by a particular stratum
which becomes its characteristic bearer and from whom it
receives its "stamp."

Before proceeding to a discussion of that step in the social
history of a religious idea, however, let us state more directly
the contrast of this position to Durkheim's theory of the genesis of religion. For Weber and Radin, religion is obviously
not symbolic of society itself, nor is it a simple reflection of
social structure. Rather, religious ideas are the products of
(1) specific individuals with specific characters, inclinations,
and abilities intellectually coming to terms with (2) some
combination of the particular empirical and ideal conditions
under which they live. These conditions are not restricted to
a social referent but extend to incorporate "the whole life of
man." Because the range of possible combinations produced
by these two broad sets of factors is obviously limitless,[3] no
reductionist formula could possibly account for the infinite
variations in the form and content of religious expression.

The Reception of Religious Ideas (I):
Adoption by Carriers

Implicit in Durkheim's account is that the production and
reception of a religious idea are simultaneous occurrences.
Religion is collectively received in the very same effervescent
rites by which it is socially produced. By definition, then, the
birth of a religion is inseparable from its diffusion to all members of the society in which it originates. As a component of
the *conscience collective*, the religion is necessarily shared by
virtually all members of the society, and presumably with
more or less the same intensity. For Durkheim, every religion
is orthodox by virtue of its very existence.

For Radin and especially Weber, on the other hand, the fact that a religious ideology has been suggested by a specific formulator or intellectual stratum neither ensures its survival nor guarantees its social effect. These outcomes, which in no way are characterized by the inevitability that pervades Durkheim's argument, can be realized only if the ideology is accepted by some receiving audience which "carries" or "bears" the religion and provides it with its characteristic "stamp." In any given case, the ultimate social effect of a religion will be realized through the particular audience that adopts it.

According to Weber's well-known work in the sociology of knowledge, if a religious idea or ideology is to be adopted, there must exist an "elective affinity"[4] between the contents of the religion's annunciation and promise on the one hand and the social character and especially the "religious needs" of the receiving stratum on the other. These needs, unlike the "intellectualism as such" referred to earlier, do not constitute metaphysical concerns in Weber's scheme, but rather are "strongly influenced by the nature of the external interest-situation and the corresponding way of life" (1946, pp. 286-87) of the group in question. No matter how important these influences may be in a given case, however, Weber insists that the religious needs themselves are usually primary in establishing a stratum's affinity with certain religious ideas.

At a general level, Weber suggests that the religious needs of a group are largely determined by its relatively privileged or unprivileged position in the order of stratification. Thus, he observes, economically and politically advantaged groups require that religion justify their good fortune. Though with different degrees of need, such groups "assign to religion the primary function of *legitimizing* their own life pattern and situation in the world" (1968, p. 491). Accordingly, except in unusual circumstances, such groups display little affinity for salvation religions. Underprivileged groups, on the other hand, are much more inclined toward religious ideas that promise future compensation for present unhappiness, and thus for salvation religions in general. Although the type and means of compensation may assume endless variations, all such conceptions involve "reward for one's own good deeds and punishment for the unrighteousness of others" (1968, p. 492).

In particular cases, of course, religious needs are linked to far more specific social conditions than these broad contrasts suggest. Thus, for instance, peasants whose lives are bound to the land and nature display a general propensity for "weather magic and animistic magic or animism" (1968, p. 470). Bureaucrats are generally carriers of a "sober rationalism," disdaining salvation needs and all irrational religion while at the same time recognizing its utility as a means of mass control (as with Chinese heterodox religions). Petty-bourgeois strata, while displaying a variety of religious tendencies, are generally inclined by their economic way of life to embrace rational, ethical, inner-wordly religious ideas. These and other affinities analyzed by Weber are too well known to merit more detailed discussion.

In primitive societies, Weber and Radin agree, religion is always carried by a priesthood of sorts, which emerges whereever economic conditions permit. To the degree that the priesthood consists of men of action, Radin suggests, it will usually adopt whatever ideas the formulators offer, conditional on only two considerations. First, "adoptable" ideas must be amenable to the magico-folklore background or traditional lore of the community. Innovations that violate tradition, as Weber points out, could easily threaten priestly authority, thereby rendering them unsuitable for adoption. Second, Radin strongly implies, those religious ideas most adaptable to professional exploitation stand a better chance of being received by the priesthood. A considerable range of adoptable ideas is possible in either case.

The same aspects of a group's social character which gave it an affinity for certain religious ideas in the first place are also most responsible for the "stamp" subsequently displayed in the religion's practical ethic. The unique features of the religion are derived from the unique character of the adopting stratum. As Weber argues:

> The various great ways of leading a rational and
> methodical life have been characterized by irrational
> presuppositions, which have been accepted simply
> as "given" and which have been incorporated into
> such ways of life. What these presuppositions have

been is historically and socially determined, at least
to a very large extent, through the peculiarity of
those strata which have been the carriers of the ways
of life during its formative and decisive period. The
interest situation of these strata, as determined socially and psychologically, has made for their peculiarity, as we here understand it. [1946, p. 281]

The most important of these interests, again, are the religious
needs of the group in question, and Weber insists that the stamp
is derived "primarily from religious sources." Other interests
are often influential, however, and "sometimes decisive."[5]
    In the case of primitive religions, Radin asserts that other
interests are in fact generally primary in the stamping process.
Apart from the substantial influence of the formulators themselves, peculiarities of a given religion are generally determined
by the economic interests of the priesthood, especially as it
seeks to secure the benefits of its profession and authority. In
this case, the priestly stamp is set most clearly on important
rituals rather than on practical ethics, as shall be demonstrated
in a later chapter.
    However a particular stamp has been first determined, and
however extensive its influence, the religion may be continuously adapted in accordance with the religious needs, world images,
and interests of its carrying stratum. Indeed, Weber suggests,
"frequently the very next generation reinterprets these annunci-
ations and promises (of a religion) in a fundamental fashion"
(Weber, 1946, p. 270) in order to accommodate its own changed
interest situation. Thus, for instance, the second and third generations of Puritans in America were increasingly confronted by the
temptations of wealth, which accrued as a result of Protestant economic virtues. Accordingly, the Protestant tenets were compromised over several generations, first by seeking to "make the best
of both worlds," later in the belief that "a good conscience [was]
simply . . . one of the means of enjoying a comfortable bourgeois
life," and finally by abandoning the religious principles entirely.[6]
    Given sufficient time, not only may religion be casuistically
adapted, but the carrying stratum itself may change, thereby

producing further, perhaps more general, alterations in the religious stamp. The genteel intellectuals (literati) who originally "set their stamp" on Confucianism, for instance, increasingly adopted bureaucratic attitudes that accorded with their administrative positions. Similarly, American Puritanism was transferred from qualified saints to entrepreneurial, middle-class businessmen. Both the ideas and their bearers are subject to changes in historical circumstances.

The Reception of Religious Ideas (II): Diffusion to the Masses and the Emergence of Orthodoxy

That a given religion is adopted and stamped by a particular stratum in no way ensures its diffusion beyond the stratum itself. Social orthodoxy is not automatic. Weber mentions several religions which, for one reason or another, were not widely received.[7] The sociological problem, then, is to determine the specific means by which a religious idea is widely diffused, that is, to determine the substantive bases of orthodoxy.

If a given religion is to find a mass audience, it may be generally presumed that the carrying stratum has an interest in its diffusion. That interest may be purely ideal, such as a sincere belief in the religion's truth or validity, which inspires an attempt to rationalize the world in accordance with its ethic and promise. Or it may be a material interest since, in bearing their stamp, a religious ideology often justifies the monopolization of certain rights and privileges for its carriers. The priesthood especially, Weber argues, seeks "to aggrandize its status and income" by addressing its religious message to the masses. To the degree the masses are receptive, the priesthood is able to secure for itself on a stable basis the considerable benefits of "ideal and material mass-patronage." Radin, while placing greater emphasis on the material advantages that accrue to primitive shamans and priests, makes essentially the same point. Carriers stand to gain in the mass reception of their "stamped" religious ideology.

Of course, the fact that interests are involved in the propagation of a religious ideology neither guarantees nor explains its popular reception. In a given society, several different religious ideologies may be simultaneously propagated by their respective carriers, each competing for the ideal and material advantages to be gained therefrom. If an orthodoxy is to be created at all, one carrying group must emerge victorious, on the basis of which its religion or ideology achieves social dominance. The related problems of ideological diffusion and legitimation of authority are thus addressed to the specific means by which, in a given case, ideological dominance is achieved. Weber and Radin suggest several possibilities in this regard, all of which connect the sociologies of knowledge and religion to issues of stratification and social competition.[8]

According to Radin, in those primitive societies where religion is largely unsublimated and hence magical, the efforts of magicians, shamans, medicine-men, and similar practitioners to extend their craft are based largely on the manipulation of lay fear and insecurity. All primitives share such fears, he suggests, because of the tenuous and difficult economic conditions on which they depend for survival. In particular, "the more uncertain is the food supply, the less man is technologically prepared, the greater naturally will be the feeling of insecurity and the more intense, consequently, will be the fear" (1957, p. 23). Around precisely those events and values most important in primitive life—food and its procurement, the physiological life-crises, happiness, long life, and so on—the magician raised magical barriers to success which usually he alone, for a fee, could overcome. In other words, due partly to his professional interests and partly to his own insecurities, "the religious formulator developed the theory that everything of value, even everything unchangeable and predictable about man and the world around him, was surrounded and immersed in danger, that these dangers could be overcome only in a specific fashion and according to a prescription devised and perfected by him" (1957, p. 25). In this case, diffusion largely took the form of professionalization. And since, as Radin and Weber agree, primitive peoples are everywhere dominated by magical interests,[9] especially in practical results, diffusion met little resistance as long as the traditional folklore was not harshly violated.

The situation was somewhat different whenever the religious thinker found enough time and economic security to sublimate or intellectually rationalize his own formulations. The interests of the now-priestly carriers in the diffusion of their formulations were not much changed by this development. Their professional security depended upon convincing the laymen that they held an intermediary position between the gods and man. At this point, the priesthood's religious ideology was confronted by the continued interests of the laity in magic. Men of action were concerned only with tangible results in their worldly affairs rather than with matters of abstract belief and cosmic meaning. The strictly religious formulations propagated among them were therefore almost always adapted in the direction of magical usage. From the viewpoint of the priesthood, successful diffusion of the religious ideology, and thus the maintenance of their positions, required that certain concessions be made to mass needs. Magical elements were therefore retained, and even where supernatural agencies were popularly received, they normally were required to contribute to some pragmatic enterprise.

    Weber also finds concessions to the religious needs of receiving audiences to be a potentially successful and even necessary technique of diffusion. He notes, for example, that salvation religions borne by socially privileged groups are almost always adjusted when transferred to the masses to include a savior or redeemer. Indeed, excluding Judaism and Protestantism, "all religions and religious ethics have had to reintroduce cults of saints, heroes or functional gods in order to accommodate themselves to the needs of the masses" (1968, p. 488). Buddhism, for instance, ultimately "had to meet halfway the needs of the laity, which in ancient Buddhism, given its nature, had essentially played an incidental role. Hence, soteriology had to be bent in the direction of faith in magic and saviors" (1958, p. 243; see also p. 234). Thus, if a religious ideology is to be successfully diffused and, equally important from their point of view, the carrying stratum is to retain its ideal and/or material privileges, certain ideological compromises must be made. If the concessions did not go far enough in addressing the religious needs of the masses, heterodox salvation religions usually emerged to compete for and often capture popular attention. In China, for instance, the unbending intellectualist orientation of Confucianism could not prevent the mass acceptance of magic and Taoist salvation promises. Generally, however, the threat that competing religions might emerge to capture mass affections was doubtless a sufficient incentive to making concessions.

A religious ideology may also be successfully propagated, Weber and Radin suggest, by an alliance between the carrying stratum and political rulers. In such cases, an established political power may itself become the agent of religious diffusion, both by active propagation and by restricting competition. In return for support and protection, a religious ideology and its adherents may provide the prince with various useful services. Not the least of these, of course, is the provision of religious legitimation to princely authority, be it in terms of deification, ritual correctness, priestly blessing, or some other legitimating principle. In more specific terms, supporting certain religious ideologies may also serve as a means of "mass domestication," and hence of lowering the costs of domination. Prior to the Hindu restoration, for instance, Buddhism served the kingships of India and Ceylon in precisely this capacity (Weber, 1958a, pp. 240, 257). In China also, despite the existence of an official Confucian orthodoxy, Buddhism was imported by the emperor as a means of "taming the masses." As opposed to Confucianism, which emphasized the here and now, Buddhist promises of Heaven and threats of Hell provided far more effective inducements of mass discipline (Weber, 1958a, p. 265). Taoism and magic were retained for similar political reasons. In other cases, the prince's support of certain religious ideologies could serve his interests not only against the generalized masses, but also against more specific usurpers of power. Thus, princely support of Jainism in India was motivated primarily by "the wish of these princes to be free of Brahman power" (Weber, 1958, p. 202). Later, in a move crucial to the successful restoration of Hindu orthodoxy, the princes reestablished their support of the Brahmans and the caste order "over and against the ancient Buddhistic monkdom and the guilds" (Weber, 1958a, p. 292). In any case princely support is often a decisive factor in establishing a religious orthodoxy.

The usurpation by a carrying stratum of status honor and of its ritual guarantees (which may also depend on political

support) provides another technique by which a religious ideology may be diffused. Prestige is appropriated in the first place
on the basis of the stratum's distinctive style of life, which includes and is legitimated by its religious ideology. This prestigious style of life then "sets the example" for the rest of the
society. Insofar as a group is successful in appropriating the
standards of status in a given society, all other groups must
base their own claims for prestige on the usurping stratum's
style of life. In other words, the more successful is a stratum's
attempt to usurp status honor in a society, the more its religious ideology will be diffused by emulation. Early Protestants
in America, for example, successfully defined the ethical virtues
on which esteem could be claimed, as did the literati in ancient
China. In both cases, other groups could not claim respectability
without first accepting the religious ideology of the dominant
group.

Where a particular stratum succeeds in completely monopo-
lizing access to the highest status, diffusion of its religious
ideology depends upon other techniques. In India, for instance,
since the prestigious Brahmanical style of life was ritually and
hereditarily closed to all but Brahmans themselves, status could
not be claimed and, hence, Hinduism could not be diffused by
emulation of Brahman styles. In this case, the Brahmans managed
to propagate their religious and status ethic by offering various
"rewards" to groups that accepted the caste and karma to which
they were assigned. Lower, impure castes, for example, were
rewarded materially for their cooptation. In terms of prestige,
they were "impure anyway, and obliged by restrictions to keep
their place." In accepting Hinduism and its caste designation,
however, they secured a monopoly over certain occupational
opportunities which, however lowly, were not available to alien
peoples. The price of cooptation for the Kshatriya warriors was
considerably higher, consisting of nothing less than second
ranking in the religious and social hierarchy.

These somewhat typical techniques of ideological diffusion
are identical with the means by which groups and individuals
claim and gain privileged access to scarce ideal and material resources. Thus, in India, "Hinduization" is virtually synonomous
with the monopolization of spiritual dignity and authority by

the Brahman priesthood, on the basis of which they formed a
stable center for the orientation of the status stratification they
controlled. Ultimately, the Brahmans appropriated the lion's
share of prestige and privileges in the entire Indian society. The
Confucian literati in China were able to institute an examination
system based on their own way of life and through which they
completely monopolized access to government offices. From
this powerful position they were able to exert enormous influence on the social character of all of China while at the same
time reserving certain economic and status opportunities for
themselves. Similarly, among the Eskimo, the Nupe, the Zande,
and most other primitive groups, Radin reports, religion and
magic are almost always connected to economic and political
usurpations (Radin, 1971, pp. 137-50).

As these examples clearly illustrate, orthodoxy is not the
result of some mystical social force, nor is it a simple reflection
or manifestation of social self-awareness. Neither, for that
matter, is it an altogether "normal" or automatic social state,
as Durkheim would have it. Rather, where it exists at all, orthodoxy is the outcome of a victorious struggle by its carrying
stratum to attain its own ideal and/or material interests against
those of other social groups. It refers, in short, to ideological
dominance.

Viewed in this way, the "functions" of orthodoxy are indicated by the motives with which its carriers propagate it. Religious and other ideologies normally provide psychological
self-justification and a "myth of superiority" for the way of
life of its carriers, on the basis of which they generally claim
privileged access to certain ideal and material values. Insofar
as the religious ideology is diffused, that is, insofar as ideology
is transformed into orthodoxy, their myth and claims are legitimated by other groups and their privileges can be enjoyed
without serious challenge. In a purely pragmatic sense, a stable
orthodoxy lowers the costs of domination and of sustaining
social advantages. Clearly, this does not suggest the sort of
mystical and moral social unity envisioned by Durkheim. What
is suggested instead is that each religion possesses an economic
or status ethic that is tailored to serve the needs and interests
of certain individuals, groups, or ceremonial units rather than

the mystical urge of the social whole. Religion, in short, serves not society, but specific people.

Orthodoxy and Social Order: Foundations of Compliance Compared

Despite their obvious differences, it is precisely at this point—once a stable orthodoxy has been established—that Durkheimian and Weberian ideas converge to some degree. Like Durkheim, Weber recognizes that social order may result from the establishment of a legitimate orthodoxy, whether religious or otherwise.[10] Nonetheless, their agreement is largely superficial, for they had very different understandings of the nature of that social order and of the means by which it is sustained.

According to Durkheim, social unity is maintained by the constraining force of moral rules, both the source and object of which is society itself. As such, these "imperative rules of conduct" speak with the sacred and authoritative voice of society itself, thus overcoming the individual's purely personal and egoistic interests and ensuring that he act "in terms of the collective interest." Moral rules inspire awe and respect in the individual, who experiences them as duty and obligation and who is thereby compelled to act in the prescribed manner. Indeed, so authoritative and obligatory are moral rules that compliance is "withdrawn from individual discretion." Conformity to orthodox rules of conduct is required "without regard for any consideration relative to their useful or injurious effects," self-interested conduct being the very opposite of moral conduct. Durkheim does observe that the individual regards compliance as desirable, owing to the superiority of society, even as it is obligatory. Even this, however, does not appear to allow him much free choice in the matter, especially since noncompliance is not considered an option.[11] By and large, subjective factors do not contribute to social order. The individual obeys moral rules because he must, inasmuch as they are invested with the authority of society, and not because, for his own reasons, he chooses to.

According to Weber and Radin, on the other hand, validation of claims to legitimate rule always involves a subjective response on the part of receiving audiences.[12] These audiences, moreover, are not identical throughout society. Different groups may (or may not) attribute legitimacy to dominant claims with widely variable degrees of commitment and on very different substantive grounds. And while a normative orientation to the dominant morality may and often does constitute one such basis of legitimation, in no way does it imply the sort of moral obligation envisioned by Durkheim.[13] Indeed, Weber suggests, many regularities of social action, including compliance with legitimate orders, "are not determined by orientation to any sort of norm which is held to be valid . . . but entirely on the fact that the corresponding type of social action is in the nature of the case best adapted to the normal interests of the actors as they themselves are aware of them" (Weber, 1968, p. 30). Clearly, recognition of the claim and powers of dominant groups may constitute an essential factor in calculations of self-interest.

Of Weber's three types of legitimate domination, charismatic authority is most suggestive of Durkheim's theory of moral obligation. Although charisma is a personal rather than social quality, it too is based on the *duty* of those subject to its authority to recognize the charismatic leader and his mission and to comply with his demands. Even so, dutiful obedience is always supplemented by and is often less important than a pragmatic evaluation of self-interest on the part of the followers. Psychologically, Weber contends, the willingness to accept a charismatic leader arises out of enthusiasm or despair, for which the leader presumably promises a remedy. In practice, the charismatic leader must continuously earn his followers' obedience by offering proof of his powers. This proof could be accomplished by means of miracles and heroic deeds, but "most of all, his divine mission must prove itself by bringing well-being to his faithful followers; if they do not fare well, he obviously is not the god-sent master" (1968, p. 1144), and his authority quickly dissipates.[14]

Evaluations of self-interest are no less important determinants of compliance with respect to traditional and legal authority, Weber's two more stable types of legitimate domination. In these cases, compliance may be based on fear, hope, expedience, opportunism, and a wide variety of other subjective motives.

The individual may fear magical vengeance, physical punishment, or, as Radin demonstrates, economic extortion.[15] He may hope for worldly or divine salvation. He may comply to achieve economic or status gains, as implied by the Brahman reward system, or because his tribal customs have "worked" in a pragmatic sense for his elders (Radin, 1971, p. 223). In still other cases, he may obey because he is helpless to do otherwise, lacking both an acceptable alternative and the means of achieving it. Indeed, the powerlessness of subordinate groups may be so extensive that legitimacy is not required at all either in sustaining the domination or in eliciting obedience (Weber, 1968, p. 214).

Once the distribution of power and status has been stabilized, groups may also comply habitually or apathetically, rather than in accordance with calculations of interest. "Such a situation exists," Weber maintains, "as long as the masses continue in that natural state of theirs in which thought about the order of domination remains but little developed, which means, as long as no urgent needs render the state of affairs 'problematical'" (1968, p. 953). In this case, neither personal motives nor moral obligation can be said to matter. Obedience becomes routine, requiring almost no subjective judgment at all (legitimacy of fact). Yet, if in some way the structures of domination are rendered "transparent," the very same symbolism and orthodoxy that legitimated dominant privileges and helped to sustain social order may also become the hated focus of revolt. Orthodoxy, therefore, need not play only an integrative role.

In any event, according to Weber and Radin, compliance does not necessarily involve the sort of positive commitment suggested by Durkheim's notion of moral obligation. Accordingly, neither does it necessarily result in moral integration and social solidarity. This does not mean, of course, that the kind of solidarity envisioned by Durkheim cannot exist. Clearly it can, at least for many groups within a society. In the Weberian scheme, however, it constitutes only one possible outcome of historical and social developments on a scale of possible outcomes, ranging from powerless opposition to reluctant accommodation to calculated (and thus opportunistic rather than "moral") support, and finally, to normative solidarity and spontaneous integration. All outcomes are empirically possible, and, indeed, in any given society, all are likely to be present as the levels of commitment for different groups. No single outcome can be considered any more "normal" or "pathological" than any other. Thus, both sacred orthodoxy and social solidarity, where they exist at all, are the results of specific, substantive causes; they are not the spontaneous products of social life.

Synopsis of Conception and Approach: Fundamental Differences Compared

The many and major differences between Weberian and Durkheimian interpretations of religion—what it is, what it does, and how—are derived largely from the very different perspectives and presuppositions with which they approach the subject matter. It therefore seems worthwhile to briefly summarize the major components of each approach.[16]

In the Durkheimian conception, the primary units of investigation are "social facts," collective determinants of individual conduct. Social action is neither examined nor explained in terms of subjective motives, but with reference to social forces and moral obligations, a focus that allows specific groups and individuals to be largely ignored or treated only abstractly. Society is clearly the star actor in Durkheim's play, whereas individuals play only supporting roles.

For Weber and Radin, on the other hand, concrete and specific individuals are never far from center stage. Weber states that social action "exists only as the behavior of one or more individual human beings," and its study "is restricted to subjectively understandable action" (Weber, 1968, p. 13).

A second major point of disagreement between the two perspectives concerns the methodological stance from which the subject matter is viewed. In Durkheim's work the stance is one of social functionalism, the inadequacies of which have been often noted.[17] While, accordingly, a comprehensive critique of that method is quite unnecessary here, its characteristic "attitude" toward empirical and historical materials does merit some attention.

Henri Bergson, a fellow student with Durkheim at the École Normale Supérieure, once reflected that "one never encountered a fact" with his former classmate. "When we told him that the facts were in contradiction with his theories, he would reply: 'The facts are wrong'" (quoted in Lukes, 1973, p. 52). While exaggerated as a criticism, Bergson's anecdote does point to one of the central failings of Durkheim's approach and of functionalism generally. Durkheim proposed an *a priori* theoretical framework contending that every society has a collective religion that functions to ensure social solidarity. The validity of the theoretical proposal itself was never allowed to become an empirical question. As a research strategy, this approach begins with the theory and then attempts to assimilate historical materials into it. In Durkheim's work, history is in fact subsumed within a typology of mechanical and organic types, leaving him unable to explore similarities and differences between specific religions. Concrete events and situations are significant only insofar as they fit the predetermined pattern. They become important not for their specific content, but only for their generalized significance to the model. The theory becomes the fact, and history is selectively culled to provide supporting evidence. As Lukes points out, for instance, whenever Australian materials failed to support his thesis, Durkheim turned to American evidence. "In brief, not only did Durkheim implausibly rest his entire theory on his single [Australian] experiment; he used data from outside that experiment whenever it failed to furnish him with the evidence he needed" (Lukes, 1973, p. 480).

The approach to empirical and historical materials recommended by Weber and Radin turns the Durkheimian conception upside-down. For them, events and activities should never be analyzed in terms of the investigator's model; rather, they are allowed to establish an open-ended pattern of their own. Events are important only for their causal significance in relation to the subject under investigation; they are allowed to become histories. Thus, a religion is to be studied in terms of its own unique history and not in reference to some imposed theoretical model. Whereas Durkheim postulates an *a priori* functionalist model and subsumes history in society, the Weberian approach is characterized by empirical, historical investigation.

These very different approaches to historical and empirical materials are perhaps best illustrated, at least on a theoretical level, by the way in which each regards its conceptual tools. As can be demonstrated by the concept of "religion" itself, Durkheim embraced what might be termed conceptual realism. In his work, religion is treated as a real entity, as a reality *sui generis*, and can therefore be discussed as something real rather than as an abstract concept. Thus, Durkheim can invest religion with a specific meaning (it operates functionally to provide moral integration, social solidarity, and order) despite the many differences between various religions. And since conceptual meanings are decided in advance of empirical investigation, they often display Procrustean selectivity in dealing with empirical realities.[18]

In contrast, for Weber, concepts provide only a means by which the infinite contents of the world may be ordered and studied. Ideal types may be regarded as "attempts on the basis of our present state of knowledge and the available conceptual patterns, to bring order into the chaos of those facts which we have drawn into the field circumscribed by our interest" (Weber, 1949, p. 105). Despite their obvious importance, conceptual tools provide no answers to the researcher's questions; they are instead themselves questions to be asked of empirical reality (hence Weber's statement of ideal types as probabilities). Concepts are heuristic devices by means of which the world may be investigated, and they are never the end or a substitute for the investigation itself. Thus, to Weber, religion remains only a concept referring to a broadly conceived institutional order roughly defined by its specific orientation toward and claim of access to the deity or divine values. The term gains more substantive contents only in reference to some empirical reality. Religion, therefore, can have no *a priori* meaning or social role. This is what is meant when Weber states that a definition of religion must await empirical investigation in a specific case.

For present purposes at least, the final major difference between Durkheimian and Weberian perspectives on religion concerns their respective conceptions of the religious domain. For Durkheim, as noted earlier, the sacred and profane represent dichotomous poles of experience. The sacred, in this conception, constitutes a realm apart from and unconnected to the concerns of everyday life. It is elevated by its own qualitative superiority to the profane well beyond contaminating contact with the petty concerns of routine existence.

As against Durkheim's division of experience, Weber and Radin suggest that religion is closely bound up with the "whole life of man," including its more mundane aspects. Durkheim's separation, Radin argues, eliminates the applicability of "history and economics . . . and religion becomes an entity in itself utterly divorced from the other aspects of individual and corporate life" (Radin, 1957, p. 157). Having dissolved the individual in history and subsumed history within society, Durkheim is unable to deal with specific religious actors or with the relationship between religion and the specific, historically developed characteristics of specific social structures. For Weber and Radin, on the other hand, religion is not something set above profane concerns but may itself constitute an arena in which conflicts over (profane) ideal and material interests are played out. Religion comes from life and is directed toward it; it serves not society but particular groups and individuals.

As a result of these premises—the societal level of analysis, the Procrustean use of theory, and the elevation of shared values beyond the sphere of profane struggles—the Durkheimian theory of religion and social order tends to neglect a whole range of empirical phenomena important to the subject. The empirical validity of the theory, in other words, is quite limited.

In the remainder of this study, several empirical applications of Durkheim's ideas are examined with reference to the historical and institutional context to which they refer. Since Durkheim himself did not undertake the empirical study that could make this kind of analysis possible, his own work is unsuitable for our purpose. However, Durkheim's ideas have been deeply influential, establishing an apparent elective affinity with the intellectual needs and interests of later thinkers who have in one way or another dealt with similar substantive and/or ideological concerns and who in doing so have given empirical substance to his general theory. It is to the work of some of these thinkers that we now turn.

Durkheim's intellectual heirs have not, of course, followed his lead blindly. Rather, they have modified his ideas, in some cases investing them with quite original emphases. Nonetheless, those of Durkheim's heirs to be considered have accepted, to greater and lesser degrees, major elements of his theory and approach, thereby incorporating into their own empirical studies the inherent limitations of each. By reexamining their empirical applications in historical and institutional context, not only can some of these theoretical limitations be demonstrated, but more important, a more complete and thus more empirically adequate understanding of the same phenomena with which they deal can be offered.

PART **II**

"CIVIL RELIGION" IN PRIMITIVE AND MODERN-INDUSTRIAL CONTEXTS

RELIGION AND RITUAL IN PRIMITIVE CONTEXT: RADCLIFFE-BROWN AND ANDAMAN FOOD RITES

Although Durkheim found his greatest following in sociology, the discipline he helped to create, he was also profoundly influential in the field of social anthropology. Within the latter field, perhaps no one has made greater use of Durkheim's general theoretical framework than A. R. Radcliffe-Brown.

Following Durkheim, Radcliffe-Brown contends that if a social group is to possess solidarity and be enduring, it must be "the object of sentiments of attachment in the minds of its members" (1952, p. 124). Rituals give periodic collective expression to such sentiments, for although organized around some "more or less concrete object" or symbol, "the primary object of the ritual attitude is the social order itself" (1952, p. 124). Thus, as the "regulated symbolic expressions of [social] sentiments," rituals "reaffirm, renew and strengthen those sentiments on which the social solidarity depends" (1952, p. 152), and transmit them from one generation to another. Indeed, Radcliffe-Brown insists, it is precisely "because they are part of the mechanism by which an orderly society maintains itself in existence [that] the rites of savages exist and persist" at all (1952, p. 152).

Radcliffe-Brown accepted this Durkheimian theory of rituals not simply as an orientation to empirical study, but as datum. Thus, for instance, he concluded beforehand that no primitive society could endure without some ritual mechanism to rekindle social sentiments in the minds of its members. As a result, the problem of social order is reduced to one of discerning and describing the particular rites, already known to exist, which perform this function for any given society. Among the Andaman islanders, Radcliffe-Brown suggests in his classic study (1964), the most important of these rites were those most closely associated with food.

The single most important social activity among the Andamanese, Radcliffe-Brown states, is obtaining food. The effort is a day-to-day activity in which all able-bodied members of the community are required to participate, either by hunting, fishing, or simple gathering. Not only is this collective effort obviously crucial to the physical survival of Andaman society and its members, but also the type and availability of food profoundly affect even their emotional life, constituting "the chief source of those variations or oscillations between conditions of euphoria and dysphoria" (1964, p. 270). Thus, food obtains a social importance not simply in the sense that it satisfies hunger, but in that during efforts to obtain it, "with their daily instances of collaboration and mutual aid, there continuously occur those inter-relations of interests which bind the individual men, women and children into a society" (1952, p. 151).

Because of the central and social importance of food to the Andamanese, Radcliffe-Brown argues, it is in connection with it that social sentiments are most frequently called into play. It therefore seems appropriate that "it should be through his relation to food that the child should be taught his relation to the society, and thus have those sentiments implanted in him or brought to the necessary degree of strength" (1964, p. 277). This, of course, involves rituals, the specific means by which social sentiments are transmitted.

During their early years, Andamanese children experience few restraints over their behavior and endure few social obligations. They are freely provided with food and, being the last to go hungry, are largely unaware of its social importance or of the fact that it is obtained only by the skill and effort of others. At some point, however, usually puberty, the child enters *aka-op*, a period during which he or she ritually abstains from eating each one of the community's most important foods. These restraints, Radcliffe-Brown indicates, "are not imposed by one person, but by the whole society backed by the whole force of tradition" (1964, p. 277). *Aka-op* may last "only one or several years," depending on the restricted food and, in some cases, the judgment of the older men.

As the period of abstention ends for each food, the initiate (for these are rites of passage) is required to observe certain ritual customs. For some foods these are relatively minor affairs, the only ritual observed being "that the food must be given (to the initiate) by an older man, who is himself free to eat it" (1964, p. 97). Rites involving other foods, particularly pork and turtle, are "fairly elaborate." Of the latter rites especially, "some . . . are painful, and all solemn and awe-inspiring." As a result of these ceremonies, Radcliffe-Brown concludes:

> Through a series of years, just at what is, for physio-
> logical reasons, the most impressionable age, the
> individual learns to subordinate his own desires to the
> requirements of the society or of custom, as explain-
> ed to him by his elders. He is thus impressed, in a
> forcible manner, with the importance of the moral
> law, and at the same time he is impressed with a
> sense of the social value of food. The ceremonies
> thus afford a moral education adapted to the re-
> quirements of life as it is lived in the Andamans.
> [1964, p. 177]

Hence, through Andaman rites of passage the initiate is impress-ed with the social value of food and is made to feel the moral force of society, thus keeping alive the sentiments on which social order and cohesion depend. In this connection also, Radcliffe-Brown mentions, almost as an afterthought, the initi-ate is instilled with "the respect for elders which is a most important element in the regulation of social life in all savage communities" (1964, p. 278).

Radcliffe-Brown adopted the functionalist method in his studies in large part as a self-conscious effort to overcome the defects of social evolutionism, the approach favored by most of his contemporaries. Their efforts, he contended, amounted to little more than descriptions of the origins and development of observed phenomena derived from conjectural reconstruc-

tions of history.[1] Social functionalism overcomes that problem
by dispensing with the historical record (which in primitive
societies is largely unavailable anyway) and by viewing presently
existing phenomena in terms of the contributions they make to
the society of which they are a part.

Radcliffe-Brown's adoption of functionalism was regarded at
the time as a decided advance over social evolutionism. Yet,
his own theoretical framework also entails limitations, particularly in its neglect of a range of empirical information about,
for instance, primitive puberty rites which is obtainable without
conjecture. The greater empirical depth that is possible contributes significantly to our understanding of the social importance
of such rites, as can be demonstrated through the work of
Paul Radin.

As seen from Radin's perspective, the Durkheimian approach
to religion incorporates two related deficiencies. First, it neglects
the concrete, specific individual, tending to deal instead only
with abstract or generalized individuals, or man in general. As
a result, the points of view of particular people in particular
situations are ignored in favor of abstract generalizations. Moreover, Radin would contend that the Durkheimian approach
tends to neglect the socioeconomic context in which points of
view are shaped, focusing instead on religion as in some way
set apart from and above ordinary life. Yet, "if an analysis of
religion is to mean anything, it must envisage the manner in
which religion is embedded in life and not examine merely the
beliefs, rituals, and speculations as such" (Radin, 1957, p. 58).
Most important of the exigencies of life in which primitive
religions are embedded, moreover, are those most important
to the struggle for survival: the economic and material. In sum,
Radin contends, the more important question to ask of a primitive rite is not its social function, but who in the community
benefits most from its exercise. Who controls the rites and is
most committed to them?

In the Andaman case, as in most hunting and fishing societies,
the answer to these questions is rather obvious: the older males
derive greatest benefit from religious rites. We should recall that
the restrictions that prohibit Andaman youth from eating certain
choice foods last for a number of years, during which time more
is available for others, and that the rites are controlled by older

males to whom the youth "subordinates his desires" in the present in the hope that he will occupy the privileged role later in life. Although Radcliffe-Brown does not mention this practice among the Andamanese, in similar rites in other societies (the Arunta, for instance), the initiate is often required to make regular gifts of food to the older men.

"To judge from the situation in the majority of hunting tribes," Radin indicates, the elders "concentrated their efforts upon securing control of whatever religious and magical machinery the community happened to possess" (1971, p. 213) in order to retain the prerogatives and privileges accompanying their social dominance. They were aided immeasurably in this effort by religious formulators, who developed into a priesthood of some sort wherever economic conditions permitted and began to pursue a twofold purpose. The first of these was to "elaborate and manipulate the religious beliefs [so that] they would strengthen the authority of the elders, in this manner also strengthening their own, for they generally belong to the same group" (1957, p. 18). Second, they sought to attain and enhance their own economic security, which generally meant having food provided for them, thereby increasing their leisure time for further religious pursuits.[2]

For Radin, it is quite apparent that in such rites as the Andaman puberty ceremonies facets of the magico-folkloristic background of the society have been integrated into a consistent whole by religious formulators and manipulated "to serve direct social-economic purposes." Moreover, it is apparent

> that these economic purposes do not always or even generally have only the good of the community as their primary objective and that, not infrequently, they directly serve the interests of certain groups or classes. . . . Manifestly this is not the work of the group as such nor the folk-soul expressing itself unconsciously in obedience to some mystical urge. Rather it is the accomplishment of specific individuals banded together formally or informally, of individuals who possess a marked capacity for articulating their ideas and for organizing them into coherent systems, systems naturally which would

be of profit to them and to those with whom they
are allied. [1971, p. 171]

In this sense, the ceremonies in question appear primarily as
rituals of dominance and deference and legitimation, depending
on the participant's perspective.

None of these comments, of course, serves to refute Radcliffe-
Brown's argument that Andaman puberty rites are socially
functional. Indeed, the rites in question clearly do seem to have
the result Radcliffe-Brown attributes to them. What Radin's
discussion indicates, however, is that primitive rites involve a
practical dimension as well as the purely religious aspects emphasized by Radcliffe-Brown, and that the rites serve the specific needs of specific people. When these features of the rites
are taken into consideration, it becomes possible to suggest
that different participants are differently committed to the
rituals for different reasons. Moreover, neither the "social sentiments" nor the "ritual attitude" itself are necessarily even
experienced by all participants, as Radcliffe-Brown at least
implicitly assumes. Rather, owing to their different substantive grounds for participation, different groups may experience
collective rites in quite different ways. Even though Radcliffe-
Brown's general conclusion is indisputable, by considering the
participants' points of view, greater empirical depth is possible
concerning the mechanisms by which primitive rituals operate,
and thus, by which they contribute to social order.

And yet, it is at least possible to understand Radcliffe-Brown's
neglect of the materials we have sought to recapture. The primitive world remains enchanted, full of mystery and awe. It is not
at all difficult to envisage a relatively small and isolated group
of people, whose lives are otherwise lacking in spectacle, collectively losing themselves in ritual euphoria and thus renewing a
sense of their own "peoplehood." To imagine a similar basis
for the renewal of social order in a diverse, rationalized, disen-
chanted, modern-industrial society, however, seems a far less
tenable prospect.

While Durkheim formulated his theory of religion on the
basis of information about primitive societies he had never
visited, Radcliffe-Brown accepted that theory as established
and applied it as an explanation of a society he had actually

visited without considering that he might collect new data to refine or refute the theory. In this sense, he seems to have treated Durkheim more as a prophet who supplied him with a vision of the world than as an investigator who had raised some intriguing questions. This quirk in the history of social theory has led to ironic consequences. Radcliffe-Brown's work later supplied theoretical support for the application of Durkheim's theory to the analysis of modern industrial society. It was assumed that the study of "simple" societies could reveal the fundamental dimensions of more "complex" societies because, at bottom, the essential foundations of all societies were similar. And given these essential similarities, it could be further assumed that the same theory which seemed so useful in explaining social cohesion in primitive societies could also be successfully applied to modern industrial types. In this sense, Durkheim is brought full circle in the work of Lloyd Warner, Talcott Parsons, and Robert Bellah.

HEIRS OF DURKHEIM IN AMERICA: WARNER, PARSONS, AND BELLAH

In their studies of American society, Warner, Parsons, and Bellah take for granted the Durkheimian proposition that to remain viable the society requires a set of common values and symbols that are invested with religious significance and that serve as a focus for moral integration. However, in applying Durkheim's proposition, they have emphasized different features of his ideas and interpreted them somewhat differently in accordance with their own substantive and intellectual problems. That is, in applying the ideas of their common intellectual ancestry, each examines a different feature of American society.

Tribal Townsfolk: Civil Religion in Newburyport

W. Lloyd Warner's intellectual kinship with Durkheim can be traced through the lineage of Radcliffe-Brown, with whom he studied at the University of Chicago. In 1926, at Radcliffe-Brown's suggestion, Warner went to Australia to study the Murngin, an aboriginal tribe still relatively "uncontaminated" by contact with industrial civilization (Warner, 1977). Applying the theoretical insights of his intellectual heritage, there Warner found a well-integrated society whose moral solidarity was established and sustained in part by the symbolic constraints of totemic beliefs and rituals. Elaboration of this point is unnecessary, for while Warner did offer novel interpretations of some findings, the study essentially affirms Durkheim's own general conclusions regarding Australian aborigines. He found the same functional links between religion and society that both Durkheim and Radcliffe-Brown had claimed were characteristic of mechanically integrated societies.

After completing his work with the Murngin, Warner returned to the United States and began to direct research on an extensive study of Newburyport, Massachusetts. Assuming that the same methods would again be applicable, he sought to "interpret the meanings and social functions of . . . American symbol system" (1959, p. 4). Warner did recognize that American society was neither segmental nor homogeneous, and that it was characterized by considerable structural and symbolic diversity. Nonetheless, he assumed that "complex societies must have a common core of basic understanding known and used by everyone or their complex and diverse symbolic superstructures will not stand. They need general symbol systems that everyone not only knows but *feels*" (1959, p. 4). This being the case, he argued, the increasing differentiation of American society is accompanied by "increasing generalization and standardization of public symbols understood by all levels of the society and by every kind of person." Despite "the increasing tendency of American society to form each individual into a semiautonomous unit and private social system of his own, the second, or unifying tendency is directly related to the social need to maintain minimum cohesion and the larger solidarity. Over-all integrative symbol systems which everyone understands and which evoke common sentiments, values, and beliefs in all members of the society are expressions of this second tendency" (1959, pp. 232-33).

Although Warner clearly recognizes structural and symbolic differentiation, he insists that the unity of society is achieved by evoking similar responses to certain generalized (sacred) symbols in widely dissimilar groups and individuals (that is, "all members"). That is, while he recognized Newburyport to be "organized," in Durkheim's sense, he treated it as though it were integrated mechanically. Emphasis was placed not on organic interdependence, but on solidarity based on moral consensus and likeness. Instead of looking for moral individualism, Warner sought a mechanical, monolithic symbolic belief system capable of integrating the whole tribe at once.

Having already determined the existence of a common core of symbolic meanings capable of providing a cultural unity over and above the everyday differentiations of class, ethnic, status, and sectarian loyalties, Warner sought to locate the ritual mechanism of integration in one of the few public events in which "the whole town" participated: the events surrounding the Memorial Day parade.

Value Consensus and the Social System

Despite the widespread dissemination of his use of Durkheim's ideas on common values, collective ritual, and social integration, Lloyd Warner represents only one strand of the interpretation of Durkheim by American sociologists. Talcott Parsons supplies another major line of interpretation.

Parsons was introduced to Durkheim's work partly under the direct tutelage of Bronislaw Malinowski and, apparently more important, through the indirect influence of Radcliffe-Brown, whom he cites with approval (1937, p. xi). His interpretation of Durkheim's ideas is nonetheless distinctly his own, having found it necessary to "unlearn" many initial impressions of Durkheim's work (1977, p. 25). It was ultimately through Parsons's extremely influential interpretation of his work that Durkheim found his widest American audience.

According to Parsons, Durkheim's ideas underwent a fundamental change during the course of his career.[1] *The Division of Labor in Society*, as Parsons sees it, was only a formative work that sketched out inchoately the basic problems which Durkheim would later look upon with a more mature eye. This interpretation allowed Parsons to assign little weight to that book. As a result, he generally neglects Durkheim's arguments regarding the division of labor, the forced division of labor, the relationship between the state and occupational associations, and other features of institutional structure. That is, he neglects Durkheim's larger concern for the moral and institutional change from mechanical to organic solidarity. Thus, Durkheim's original emphasis on the problem of order *within* a broad context of moral and institutional development is interpreted by Parsons to be simply an abstract problem of order.

This deemphasis of institutional structure is carried over fully into Parsons's own treatment of the problem of order. In the absence of a structural referent, Parsons can contrast moral consensus and anomie only at a purely abstract, conceptual level. But since these opposing states can be properly assessed only with regard to the changing institutional structure of society, Parsons is left with only the abstracted common or core values of a society divorced from existing institutional arrangements. Value consensus is made a system property regardless of structural features, which are examined separately. In this sense,

> the value-standards which define institutionalized
> role-expectations assume to a greater or less degree
> a moral significance. Conformity with them becomes,
> that is, to some degree a matter of the fulfillment
> of obligations which ego carries relative to the in-
> terests of the larger action system in which he is
> involved, that is a social system. The sharing of such
> common value patterns, entailing a sense of respon-
> sibility for the fulfillment of obligations, then creates
> a solidarity among those mutually oriented to the
> common values. . . .
> [W]ithout the attachment to the constitutive
> common values the collectivity tends to dissolve.
> [1951, p. 41]

Common values are, therefore, crucial to the effective function-ing and continued integration of the social system. This notion more than any other connects Parsons to the "civil religion" theme with which we are interested.

Having determined at a theoretical level that common values are functionally indispensable for social systems, Parsons was led to indicate just what these values might be in particular cases. For the most part, when addressing this issue, Parsons was con-tent to remain at a rather abstract level, referring to a typology of general pattern variables rather than offering specific empiri-cal details. With reference to American society, however, Parsons did provide more substantive suggestions, thereby adding spe-cific content to his theory of core values.

The National Village: Civil Religion in America

For the most part, Robert Bellah's work on civil religion may be viewed as an effort to explain, in the specific case of America, the details of social coherence and viability in highly specialized societies. Strongly influenced by Parsons, his teacher and colleague, Bellah also finds in value consensus the key to social solidarity. Thus, he argues that "any coherent and viable society rests upon a common set of moral understandings about good and bad, right and wrong, in the realm of individual and social action. . . . (T)hese common moral understandings must also rest in turn upon a common set of religious understandings . . . that provide a picture of the universe in terms of which the moral understandings make sense" (1975, p. ix). To this initial assumption, Bellah adds emphases derived from his own rather sophisticated interpretation of Durkheim's arguments.

According to Bellah, Durkheim finally resolved the inconsistencies involved in his contention that the *conscience collective* is progressively enfeebled by the advance of the division of labor. While he retained the structural typology of segmental and organized societies, Bellah asserts, in his later work "the contrast of the two types of society at the moral level has become the contrast of two types of common conscience rather than the contrast between the strength or weakness of the common conscience" (1973, p. xli). Moreover, as a different type, the modern *conscience collective* operates in a different way to sustain social solidarity. Specifically, while external discipline remains a feature of the new secular morality, it is now tempered by the *rational* exercise of individual autonomy and self-determination in accordance with the principles of moral individualism.[2] And because rational individual judgment is now possible, the attachment to society and social groups "is no longer . . . blind and uncritical." Rather, integration and solidarity are dependent upon the groups' regard for human dignity and justice, the key components of the emergent value consensus.

Under this new secular morality, the state has attained a position of special importance. According to Bellah, following Durkheim,

> Since the state is the organ of consciousness of so-
> ciety, it must have a relation to that common
> conscience which is at the same time moral and
> religious. The state must be ultimately related to the
> deepest level of value consensus in the society, what
> I have called . . . the civil religion. And so here . . .
> Durkheim brings in the religion of humanity and the
> cult of the individual. Since the cult of the individual
> is the highest moral ideal of society and the state is
> society's organ of consciousness, Durkheim says
> that it is the role of the state to "organize the cult,
> to be the head of it and to ensure its regular work-
> ing and development." [Bellah, 1973, p. xxxv]

Consequently, insofar as the state embodies the principles of
moral individualism, it enjoys "a certain moral primacy in the
new secular morality (in this way replacing the church)" (1973,
p. xli). It is the universal, humanistic values which transcend
the state, however, and not the state itself which is important.

It is essentially this background of ideas, especially the emphasis on shared, transcendent values, that Bellah brings to his
studies of civil religion in America. Generally, Bellah does on
a national scale what Warner did to Newburyport: he looks for
a set of values and symbols which nearly everyone holds in
common and to which everyone responds similarly. Consequently, at some points Bellah's analysis implies the image of a national
village, transcending all religious, racial, and class differences.

The American Creed Reexamined: Questions
and Considerations

As these summaries indicate, Warner, Parsons, and Bellah all
accept the proposition that the stability or viability of a society
rests upon its possession of a set of common values and symbols
around which the society is integrated. The proposition is taken
as an article of sociological truth, as a matter already concluded,
and, thus, as a resource in their subsequent studies of the "common faith" of Americans.

In following chapters, their accounts of American "core
values" are reexamined by placing them within the historical

and institutional context to which they refer. In this way, a more empirically grounded understanding of these values and their relation to American social order can be offered. Since Warner, Parsons, and Bellah are participants in that context, we also move from the intellectual antecedents of their thought, via Durkheim, to the social and historical influence on their own intellectual productions.

This effort certainly is not meant to suggest that the values and symbols to which Warner, Parsons, and Bellah refer do not exist or that they are socially unimportant. To the contrary, these values have unquestionably been prominent throughout American history, and remain so. Much less acceptable is the argument that they have achieved transcendence, that they stand apart from and above the nation itself and its institutions, or perhaps even that they are genuinely common. To make such an argument is quite different than attributing social dominance to these values. It is rather to contend that they exist almost independently of, or at least are only tangentially connected to, social structure. As all three suggest and Bellah makes explicit, American civil religion exists, so to speak, "out there," as a motivating orientation for Americans and as an objective yardstick by which the performance of groups and institutions can be measured. By this argument, the ideology is detached from its historical location among the specific groups in society who have served as its carriers.

Like any morality or religious ideology, American civil religion must have specific origins and a specific history; it must express the experiences and aspirations, the ideal and material needs and interests of certain groups. In a nation as diverse as our own, "the experience of the American people" seems far too broad to serve as a reasonable referent. Indeed, as Bellah himself acknowledges, American civil religion

> has never been shared by all Americans. At the very
> beginning it is estimated that about a third of the
> colonists subscribed to its tenets, another third were
> loyal to Britain and the rest remained indifferent.
> In the late 1850's it is clear that the articulate
> spokesmen of the south had abandoned the faith
> and that the Douglas Democrats in the north were

> indifferent to it. Lincoln's effort to recall the nation
> to its "ancient faith" was a long uphill battle. [Bel-
> lah, 1976b, p. 154]

This passage suggests that the history of American civil religion is not the story of the march of the American spirit, its
travels and travails, but rather is the story of groups competing
to define what the nation should be and which morality should
prevail. Throughout American history, what Bellah calls our
"ancient faith" was only one among several ideologies that
competed at various times. There appears to be no good or
just reason to declare that any one such ideology embodies the
"highest values" of the society (except from the perspective
of these values themselves), but only that at most points in
American history it has achieved dominance. The champions
of various aspects of American civil religion have changed over
time; they have lost some battles but, until recently, won most.
And therein is our problem.

From this point of view, we shall wish to know, to paraphrase Weber, whose "intellectual child" is that constellation
of beliefs, values, and symbols referred to as American civil
religion? Through which particular agents and by what particular means have its contents been championed? How has it
been developed, modified, and adapted to meet the demands
of changing historical and institutional circumstances? How
were the principles of American civil religion made dominant,
and, once dominant, how have they been sustained? Finally,
what is the status of American civil religion today? If, as Bellah
suggests, it appears now as a "broken shell," what has caused
the egg to crack and why?

Analyzing the work of Warner, Parsons, and Bellah in terms
of these questions enables us both to reexamine the foundations
of the Durkheimian theory of religion and to examine the notion of civil religion as it has been derived from Durkheim's work.
In addition, it provides an opportunity to trace through some
transvaluations of original Puritan values to their later secular
manifestations in a theory of civil religion that has come to
connect religious and national values.

SAINTS AND CITIZENS: THE PROTESTANT FOUNDATIONS OF AMERICAN CIVIL RELIGION

Covenant and Community: Theological Foundations of Puritan Civic Morality

Like so many other of America's cultural components, its traditional ideology of civic unity as a delicate balance between individual freedom and collective obligations has its origins among the New England Puritans. By and large, the entire corpus of Puritan political thinking rested upon just such a conception of society, characteristically expressed in the form of a covenant.

Of course, theological doctrine, not political theory, provided the source of the covenant philosophy. The kind of individual freedom sought by the Puritan had nothing to do with escaping political repression per se, and was only secondarily connected to the attainment of political rights and privileges. The later-developed principles of Jeffersonian democracy could not have been further removed from the thought of those who sought to construct a City of God. Any contributions Puritanism might have made to American democracy were most certainly the result of accident rather than intent. The Holy Commonwealth was a dictatorship of saints and, as Perry Miller submits, was never intended to be anything else. Hence, for the Puritans individual freedom meant something entirely different from that suggested by later democratic notions. Theirs, after all, was a universe dominated by religious ideals and ultimate truths, next to which political liberties could attain only secondary significance.

Perhaps the most fundamental of Puritanism's religious truths, and the one upon which the covenant philosophy is premised, is the doctrine of original sin. Adam's apostasy, the Puritans held, placed a burden of inherent sinfulness upon all his descendants. Thus separated from God and enslaved to their own sinful inheritance, people in nature were thought capable of any evil, thus raising for the Puritans a spectre of natural social and moral anarchy which, if anything, was even more harsh than the Hobbesian vision. Natural man holds much in common with "brute beasts," as one Puritan divine put it, and "hath liberty to do what he lists" in his relations with others. The imagery of New England parson John Barnard is even more striking. In the absence of any restraints on their sinful natures, he wrote,

> the different Views and Interests, Humours and Passions of Mankind, and these often excited by false Principles, and strongly moved by a corrupt Bias on the Mind, would unavoidably produce a continual Jarr and Strife, a constant Endeavour in every one to promote his own, and gratify Self, and so a perpetual Preying of the Stronger upon the Weaker; and no Man would be able to call any Thing his own, nor be secure of his Life and Limbs, from the Rapine, and Violence, of his fellow Creature; and by how much the Views, Interest, and Passions of Men, are more numerous, appropriated, and strong, by so much would they become fiercer upon one another than the Beasts of Prey. [Quoted from Miller and Johnson, 1938, p. 272]

As long as this pessimistic doctrine was taken seriously, it could only be from his own inherent moral depravity and distance from God that the Puritan sought relief. But although freedom from bondage to sin was the goal, individuals were unable to acquire it by their own efforts alone. The conditions for its attainment were, first of all, the arbitrary contribution of grace on God's part and, second, the voluntary reception of God's spirit on the part of those He elects. In receiving the spirit of God, or entering into the "invisible covenant," the individual essentially struck a bargain with Providence, receiving assurance of his own redemption in return for a pledge to fulfill God's will.

The freedom attained by a person's participation in this covenant was of two distinct kinds, though to the Puritan mind they were inseparable. The regenerate was first released from his "natural" condition and liberated from his enslavement to sin. To be sure, this emancipation could not be completed as long as he retained the creaturely longings and carnal desires that were the curse and bane of every saint, but the internal covenant imparted courage and strength so that, with constant diligence, the tendency to sin could at least be resisted. Release from his sinful nature, in turn, provided the regenerate with the freedom to serve God and do *only* as He commands. Obeying God's commands was perceived not as an obligation, but as a genuine liberty to do "that only which is good, just, and honest." And even though, as Winthrop remarked, such freedom could be maintained only "under the authority of Christ . . . his yoke is so easy and sweet . . . as a brides ornaments." Liberty was possible only under the authority of God.

Under the terms of the invisible covenant, each saint was to serve God and enhance His glory to the best of his or her ability. God's glory was more greatly augmented, however, not by so many individual worshippers each making their separate contributions, but through concerted effort. Consequently, a fundamental responsibility (or freedom) of the elect was to join together in churches where they would jointly covenant with the Almighty and form a visible union of saints.[1] The logical extension of the "internal covenant" between each saint and God was thus an external church covenant between God and His elect combined. The church covenant was "not another Covenant contrary to the Covenant of Grace, which every beleever is brought into at his first conversion, but an open profession of a mans' subjection to that very Covenant, specially in the things which concerne Church estate" (quoted in Miller, 1954, p. 446).

The church covenant, therefore, offered each saint the opportunity to publicly profess his faith, to make visible his internal covenant with God. It also required of God's Chosen further responsibilities not only to God but, under His auspices, to each other and to their communion as well. Church members were jointly obliged, for instance, to limit their congregation to genuine saints (at least as far as this was possible), to raise their children in the ways of the Lord, and to live together in peace, fellowship, and "brotherly affection" according to God's plan. In the churches, Winthrop admonished, "wee must bring into familiar and constant practice, as in this duty of loue wee must loue brotherly without dissimulation, wee must loue one another with a pure hearte feruently wee must beare one anothers burthens, wee must not looke onely on our owne things, but allsoe on the things of our brethren . . . " (quoted in Miller and Johnson, 1938, p. 198). Thus, to the liberation from natural sinfulness, the church covenant added a freedom (responsibility) of self-sacrifice and community service.

In these two covenants, the Puritans had agreed to abide by God's rules both individually and collectively. Yet, as they knew, the rigors of God's service were difficult, even impossible, to sustain at all times. Not every person was a saint, and even those who were could be occasionally slack in resisting temptations and fulfilling their obligations to God. Moreover, the unregenerates, who constituted perhaps 80 percent of New England's population, could not even be counted on to try. They, after all, lacked the benefit of conversion and unless restrained could be expected to pursue their natural sinful inclinations to the shame of the whole community and detriment to the glory of God. In addition to their private and collective agreements with God, then, the Puritans further required some instrument with which to enforce their terms. For surely, as it is stated in the Cambridge Platform, "Idolatry, Blasphemy, Heresy, venting corrupt and pernicious opinions, that destroy the foundation, open contempt of the word preached profanation of the Lord's Day, disturbing the peaceable administration and exercise of the worship and holy things of God, and the like, are to be restrayned, and punished by civil authority" (quoted in Schneider, 1958, p. 24). To this end, once again adopting the pattern of God's association with mortals, the Puritans established a third compact, a governmental or civil covenant[2] to whose discipline all of New England would be subject. The Holy Commonwealth would set an example of God's plan which the rest of the world would do well to follow.

Theoretically, under the civil covenant, church and state, ministers and magistrates, were to exercise separate responsibilities. In churches God's word would be preached; in courts it would be enforced. Both spheres of order, however, were conceived to be under the same divine authority and guidance. It could make little difference, therefore, if the distinction between political and theological authorities was blurred since both were concerned "to take care of matters of religion . . . of righteousness and honesty . . . of all godliness" (quoted in Schneider, 1958, p. 24). Hence, in practice the church and civil covenants were often indistinguishable both from each other and from the invisible covenant of which they were but logical extensions. Separate in theory, they were married in fact as pillars of the City of God.

Within the Commonwealth, their unity was furthered by the fact that, generally, only church members could vote for or be elected as magistrates or other officials. Such limiting conditions posed no problems for the Puritans. For them, democracy could be reasonably extended only to the converted. Otherwise, it would surely prove to be the means by which unregenerates could assume power, a clear danger to be avoided at all costs. John Cotton's remarks were typical in warning his people "to give mortall men no greater power than they are content they shall use, for use it they will; and unless they be better taught of God, they will use it ever and anon" (quoted in Miller and Johnson, 1938, p. 212) to the detriment of God's work and the common good.

Despite what to the contemporary mind appears as a distinctly authoritarian, undemocratic means of self-governance,[3] each of the three compacts, the internal as well as church and civil covenants, was framed within that context of intense individualism and "inner-directedness" for which the Puritan Ethic is famous. The participation of any individual was thought to be entirely voluntary. Each person bargained with the Almighty for his or her own soul, and God would certainly not force conversion on anyone unwilling to seek it. As mentioned previously, membership and active participation in the church covenant were regarded as positive freedoms resulting from regeneration. Even outward obedience to the rules of the Commonwealth was regarded as voluntary. Those unwilling to abide by the laws of the civil covenant, and especially those of contrary faiths, were, as Nathaniel Ward warned, at liberty to stay out of New England or to suffer the consequences of their insubordination.[4] Puritan individualism was very much alive, then, even under the authoritarianism of self-righteousness.

Clearly, however, individualism as conceived by the Puritans makes sense only within a collective context. Once voluntary choice was exercised and a bargain with God was struck, the individual was free only to follow the Lord's ways, and those ways emphasized social as well as personal duties. Although the rights and dignity of the individual were sincerely respected by Puritan opinion, their strong sense of common purpose, collective obligations, and joint accountability to God committed each person to serving the community as best as he or she could.

The terms of the covenant made personal wants nearly synonymous with communal needs, thus effectively harnessing individual activities to the attainment of collective goals and the common good. In turn, the community as a whole was also obligated to maintain certain standards of performance, failure of which would be considered a breach of the social covenant certain to invite divine desertion or even retribution. In their individual and collective lives, the saints of New England both desired and were required to become "models of Christian charity" whose primary concern was for the collective welfare, both spiritual and material. Hence, the solidarity of brotherhood was both a privilege and a responsibility.

This delicate balance of individual freedom and community obligations, or individualism within a collective moral and religious framework of fellowship and brotherhood, constitutes the core of a civic morality that would greatly influence the subsequent social and cultural development of American society. No better summation of the manifold themes of this morality can be offered than John Winthrop's reminder to his fellow voyagers aboard the *Arabella* of the tasks that would soon confront them and of "the cause betweene God and us." The eloquence and imagery of Winthrop's sermon (quoted from Miller and Johnson, 1938, pp. 198-99) make their own apology for the length with which it is repeated here:

> Thus stands the cause betweene God and vs, wee
> are entered into Covenant with him for this worke,

wee haue taken out a Commission, the Lord hath
giuen us leaue to drawe our owne Articles wee haue
professed to enterprise these Accions vpon these and
these ends, wee haue herevpon besought him favour
and blessing: Now if the Lord shall please to heare
vs, and bring vs in peace to the place wee desire,
then hath hee ratified this Covenant and sealed our
Commission, [and] will expect a strickt performance
of the Articles contained in it, but if wee shall neglect the observacion of these Articles which are the
ends wee haue propounded, and dissembling with
our God, shall fall to embrace this present world
and prosecute our carnall intencions seekeing greate
things for our selues and our posterity, the Lord will
surely breake out in wrathe against vs be revenged of
such a periured people and make vs knowe the price
of the breache of such a Covenant.

Now the onely way to avoyde this shipwracke and
to provide for our posterity is to followe the Counsell
of Micah, to doe Justly, to loue mercy, to walke
humbly with our God, for this end, wee must be
knitt together in this worke as one man, wee must
entertaine each other in brotherly Affeccion, wee
must be willing to abridge our selues of our super-
fluities, for the supply of others necessities, wee
must vphold a familiar Commerce together in all
meekenes, gentlenes, patience and liberallity, wee
must delight in eache other, make others Condicions
our owne reioyce together, mourne together, labour,
and suffer together, allwayes haueing before our eyes
our Commission and Community in the worke, our
Community as members of the same body, soe shall
wee keepe the vnitie of the spirit in the bond of
peace, the Lord will be our God and Delight to dwell
among vs, as his owne people and will commaund
a blessing vpon vs in all our wayes, soe that wee shall
see much more of his wisdome power goodnes and
truthe then formerly wee haue beene acquainted
with, wee shall finde that the God of Israell is among
vs, when tenn of vs shall be able to resist a thousand

of our enemies, when hee shall make vs a prayse and
glory, that men shall say of succeeding plantacions:
the lord make it like that of New England: for wee
must Consider that wee shall be as a Citty vpon a
Hill, the eies of all people are vpon vs; soe that if
wee shall deale falsely with our god in this worke
wee haue vndertaken and soe cause him to with-
drawe his present help from vs, wee shall be made
a story and a by-word through the world. . . . Be-
loued there is now sett before vs life, and good,
deathe and euill in that wee are Commaunded this
day to loue the Lord our God, and to loue one another to walke in his wayes and to keepe his Commandments and his Ordinance, and his lawes, and
the Articles of our Covenant with him that wee may
liue and be multiplyed, and that the Lord our God
may blesse vs in the land whether wee goe to possesse
it: But if our heartes shall turne away soe that wee
will not obey, but shall be seduced and worshipp . . .
other Gods our pleasures, and proffitts, and serue
them; it is propounded vnto vs this day, we shall
surely perishe out of the good Land whether wee
passe over this vast Sea to possesse it;

> Therefore lett vs choose life,
> that wee, and our Seede,
> may liue, by obeyeing his
> voyce, and cleaueing to him,
> for hee is our life, and
> our prosperity.

Sects and Citizens: Institutional Supports for Protestant Civic Morals

The historical significance of Puritan contributions to America, including its conception of civic virtue, may be at least
partly attributed to several unique circumstances. As "the first
new nation," America lacked any strong traditions built up
over centuries past. There existed no established social structure
with which the first settlers would have to contend. No stable

aristocracy, or even a class structure, waited to exact deference
and tribute, and no national church stood intolerant of heter-
odoxy. The New World offered both escape and opportunity
for the disgruntled of Europe, most notable of whom were the
Puritans themselves. Little wonder, then, that they beheld in
America the promise of potential paradise.

In the absence of any indigenous ways of life, at least as far
as they were concerned,[5] the Puritans eagerly instituted their
own. Precisely because of America's cultural barrenness, the
cultural patterns established by its earliest settlers were endowed with an historical significance unwarranted by their numbers
alone. The mere fact that the Puritans were among the first to
reach American shores, and were surely the best organized,
thus contributed greatly to the pervasiveness of the cultural
legacy they bequeathed to later generations. Their inner-drive
and self-righteous surety of a God-given task to master the
world, which Weber thought so important, no doubt also contributed to the endurance that inheritance has displayed.

Owing to these conditions, the New England Puritans stood
in good position to ensure the survival of their ethos. Nonetheless, even with so many unique supports, that Puritan theological doctrine in itself could account for its own subsequent
secular influence is doubtful at best. No idea or ideology is
guaranteed survival, much less continued significance, by virtue
of the inherent persuasiveness of its contents alone. To emerge
as a force in history, to become a relatively autonomous principle, and to acquire, as it were, a life of its own, any idea, ideology, or morality requires institutionalization and a set of "carriers" to champion its cause. For the Puritan ethos, including its
civic morality, both were ensured through the agency of the Protestant sect, especially by its techniques of admission and
discipline.

Like virtually all the other Protestant groups who settled in
America, the Puritans organized themselves according to sectarian principles or, in Weber's (1946, p. 306) words, as "a
voluntary organization of only those who . . . are religiously
and morally qualified."[6] On the one hand, a fundamental responsibility of the converted was to seek and gain admission to
a church, thereby forming a visible union of saints. On the
other, because the church was to be based on a mutual cove-

nant, membership could logically be extended to saints alone, to those who had already undertaken the internal covenant with God. This latter requirement proved to be a matter of great concern, for the Puritan divines were convinced—and rightly so since church membership entailed obvious personal and social advantages—that true saints would not be the only applicants. Hence, their problem was to establish recognizable and "infallible signes" of grace, application of which could serve to separate sheep from goats.

Ideally, spiritual quality alone would provide the criteria for membership. Yet, establishing an applicant's spiritual credentials was a matter of no small difficulty when, according to John Cotton (quoted in Miller and Johnson, 1938, p. 316), "even Eagle-eyed Christians will have much adoe so to discern of sanctification in themselves, before they see their justification, as to cut off all hypocrites from having the like in them." The difference between outward respect for and obedience to the law and genuine "Sanctification . . . which is of the Gospel, is a matter so narrow, that the Angels in Heaven have much ado to discern who differ" (quoted in Miller, 1954, p. 52). Unlike the more fortunate angels, however, the Puritans were required by the terms of the covenant to make just such a distinction.

Contributing to the urgency of resolving this problem was a basic structural feature of the Protestant sects: Responsibility for restricting membership was shared equally by all members and could not be escaped by deferring to clerical opinion. "The sect," wrote Weber (1946, p. 317), "placed disciplinary power predominantly into the hands of laymen. No spiritual authority could assume the community's joint responsibility before God." Thus, sect members exercised a collective duty to God to ensure that their body be kept pure and exclusive of the sinful, whose presence could prove both contaminating and embarrassing to their union. Every member was a judge whose judgments were judged in turn by God. There can be little wonder, under the circumstances, that so many New England sermons were concerned with the identification of God's chosen.[7]

The first indication of chosenness required was, of course, those signs of grace the individual hoped to find in himself. How was one to know of his own justification when neither good morals nor good works were reliable indicators? Even a hypocrite, after all, could lead a commendable life. In effect, the clergy answered, the Elect can find signs of their own grace only in the strength of their faith and the purity of their motives. Although the two might appear externally similar, true sheep are guided by the desire to enhance the glory of God, whereas goats will perceive in themselves less admirable motives. Not good deeds, then, but earnest intentions are characteristic of the genuine saint. Still, measuring the purity even of one's own intentions was no easy matter. Constant introspection was required as well as continuous self-control.[8] And following all his efforts at self-mastery, the true saint, upon recognizing his salvation, could take no credit for success. "[T] here is a reall difference in the presence of the Spirit," wrote John Cotton, "so also in the worke of faith in hypocrites, and the children of God, for one putteth confidence in himselfe in the gift received, and the other in Jehovah" (quoted in Miller and Johnson, 1938, pp. 316-17).

The individual, then, through great patience and diligence, might be reasonably certain of his own state of grace, but how were others to recognize it? Members of the sect, in deciding upon an applicant's spiritual credentials, obviously lacked access to his inner motives. On the other hand, they reasoned, if those motives were truly pure, the applicant's salvation would surely be revealed in his behavior. Proper conduct and good deeds, though useless in the attainment of salvation, might at least be recognized as evidence of its possession. Thus, the ethical responsibility of every saint was to maintain constant vigilance over the conduct of his brethren. The principle that each was his brother's keeper was firmly institutionalized.

Of course, conduct was hardly a completely reliable index of grace. The Puritans were never so confident of their methods, either in judging themselves or others, as to claim absolute certainty, for the Elect were known ultimately only to God. Mistakes would be made, and some unregenerates would inevitably deceive their judges into granting them sect membership. Yet, even God would expect as much from His imperfect servants. From the beginning the Visible Church of Saints was an ideal they knew could never be completely realized, but neither could they cease struggling to attain it. In offering His internal covenant to the fortunate Elect, God could look into the hearts of individuals; the Puritans could only rely on external evidence that the covenant had been made. Thus, whether truly saintly or not, any individual hoping to attain church membership would be required to display the appropriate conduct.

The admission and disciplinary mechanisms of the Protestant sects did not, however, merely restrict and direct external conduct. If that were the case, Puritan influence in America would have survived no longer than the Puritans themselves. Rather—and this was Weber's great contribution—the Protestant sects proved enormously successful at producing a particular personality type or "social character" by means of establishing and controlling the distribution of certain psychological "premiums." The result was not simply to emphasize various concrete activities, but to induce and sustain a whole way of life with its attendant ethos and morality. The Puritans set their "stamp" irrevocably on American society by means of their sectarian organization.

To be admitted to a Protestant sect, the applicant was required during a probationary period to demonstrate in conduct his possession of the ethical and characterological virtues which the sect demanded of its members. Of crucial significance, Weber felt, was the fact that the applicant must prove in advance of admittance his possession of those qualities, for this demanded of him that he consciously make himself over in conformity with sect requirements. Whereas for most people in all ages the rules of conduct for everyday life are a matter of habit seldom raised to the level of conscious awareness, for the sect applicant they were the object of intense scrutiny. His every action, however routine, had to be considered in advance in order to ensure its congruence with the sectarian ethos. Before the wary eyes of his judges, the applicant sought to master his own impulses, to systematically orient his actions, thoughts, and feelings toward the principles on which his admittance would depend. By means of such a thorough self-rationalization,[9] the individual anticipated and participated in his own socialization, self-consciously internalizing the group morality. He accomplished his own psychological and emotional adjustment, a transformation of his own character and personality.

That this transformation would not be reversed was further

ensured by the fact that, even following his admission, the sect member could never be relieved of these intense pressures toward self-control and self-conscious conformity. Because his standing and respect within the community were dependent upon his possession of the proper virtues, "the member had to prove repeatedly that he was endowed with these qualities" by constantly displaying them in his conduct. The character structure constructed by the Protestant sects was thus sustained by the requirement of continuous peer approval, the crucial condition from which its subsequent historical importance is derived. "According to all experience," Weber (1946, pp. 320-21) argues,

> there is no stronger means of breeding traits than through the necessity of holding one's own in the circle of one's associates. . . .
> The Puritan sects put the most powerful individual interest of social self-esteem in the service of this breeding of traits. Hence *individual* motives and personal self-interests were also placed in the service of maintaining and propagating the "bourgeois" Puritan ethic, with all its ramifications. This is absolutely decisive for its penetrating and powerful effect.

As Weber's arguments make clear, the specific features of the Protestant social character were determined far less by the Puritan ethical doctrines than by "the form of ethical conduct upon which premiums are placed." The sort of ethical conduct in which Weber was interested, and upon which the Protestant sects promised premiums of knowable grace and social self-esteem, was, of course, that "certain methodical, rational way of life which paved the way for the 'spirit' of modern capitalism." The Protestant sects provided for him the institutional mechanisms by which an individualist economic ethos became part of the character structure of "the modern bourgeois middle classes." Precisely because this was the focus of his problem, however, Weber paid much less attention to other consequential components of the ethos which were also bred within the Protestant sects.

The most important of these components, at least for present purposes, was the communal ethos or civic morality characteristic of Protestant sectarians. The sect member was expected to be helpful to his brethren, whether individually or collectively, and all individual activities were to be willfully bounded by considerations of fellowship and community welfare. Of course, this demand alone is by no means unique. Such qualities as neighborliness and helpfulness are generally valued by villages and small settlements everywhere as indigenous, perhaps even necessary, to their way of life. It is of decisive significance, however, that within the Protestant sects these general demands for fellowship and community service were transformed into everyday ethical duties. Christian stewardship, a charitable disposition, and a willingness to work for community betterment were exalted as moral virtues, the possession of which was required of every sect member. Moreover, as in Weber's example, the continuous display of these civic morals was accepted both as evidence of one's spiritual credentials for membership and as a means of "holding one's own" or even of claiming prestige.

There is support for these contentions in the Puritan concept of the "calling," diligence which Weber rightly found to be among the individual's most highly premiumed ethical duties. Again, however, Weber's own interest in the calling was strongly circumscribed by his overriding concern to identify the ethical foundations of the emerging spirit of rational capitalism. That honesty and diligence in one's calling did not exhaust its requirements was of little consequence within the framework of his problem.

To improve the world in his calling for the glory of God was the vocation of every Puritan, and there could be no better place to begin than in one's own community. The very idea of the calling was bound up with serving and bettering the collectivity. Hence, a Puritan's work had also to be "warrantable" by aiming "not only . . . at our own, but at the public good . . . (True faith) will not think it hath a comfortable calling, unlesse it will not onely serve his owne turne, but the turn of other men" (quoted in Miller and Johnson, 1938, p. 320).[10] Indeed, only in being beneficial to the brethren can one's work be pleasing to God. True saints, lectured John Cotton, New England's foremost proponent of do-goodism, "live by faith in [their] vocations, in that faith, *in serving God, serves men, and in serving men, serves God.* . . . A man therefore that serves Christ in serving of men . . . hath an heavenly business in hand, and therefore comfortably as knowing God approves of his way and work" (quoted in Miller and Johnson, 1938, p. 322; Cotton's emphasis). To those, on the other hand, who failed their obligation of community service, Cotton had no reason to be respectful: "[I] f thou hast no calling, tending to publique good, thou art an uncleane beast" (quoted in Miller and Johnson, 1938, p. 326).

Those whose callings had been blessed by God with material success were thought to have a special dispensation of stewardship and community service. The virtuous rich man would devote his wealth to "pious uses," scattering Bibles throughout the community, relieving the poor of their misery, supporting the ministry, building colleges and hospitals, and so forth. At the same time, the wealthy saint found himself with the unique opportunity "to intermix a spiritual charity among (the) temporal," for the distribution of his beneficence could be used to morally improve its recipients and, by extension, the community as a whole. Two inducements, apart from the purely spiritual, encouraged the rich man to employ his wealth in this fashion.

First, the faithful steward could be assured that charitable expenditures were excellent investments, the worldly returns on which would include long life and continued business success. "History has given us many charming examples," reminded Cotton Mather (1966, pp. 110-11), "of those, who have had their conscientious decimations followed and rewarded with a surprising prosperity of their affairs." Idle and uncharitable gentlemen, Mather was further convinced, would be taking their chances with God's discretion, risking almost certain punishment.

A secular, though perhaps even more effective incentive than the promise of divine reward or punishment was the social and self-esteem that accrued to the philanthropist. The judicious distribution of his estate offered a means by which material wealth could be translated into spiritual and social reputability, a commodity at least as highly valued among the Protestant sects. Moreover, because his resources for doing good were greater than most, the wealthy man was generally able not merely to "hold his own," but to forge ahead in the competition for social and self-esteem. Thus, in addition to the fact of his wealth—presumably a sign of God's blessing—the wealthy man could, by using it wisely, display evidence of his civic virtues and thus of his spiritual credentials and qualifications for social honor.

Those with fewer resources had other avenues available by which their civic morals and community commitments could be displayed. When not engaged directly in their vocations, virtuous persons of moderate means would likely seek other ways to serve and improve the community. To this end, active involvement in "reforming societies" was thought to be especially commendable. Such societies, thought Cotton Mather, "may prove an incomparable and invalueable blessing to a town" in its efforts to do good generally and to end "raging profanity," idleness, and other vices. No less important was the fact that reforming societies provided a highly visible means of advertising one's civic commitments, making them an ideal vehicle through which prestige claims could be successfully made. Even Mather, whose concerns were limited to strictly spiritual issues, could not fail to notice this secular product of organized stewardship. "Well-inclined men," he wrote, " . . . will easily see it their *honor*, to be of a society that will pursue such excellent ends" (Mather, 1966, p. 134; Mather's emphasis).

Not everyone, of course, was capable of such dedicated community service and stewardship. Most lacked the resources, and many others were engaged in callings too demanding of their time. Nonetheless, even if most persons were unable to make claims for greater prestige, they were equally unable to afford its loss. It was of fundamental importance, Weber argued, that the premiums were set not only on gaining esteem (though, of course, this was preferred) but also on avoiding negative peer appraisals. One had still to "hold his own" even if he failed to advance in social honor. This could be accomplished, at least in the area of civic morals, by maintaining friendly, neighborly, and helpful relations with the rest of the community. One must be a good Christian and a good citizen, as defined by sectarian standards. That premiums were set on holding one's own is decisive since, by this means, the civic ethos could be extended not only to those with greater time and resources, but to every member of the sect. At every social and class level, therefore, the Protestant sects transformed civic morals into characterological virtues.

In sum, to put the matter into Durkheimian terminology, moral integration and social solidarity were ethical duties of the Protestant sectarians. Obligations of fellowship, brotherhood, and community harmony were demanded by religious doctrine and were backed by both divine and social pressures. More important, however, is that the duties of social solidarity were not merely prescribed, but transformed through sectarian mechanisms into enduring components of the Protestant social character.

Protestant Civic Morals on Main Street: The Small Town Businessman as Secular Sectarian

Despite the dreams and efforts of Puritan divines, America, or for that matter even New England, would not be home for the City of God. Indeed, by only the third generation the Holy Commonwealth of the Puritans was fast becoming an abandoned dream. Secular concerns intruded from the beginning, and the original religious principles were forced into numerous compromises.

Despite their fading religious content and the decreasing fervor of their sectarian carriers, neither the economic nor the social virtues of Protestantism were in danger of disappearing. While both the righteous commitment and unchallenged social dominance of the first generation were lost forever, the Protestant churches would continue well into the twentieth century as a strong and influential force in American society. The church, however, would no longer be primarily responsible for the continued survival of its original values. Rather, it is decisive that the civic ideology of Protestantism was adopted by the emerging bourgeois middle classes, especially by the independent farmers and small business stratum that soon replaced the sectarian Protestants as the dominant social group.

Although the religious ideas were generally retained, it is primarily as a secular ideology that Protestant values found favor with the small town middle classes, and especially its

dominant business stratum. As usually occurs when the carrying stratum of an ideology changes, the business stratum adapted
Protestant values in accord with its own ideal and material interests, most generally by gradually replacing their theological
with secular significance.

As has often been mentioned in this regard, this adaptation was
personified and articulated most eloquently by Benjamin Franklin. His transformation of the Puritan quest for spiritual self-
improvement into a more worldly, utilitarian ambition was only
a personal statement of an understanding already gaining widespread acceptance among rising social groups. The catalog of
moral virtues to which Franklin aspired as a young man—temperance, silence, order, resolution, frugality, industry, sincerity,
justice, moderation, cleanliness, tranquility, chastity, and humility—is thoroughly Protestant in character, derived from his own
Quaker upbringing. Franklin sought virtue, however, not for its
spiritual value but for its pragmatic usefulness. It was to his own
imperfect command of these traits, for instance, that he attributed his own good health, "good constitution," business success,
scholarly reputation, public prestige, even disposition, and
"cheerfulness in conversation" (1966, p. 78). Ultimately, similar
ambitions were responsible for the adoption of secularized
Protestant values by members (and those who wished to be) of
the emerging middle classes, not because they were pleasing to
God but because they were useful in secular and especially
business endeavors. Franklin, and not Winthrop or Edwards,
was to be America's foremost prophet.

Though clearly important, usefulness alone provides an inadequate explanation of the "penetrating efficiency" with
which these secularized Protestant values were received by the
emerging American commercial bourgeoisie. Such an explanation, as Weber observed, must make reference to the institutional structures and procedures through which and by which these
values are premiumed, in this case to the now-secularized
structures of sectarian organization.[11]

At the time of Weber's visit to America in 1904, he noticed
that the original purpose of the sects had been altered significantly. What was once an exclusive organization for the worship
of God had been transformed, in effect, into a credit-validating
institution. Membership in a sect had become a business neces-

sity and "moral qualification" translated into credit-worthiness. Because entry into a Protestant sect followed a probationary period during which the applicant's moral character was closely scrutinized by his peers, membership was recognized as an absolute guarantee of the moral qualities of the member, especially as those qualities pertained to his business dealings. Thus, if a sect member

> got into economic straits through no fault of his own, the sect arranged his affairs, gave guarantees to the creditors, and helped him in every way. . . .
>
> The expectation of the creditors that his sect, for the sake of their prestige, would not allow creditors to suffer losses on behalf of a sect member was not, however, decisive for his opportunities. What was decisive was the fact that a fairly reputable sect would only accept for membership one whose "conduct" made him appear to be morally *qualified* beyond doubt.
>
> It is crucial that sect membership meant a certificate of moral qualification and especially of business morals for the individual. [Weber, 1946, p. 305; Weber's emphasis]

Thus, if an individual was a sect member, prospective creditors could be fairly certain that he was industrious, diligent, honest, and frugal—an ideal specimen of Protestant virtue and therefore certain to repay his debts.

Weber also recognized that the influence of the sects themselves was "steadily decreasing" as religious concerns gave way to an economic ordering of life. At the same time, however, the economic function of the sects, indispensable for business organization, was increasingly taken over by secular associations, fraternal orders, and the like. The organizational basis and credit-validating procedures of the associations were precisely the same as those exercised by sect discipline. Their position, in fact, was "derived from the far more exclusive importance of the prototype of these voluntary organizations, to wit, the sects." The most important of these derivatives in an organizational sense included above all "the social premiums, the means

of discipline, and, in general, the whole organizational basis of
Protestant sectarianism with all its ramifications. . . . The survi-
vals in contemporary America are the derivatives of a religious
regulation of life which once worked with penetrating efficiency"
(1946, p. 313). Thus, having been found useful for the prevailing
system of business operations, the organizational framework
of the Protestant sects was retained and continued to foster
certain traits even after the religious content of those traits had
faded. Secularized sectarian structures constitute the specific
means by which useful business values were transformed into
characterological virtues.

In short, largely through "the steady progress of the characteristic process of 'secularization' to which in modern times all
phenomena that originated in religious conceptions succumb,"
the dynamics of sectarian discipline had been transformed into
what Thorstein Veblen cynically conceived of as a "test of country
town fitness" for Main Street businessmen.[12] The "test of
country town fitness" continued to foster many of the Protestant-based economic virtues in which Weber was interested,
often joining them to others of more secular origin. These economic virtues, however, were not the only Protestant value-
traits to survive with "penetrating efficiency" in small town
America. The Protestant civic morality whose origins we have
traced was also retained, both because it was useful to the business interests of the dominant carrying groups and because
surviving sect-like discipline sustained and relocated it in the
newly emergent institutional context.

The credit-worthiness conferred upon him by membership
in a sect or sect-like association was hardly the businessman's
only worry, for an estimation of his moral character was important to prospective customers as well as creditors. Indeed,
the businessman's ability to create and sustain a virtuous reputation could easily be the difference between success or failure
in his business dealings. In the small town retail trade, decent
folks would buy from decent and respectable merchants. Thus,
for instance, in accordance with Protestant values, one had to
be honest, charitable, public spirited, neighborly, friendly,
temperate, industrious, and chaste. Or, failing to possess these
virtues, the prosperous businessman had at least to convince
others that he did.[13] To have his vices and nonconformist atti-

tudes exposed publicly could prove a devastating blow to a businessman's reputation and, subsequently, to his livelihood. Like his sectarian ancestors, the businessman could not afford (literally) to relax once his good Protestant character had been initially confirmed. Rather, he, too, was required to "hold his own" in the community circle by providing constant proof of his ethical virtue.

It is with reference to this necessity for holding one's own that Veblen observes the scheme of conduct for the small town businessman to be "a scheme of salesmanship" or "salesman-like pusillanimity," the dominant aspect of which is constant circumspection, that is, self-rationalization. As a requisite for doing business, he noted,

> one must avoid offense, cultivate good will, at any
> reasonable cost, and continue unfailingly in taking
> advantage of it. . . . One must be circumspect, acquire
> merit. . . . So one must eschew opinions, or informa-
> tion, which are not acceptable to the common run of
> those whose good will has or may conceivably come
> to have any commercial value. The country town
> system of knowledge and belief can admit nothing
> that would annoy the prejudices of any appreciable
> number of the respectable townfolk. [Veblen, 1923;
> p. 159]

Thus, the self-rationalization of individual conduct came to be organized around one's answer to the usually implicit, always central, question of small town life: "What would the neighbors think?"

The businessman could be most certain, moreover, that attentive neighbors would evaluate his claims for business re-spectability. While its religious significance continued to fade, the ethical responsibility of each sect member to scrutinize his brother's conduct was generalized into an informal pattern of busybody-type nosiness. As a corollary of this pattern, sectarian lay discipline gave way to gossip and moral reproach as the primary means of ensuring social control and local conformity. And none, according to Veblen, stood readier to point out one's moral deficiencies than one's rivals in business. Since moral repute was generally essential to business success, one aspect of business competition could be played out on moral grounds. As Veblen described the rules of the game in American country towns, the truly competent businessman "should be ready to recognize and recount the possible short-comings of one's neighbors, for neighbors are (or may be) rivals in trade, and in trade one man's loss is another's gain, and a rival's disabilities count in among one's assets and should not be allowed to go to waste" (1923, p. 159). A virtuous reputation was the most fragile and treasured of business commodities, and had to be guarded at all times.

Passing the test of country town fitness in the sense of simply avoiding offense and "standing pat" was clearly insufficient to persons imbued with the notion of self-help and the ambition to "get ahead." A businessman satisfied with standing pat would likely eventually fail to hold his own. Since his rivals could be expected to work actively in acquiring prestige, no successful businessman could afford to do less, or else he would fall behind in relation to the "commercial good-will" cultivated by his competitors. The resulting business necessity of holding one's own by actively competing for prestige is at least partly responsible for the retention of Protestant civic morals by Main Street businessmen, and, by extension, by the entire old middle-class stratum, for virtually all the recognized means of doing so were related to community service.[14] One could generally gain prestige and good-will for business by outserving one's competitors and by contributing most to the community's welfare, as expressed somewhat explicitly in one of the Rotary songs: "He profits most who serves the best" (cited by Lynd, 1929, p. 302). The ambitious businessman was thus obliged to be generous to local charities[15] and to be active in his membership to one or another civic association as it helped to build hospitals, schools, libraries, and other worthy projects.[16] Civic leadership was a widely accepted claim for prestige and commercial good-will, and if a position of leadership could not be attained, one still had to hold his own in community service. "'It is just good business to be somebody civically,' said a prosperous merchant, who was" (Mills, 1951, p. 45).

With business expediency and social self-esteem operating as powerfully effective premiums, there can be little wonder that small town business classes retained as part of their characterological makeup the "respectable prejudices," including civic morals, composed of secularized Protestant values. Certainly, the business stratum understood very well, to cite Veblen once again, that "any assertion or denial that runs counter to any appreciable set of respectable prejudices would come in for some degree of disfavor, and any degree of disfavor is intolerable to men whose business would presumably suffer from it." On the other hand, "there is no (business) harm done in assenting to, *and so in time coming to believe in,* any or all of the commonplaces of day before yesterday (i.e., the secularized Protestant values). . . . And the men of affairs and responsibility in public life, who have passed the test of country town fitness, as they must, are men who have come through and made good according to the canons of faith and conduct imposed by this system of holdovers" (1923, pp. 159-60; my emphasis).

Though clearly important, the display of civic values as a means of competition among local businessmen does not sufficiently explain the passionate commitment with which these values were held on Main Street. For the latter, it is decisive that values of civic service and solidarity were essential to the prosperity of local business generally.

Business in American small towns was based primarily on real estate speculation and retail trade. Since real estate is local by nature and retail trade at the time lacked both centralized direction and access to national markets, in either case the upper limits of prosperity were established by the amount of local business traffic as it affected the demand for land and the size of local markets. In a very real sense, then, personal and group prosperity was bound up with the fortunes of the town. If the town went "bust," so did its citizens and especially its businessmen, a connection of which they were acutely aware. On the other hand, if the town continued to grow, so did land values, consumer demand, and their own opportunities for "getting ahead." Especially as competing towns grew more numerous, local business interests and the middle classes generally were class-consciously united, in anticipation of financial glory and on pain of personal failure, in an organized crusade to attract more business and encourage local expansion.

Consequently, just as local businessmen had to hold their own against one another, so, too, were they compelled to hold their own collectively against the economic competition of rival towns. In a very real sense, local businessmen were united in a second and larger test of country town fitness, the outcome of which would be shared by all. In this collective test of country town fitness, as in its more personal counterpart, a premium was placed on the values and actions demonstrating civic service, pride, and loyalty.

The collective effort to hold their own was expressed, first of all, in the shrill pitch of "boosterism," an ambitious propaganda campaign on the part of local Rotarians and Chambers of Commerce to increase the business traffic and raise land values in their area. Boosterism provided the central focus of business class consciousness in American small towns, representing by far the strongest common interest in an otherwise competitive situation. Middletown's trite but typical slogan effectively captures the sentiment behind the booster effort (quoted in Lynd, 1929, p. 487):

> United we stick,
> Divided we're stuck.
> United we boost,
> Divided we're bust.

And boost they did. With missionary zeal, local businessmen lost few opportunities to present their own town as quite probably the friendliest, most progressive, and loveliest place on God's footstool, as one supporter of "Magic Middletown" put it. Certainly, those looking for a place to settle, live, work, raise a family, prosper, buy a house, and patronize local merchants could do no better. Local citizens were also exhorted to "get behind" the effort to "put over" their town by demonstrating civic pride and loyalty,[17] and especially to say or do nothing to tarnish the image of local solidarity and cooperation. "Knockers," accordingly, were the worst sort of small town heretics, blasphemers of booster religiosity and outright dangers to local prosperity.

To be sure, booster rhetoric was by no means entirely empty, for local businessmen were concerned not only to boost their

town, but usually also to better it. Virtually every business and
civic club was involved in some effort to improve the community. In addition to providing further points for Main Street
publicists, civic improvements were a recognized means of
attracting more business. Thus, for instance, as Lynd points
out, support for Middletown College "did not mean essentially
pride in the college as an educational institution, but, as press
and merchants proclaimed, 'A live college here will mean thou-
sands of dollars annually for local business'" (1929, p. 486).
Civic improvements meant expansion, and expansion meant
economic progress—for the city, for Main Street, and for the
individual businessman. The whole complex of self and group
interests has been eloquently expressed by Booth Tarkington
as he describes the fictional boosters and betterers of Midland
City:

> They were vicariously governed, but sometimes they
> went so far as to struggle for better government on
> account of the helpful effect of good government
> on the price of real estate and "betterment" general-
> ly. . . . The idealist planned and strove and shouted
> that their city should become a better, better and
> better city—and what they meant, when they used
> the word "better," was "more prosperous," and the
> core of their idealism was this: "The more prosper-
> ous my beloved city, the more prosperous Beloved
> I." [Tarkington, 1918, pp. 388-89: quoted in Ather-
> ton, 1954, p. 330]

While the concern for business expediency always remained
an aspect of Main Street's civic values, these values were nonetheless held with apparent sincerity. As we have seen, business
interests themselves operated in both private and collective
contexts as powerful premiums for the "breeding" of civic
traits among the business stratum. So constantly and consistently were they compelled in the interests of business and
personal esteem to espouse and display civic-mindedness that
they could presently do so with genuine commitment. Even
allowing for numerous hypocrites, the typical small town businessman was a paragon of civic virtue and would remain so at

least as long as the congruence between his commercial interests and civic-mindedness was sustained by prevailing institutional arrangements.

From Business Class Civic Ideology to Small Town Orthodoxy: Strategies of Cooptation and Diffusion

Business groups were clearly and actively concerned to propagate their civic ideology. Their most immediate motives for doing so involved a clear recognition that local solidarity considerably enhanced the prospects for business profitability. More generally, however, since business groups were usually dominant locally and could thus largely define the particular sort of civic loyalty and solidarity to be attained, popular acceptance of their ideology could readily help sustain and legitimize local business class control.

The typical pattern of business class dominance in American small towns operated to identify the public welfare with business enterprise. What was good for business was good for the community as well. The Main Street conception of local harmony, meaning especially the absence of labor strife, was virtually synonymous with acceptance of business class leadership. Thus, for instance, assertions of a "partnership" between labor and capital more often served as public rhetoric for a stable domination on the part of capital.[18] Worker loyalty and cooperation (civic solidarity), and especially the advantage of being an open-shop town, were highly prized booster points almost guaranteed to attract more business.[19] Under the circumstances, civic allegiance was virtually inseparable from support for and validation of business claims to legitimacy.

Since businessmen adapted the civic ideology to suit their own ideal and material interests, not surprisingly its contents were less intrinsically compelling to other small town groups. As compared to the working classes, for instance, Lynd (1929, p. 495) observed that the business stratum

> did the "civic" thing more easily, because civic values are its values at so many points. The workers, on the

other hand, instead of yielding to and reinforcing
the pressures of this organized community life, are
more often inert, uncooperative, and even resistant. . . .
The major drives of "Magic Middletown" are not so
completely their drives, and only at second hand
do they tingle to the exhilaration of some of the
things that are living itself to the business group.

Yet, if local pride and civic virtue were more congruent with
the ideal and material interests of business classes, these values
were by no means restricted to their ranks. Along with the
legitimacy claims of business leadership generally, these values
were so extensively validated by so many small town groups
that they were generally elevated to an orthodox status. However, receiving groups, since they did not fully share the ideal
and material needs and interests of the business stratum, accepted the legitimacy claims and values of the business classes—including its civic loyalties—with very different levels of commitment and on quite different substantive grounds. Or re-
phrased, they responded with different motives and intensities
to the various strategies of cooptation utilized by Main Street
to gain and maintain compliance with its control and, consequently, with the exigencies of its ideology.
    One of the most generalized of these strategies concerns the
distribution of status in small town America. Any groups or
individuals seeking to acquire social esteem, including especially
those who had "made it" economically, discovered rather
quickly that there was only one ladder of respectability. White-
Anglo-Saxon-Protestant groups had been the first to arrive on
America's eastern shores, and by virtue of that head start, America's culture and social order bore their unmistakable stamp. As
one aspect of that imprint, virtually all standards of respectability
had been defined, established, and controlled by WASP groups.
Consequently, upwardly mobile members of later arriving
immigrant groups and "native" Americans alike had little choice
but to base their own claims for respectability on the already
existing standards, and to display their acceptance of those
standards by emulating the actions and espousing the values of
the old middle classes generally and its business stratum speci-

fically.[20] In order to gain respect in a WASP-dominated society, other groups had almost to become WASPs themselves, or even to become 110 percent WASP in an effort to escape the contaminating influence of another heritage. This meant, among other things, that such groups were often compelled to display the appropriate civic virtues as a prerequisite to gaining reputability. At least for some of the more socially ambitious groups and individuals, then, civic pride and loyalty were fostered by a desire for acceptance and respect.

Some other means by which businessmen ensured compliance with their ideology and control were more overtly coercive. As owners of stores, banks, and factories, they were equipped with a most persuasive set of economic rewards and sanctions. Employment, raises and promotions, preferential duties (for example, day or night shift), housing,[21] access to credit, and other such inducements could be regularly offered to persons on the stated or unstated condition that they not challenge business class leadership and accept certain of its demands on their conduct. Once such a conditional offer had been accepted and its benefits enjoyed for a time, the threat of losing them could be effectively plied to ensure continued compliance. Employees were frequently "urged" not only to work hard, but also to attend church regularly, to observe the norms of Protestant decency,[22] and, perhaps above all else, to be "loyal," a term which was usually defined as opposition to unions. At the very least, workers were made to understand the wisdom of publicly "knocking" neither their community nor their employer, and of demonstrating civic and worker loyalty whenever necessary.

An often neglected and therefore less familiar economic means of eliciting compliance, in this case from the unemployed and destitute, was afforded by the practice of philanthropy. The Protestant businessman was encouraged to give but never to give indiscriminately, for Protestant conceptions of charity required that the recipient be morally worthy of the gift. Defined, of course, by Protestant standards, "morally worthy" generally meant willing to work, to remain temperate, to resist carnal temptations, and generally to be a good and loyal citizen. As the brother being kept, the recipient was obliged to orient

himself to Protestant standards of decency, or if "fallen" to
reform, and, equally important, to appreciate the largesse of
his benefactor.[23] Not that either the conforming or the appreciation was necessarily insincere; compromises come cheap
when the cupboard is bare, and gratitude can be genuinely
extended to those who fill it. But in either case, acquiescence
could be secured from the impoverished in return for charitable
aid and could be sustained by the possibility that such aid
might again be required in the future. Thus, philanthropic
activity not only constituted a claim for prestige, but also was
an important component in the business class control system
in American small towns.[24]

The more general sort of civic philanthropy, of course, was
also a mainstay of business class legitimacy and control. For
instance, no one would likely dispute that building schools,
churches, and hospitals constitutes meritorious activity. By
making the greatest contributions of both time and money to
such activities, and by doing most in the way of community
betterment generally, businessmen emerged as almost natural
local leaders.

Implicit claims to legitimacy based on civic contributions
were no doubt especially successful when addressed to those
who shared the older Protestant heritage which equated civic
contributions with moral leadership.[25] No group, however,
could ignore real community improvements, so that business
class leadership was largely accepted on this basis. This meant,
in part at least, an acceptance of the business class civic ideology.

In addition to controlling important economic means of
domination, Main Street businessmen ordinarily wielded considerable influence over local agencies of information dissemination and opinion formation. Small town newspapers, for
instance, could often be coopted by their financial dependence
on local advertising and by the hope of linking their own growth
in circulation with the general expansion of the town. Newspapers, after all, were businesses themselves and typically reflected business class attitudes. Not only, for instance, did local
newspapers almost universally encourage civic pride and participation, but they would often print nothing that might tarnish

the booster imagery of the community as "one big happy family." (In the true spirit of boosterism, however, such information
could often be found in the pages of rival town newspapers.
See Vidich and Bensman, 1968, p. 31.) In any case, the press
ordinarily served as the primary mouthpiece of Main Street,
accepting and propagating the business class identification of
its own interests with those of the public. The major Middletown newspapers, for example, were typical in consistently
regarding labor "trouble" as uncivic and contrary to the public interest—one instance of a situation wherein, as Lynd (1937,
p. 378) observed, "information . . . tends to reach the public
'with the compliments of' business." The local press was thus
an important tool in the business class system of control and
did much to propagate its civic ideology.

Finally, the Protestant church also continued to provide
legitimacy to the principal carriers of its now-secularized values,
even though its role in validating the business community progressively declined as competing religious and secular concerns
grew in importance. Like the press, churches and ministers
were often financially dependent on local business contributions,
a situation that encouraged neither independence nor neutrality.
Of perhaps greater importance, however, small town entrepreneurs were the legitimate offspring of a Protestant culture.
Businessmen were Protestant heroes, diligently fulfilling the
demands of their calling, serving the community, and reaping
the benefits of God's blessing. God had so long and consistently
been their ally that the churches were quite unable to readily
forsake their traditionally close ties to the business community.
Moreover, as has already been pointed out, business interests
were expressed as an advocation of civic solidarity, secular
brotherhood, and a "Harmony of Interests." Because the clergy
typically regarded conflict and disruptions of local harmony
as un-Christian, they most often supported the business community, which favored a return to the status quo of orderly and
cooperative workers (see Pope, 1942). At any rate, the Protestant church furnished yet another support to business class
dominance and, with the others, served to propagate and diffuse the contents of its civic ideology.

In each of the ways mentioned and doubtless many others,[26] the business classes achieved and sustained their institutional and ideological domination of small town America. In denoting the means by which small town ideological domination and social control were accomplished, there is neither need nor desire to depict old middle-class businessmen *as a stratum* as money-grubbing, oppressive, power-hungry, selfish, or evil in any way. Indeed, many of the techniques of local dominance discussed here were sincere expressions of public-spiritedness on their part and no doubt were usually accepted as such by townsfolk. The secularized Protestant ideology of civic unity and common purpose certainly was not perceived by its primary carriers as but a weapon to be used in conquering and controlling the local community. To the contrary, Main Street was genuinely committed to the contents of its own civic ideology.

Nonetheless, good intentions and sincere motivations do not diminish the fact that the old middle classes generally and business groups in particular were locally dominant, nor is the cultural imprint made possible by that domination any less important. To make the point to which our discussion has been leading, it is precisely because this domination was so effective that many of the secularized Protestant values which they carried, including both economic and civic values, survived as central elements in the ideological self-image of small towns all across the country. These secularized Protestant virtues, generalized as aspects of the small town ideological self-image, included honesty (a spoken word is as good as a contract), fair play, trustworthiness, industriousness, voluntarism, good neighborliness, helpfulness, friendliness, equality, universal participation, common purpose, and willingness to work for community betterment—in short, civic pride and solidarity, individualism within a collective context.[27] All were secularized elements of the sectarian brotherhood; all were components of the small town orthodoxy; and all were values "stamped" on small town America by its dominant old middle-class stratum, the most prominent representatives of which were Main Street businessmen.

As Saints Fall From Grace (I): On the Decline of the Old Middle Classes

As we have seen, by virtue of their local control, the old middle classes attained and sustained throughout the country an orthodox status for the Protestant-based economic and civic virtues they carried. Ultimately emerging as central components in the ideological self-image of small town America, these values attained prominence through the dominance of their carrying stratum. Nonetheless, the social history of neither these values nor the old middle classes has been one of uniform success, for in truth they have found themselves increasingly on the defensive since the middle 1800s. Fundamental structural changes in American society increasingly and consistently undermined their entire way of life. Ultimately, these institutional changes effected a substantial shift in the foundation of class structures. One result of this shift has been a long but steady decline of the old middle classes themselves. For a stratum that began its existence as a self-chosen body of saints, the past century has been a sustained fall from grace.

In the decades following the Civil War, American institutional structure underwent a metamorphosis so profound that it can only be likened to a revolution, one whose consequences can hardly be considered less significant than the insurrection that gained America its independence. The post-Civil War period experienced spectacular industrial growth and expansion as the earth, after several generations of attempted mastery, finally submitted to domination by mammon. Railroads crisscrossed the country, making overland travel and commerce much more convenient and profitable. Coal, oil, and steel industries virtually exploded as more efficient means were found for extracting, refining, and distributing natural resources. Whole new industries were begun, while old ones were made vastly more productive through the invention of labor-saving machinery. All totaled, the economic growth of the period is staggering. The same nation which in 1858 had a total income of $16.6 billion had by 1900—despite the Civil War itself, a depression, and a host of financial and industrial failures—an income of $126.7 billion.[28] "The old nations of the earth creep on at a snail's pace," wrote Andrew Carnegie (1886, p. 1), who perhaps had every right to gloat; "the Republic thunders past with the rush of the express."

The enormous industrial growth of the postwar period was far from uniform or evenly distributed. Even as the economy grew, it was being consolidated and centralized into extensive corporate empires. This tendency was aided by the federal government, which maintained high tariffs and enforced patent laws, thus effectively inhibiting competition, and especially by the judiciary, whose interpretation of the Fourteenth Amendment in 1886 bestowed upon the still incipient form of business organization known as the corporation all the legal rights of individual persons. Since the corporation was not likewise saddled with the limitations of flesh-and-blood individuals, being generally immortal, less accountable, and having access to much greater sums of operating and investment capital, the overall effect was to grant to corporations a substantive advantage in the marketplace.

A generation of bold, often ruthless entrepreneurs, whose predatory inclinations were given full reign under the prevailing system of free enterprise, was quick to take advantage of circumstances. Carnegie, for instance, rose from a bobbin boy making $1.50 per week to found a nationwide corporate monopoly of the steel industry. John D. Rockefeller made an equally meteoric rise to consolidate and head the oil industry. Their efforts were duplicated in such diverse industries as railroads, farm equipment, investment banking, tobacco, meatpacking, sugar, and copper.[29]

In the century following the Civil War, this tendency toward economic centralization decimated the old middle classes. They had been a stratum of small entrepreneurs, of independent farmers and self-made businessmen, of property owners who typically worked their own holdings for a livelihood. Most independent farmers, however, were pressured into liquidation by rising operating costs (particularly in farm machinery), ordinary calamities, federal agricultural policies, and prohibitive mortgage debts. In 1820, agricultural production accounted

for almost 75 percent of the labor force; by 1900, the percent-
age was down to 35, and to 12 percent by 1950. The decline
continues today. Similarly, small manufacturers and Main Street
retailers have been unable to hold their own against competition
from mass production, mail order houses, and franchise operations. As a result, the old middle classes have witnessed a
gradual expropriation of their properties and thus of their very
basis as an independent class formation.[30]

When the Morgans and Vanderbilts and Carnegies had finish-
ed their work, America was on a different path—away from a
nation of small but independent capitalists and toward a nation
incorporated. The Captains of Industry had initiated a structural revolution of the American economy. It was not, however,
a revolution whose effects would be felt suddenly. The fundamental unit of American business was still the enterprising
individual and would remain so for years to come. But from
this point on, slowly and grudgingly, the small business stratum
would succumb to the economic developments that had been
set in motion. A new American society had begun to emerge;
it left progressively less room for the champions of the old.

As Saints Fall from Grace(II): On the Decline of the Small Town Moral Orthodoxy

Probably no ideology or morality can be nourished for
long by the intrinsically compelling force of its own contents.
To survive, at least as orthodoxy, institutional supports and a
carrying stratum are required. For the small town Protestant
orthodoxy, neither has endured. The Protestant economic and
civic ethos, having been secularized and diffused into central
features of the small town ideological self-image, was part and
parcel of an institutional arrangement in which it "made sense,"
in which its constitutive values could find some validation in
everyday experience, and, indeed, in which conduct accordant
with these values was positively premiumed. The ethos was not
designed for an urbanized, corporatized, bureaucratized, and
powerfully productive society even if, ironically, it helped usher
that society into being. Accordingly, as a new set of institutional

arrangements began to pressure and displace the old, and as the old middle classes grew progressively less able to sustain the orthodox status of the values they carried, the small town Protestant ethos began to show signs of decay in both its economic and civic aspects.

Many of the economic virtues associated with the Protestant Ethic appear to have been especially vulnerable. As Weber maintained, many of its constituent motivations were not entirely natural inclinations of human beings. The Protestant ethic was one of unlimited production, for only uncompromising devotion to labor itself could satisfy the ethical demands of God. This emphasis, in both its religious and secularized expressions, was well suited to the requirements of a developing industrial order. Once productive efficiency began to outstrip the market's capacity to absorb it, however, as Veblen tirelessly chastised, the principles of industry were replaced with those of the price system, the primary concern of which was "not productive work, but profitable business." And to the latter too much productivity, by saturating markets and reducing profits, posed a very serious threat.

Leaders of the emergent business enterprise responded to the challenge of overproduction with two strategies, both of which hastened the demise of Protestant economic virtues. The first, as Veblen argued, was to inhibit productive capacity (sabotage). Since one of the more acceptable means of doing so was to reduce working hours, one byproduct of managerial sabotage was an increase in leisure time for large segments of the population. The "idle hands" thus created kept busy by turning not to other productive labors, but to emerging industries devoted to furnishing entertainment and personal enjoyment (for example, motion pictures, touristry, autos). As a result of the transition to a vastly more productive economy, the "devil's workshop" was institutionalized.

The threat of overproduction was also met by the developing techniques of salesmanship, the most important expression of a general effort to shift the grounds of economic competition from increasing productivity to generating consumption. Professional advertisers found no end to the ways in which income could be spent and leisure enjoyed. In a largely self-conscious effort to undermine puritan thrift and self-denial, advertising encouraged spending for immediate gratification.[31] Ultimately, immediate satisfaction of the commodity fetish cultivated by salesmanship was made not only desirable but also possible as credit, formerly reserved for producers, was systematically extended to consumers. Installment buying may well have struck the decisive blow to the Protestant Ethic, especially to its virtues of thrift and frugality.[32]

The Protestant emphasis on the warrantability and dignity of labor has fared little better under these tendencies than the economic virtues just mentioned. Certainly, for instance, one can hardly imagine most modern factory and white collar workers, to paraphrase Parsons, subordinating personal needs and devoting full energies to their assigned, impersonal tasks. Ultimately, even labor in a calling, which under the Protestant ethos was considered meaningful and dignified as an end in its own right, has in contemporary society become little more than an unavoidable means of attaining a limited secular salvation at the altar of mass consumerism.

The Puritan's economic virtues had been part of a larger complex of ethical behavior, the mastery and display of which formed the foundation of his claims to social self-esteem. By using rationalized techniques, and especially by rationally manipulating the irrational, advertisers were able to extend the definition of "ethical behavior"—now thoroughly secularized— to include a high level of commodity consumption. In the process, social self-esteem came to depend largely on one's ability to maintain a certain level of consumption. Veblen's argument, though somewhat exaggerated, is that conspicuous waste and consumption—both anathema to the Protestant Ethic—finally emerged as the only measure of respectability and personal worth.[33]

Unlike their economic counterparts, the small town Protestant civic virtues were not deliberately undermined by agents of the emerging institutional structure. They have nonetheless fared little better. Protestant civic morals had attained an orthodox status in the first place through the local dominance of the old middle classes generally and the local business community particularly. In the century following the Civil War, however, their local dominance was challenged at virtually every level. Thus, for instance, the ability to make important decisions affecting the community, which had once rested almost entirely in the hands of Main Street, was gradually appropriated by agencies outside the community.[34] Absentee ownership of local companies, for example, became increasingly common, resulting in a situation where decisions of vital importance to the community were made not on Main Street, but in the board rooms of Bell Telephone, General Motors, and other large corporations. The center of political gravity, including party politics as well as political administration, also began to shift to the national level as the federal government, often reacting to changes in the economy, gradually usurped more and more authority from local, state, and private sources. And finally, within many small towns, immigrant groups eventually mounted a successful challenge to old middle-class dominance.[35] As the stratum declined, so did its ability to uphold its values.

The declining power of its carrying stratum was not alone in causing the erosion of small town civic morals. In addition, it seems, the civic virtues that were so vital to the Main Street businessman's way of life proved largely useless in the way of life that was emerging. As the new set of institutional arrangements replaced the old, small town Protestant civic virtues began to suffer from obsolescence.

As compared with their central role among Main Street businessmen, civic virtues held little relevance for the type of businessman who became increasingly prominent as a result of structural changes in the economy. Civic-mindedness on Main Street, as noted earlier, was "bred" and sustained at least partly by economic competition between local businessmen as each sought to gain respect and commercial good-will through civic contributions. These and other institutionalized premiums operated not only to ensure civic conduct but also to define such conduct as ethical and to instill it into the social character of the old middle-class business stratum. The absentee owner, on the other hand, was not subject to local standards of ethical conduct and respectability, even if his was the most important business concern in the community. He did not, for instance, typically address his claims for status to the small towns in which his factories were located, nor did his major competitors consist of local businessmen. Rather, since he usually had access to larger markets, he lived beyond the range of Main Street disciplinary procedures. He was not subject to any institutional mechanisms that would encourage in him the same civic virtues associated with Main Street. As a result, in the emerging type of corporate businessman, economic motives were able to stand alone, undiluted by the decaying framework of local competition and civic obligations.

Also largely exempt from this framework was the rapidly expanding stratum of Big Business functionaries, the white collar managers and administrators responsible for the day-to-day operation of corporate factories and other properties. Although members of this group tended to live in the smaller towns and cities where corporate properties were located, and in some cases could even exercise a considerable amount of local influence, they nonetheless differed significantly from their business colleagues on Main Street. Specifically, because their economic fates were not connected to local trade but to larger markets and economic developments, they did not share the same stake in the community's welfare and, accordingly, were not subject to the same pressures that shaped the social character and civic morals of the middle classes. As a result, the emerging stratum of businessmen would not carry the old middle-class civic morality. This morality was thus weakened as the old business stratum and its way of life gave way to the new.

Despite the increasing prominence of Big Business and the new classes it engendered, the old middle classes did not experience a complete and sudden decimation. Rather, a remnant of the old middle-class small business stratum continued to survive in American towns and cities, its economic fate remaining dependent on local trends. But if the emergent structural developments did not completely eliminate the Main Street business stratum, they were sufficient to engender a fundamental change in its social psychology, which grew more defensive and self-protective. This change found expression in the heroic efforts of diminished people who, unable to recognize that they had been defeated, sought to stem the tide of their own continuing decline by any means available. Thus, for instance, they more aggressively asserted the older values, as in the Temperance Movement,[36] Know-Nothingism, the Ku Klux Klan (a regional example), and some expressions of Protestant fundamentalism. They began offering all manner of tax breaks to large corporations if only they would set up plants in the town, thus improving local business.[37] Finally, and most important for present concerns, this defensive business culture also included an emphasis on civic celebrations, the contents and purpose of which were appropriated by local business groups and adapted in accordance with their own needs and interests—particularly, it appears, to shore up their own waning dominance and to foster local pride in order to hold people in the community. It is with reference to these defensive efforts of a declining stratum that one such ceremony must be reexamined—the Memorial Day parade analyzed by W. Lloyd Warner.

PARADES, PROTESTANTS, AND PATRIOTS: W. LLOYD WARNER AND THE MEMORIAL DAY PARADE

The Memorial Day Parade in Historical and Institutional Context

By the time Warner began his studies of Newburyport in the 1930s and 1940s, the old Protestant middle classes had already experienced gradual but persistent erosion of their local dominance. Accordingly, the traditional foundations of town unity had been undermined to a significant degree. Many causes of local disunity, such as ethnic and religious competitiveness, labor unrest, and the appearance in town of managers representing New York-based firms, are given ample attention by Warner himself in several volumes of the Yankee City series.

The Social System of the Modern Factory (Warner & Low, 1947), for instance, focuses primarily on the development of class antagonisms centering around a 1933 strike against local shoe factories. In a mythical age prior to the industrialization of these factories, Warner argued, making shoes was an honorable calling, the workman was accorded respect and dignity, and the relations between workers and managers were friendly, personal, and subject to community attitudes and traditions.[1] As the factories were mechanized, the worker became enslaved to machine discipline, which effectively stripped him of craft dignity and fostered greater class consciousness among the laborers.[2] Accompanying this change in the position of the workers, Warner observed, were two others affecting the relations between workers and management. First, factory ownership had shifted to New York City, beyond the purview of traditional community controls. Second, as a necessary response to absentee ownership, worker-management relations grew increasingly formal and impersonal, being finally mediated through manufacturers' associations and labor unions.

According to Warner, worker responses to these developments, especially to the loss of status, autonomy, and opportunities for mobility, were primarily responsible for the strike. The more significant point, however, is that class conflicts were no longer located within and constrained by a larger community context. As Warner points out, the institutionalization of manufacturer-labor operative conflicts had "in some degree set worker interests *in opposition* to community interests" (1947, p. 109), and the trend toward absentee ownership indicates much the same position for management. The process of industrialization, in other words, made class conflicts a structurally endemic aspect of community life.

Another source of conflict can be found in the town's ethnic diversity. In addition to the small black population, all of whom were "lower-lower class" with virtually no opportunities for social mobility, Newburyport had eight groups of European immigrants, each with its own distinctive set of traditions and loyalties. While for many of these immigrants ethnicity was something to be overcome in assimilating to American middle-class life, for others it provided a basis for struggling against the established system of Yankee control. Such, for instance, was the case with Biggy Muldoon, Newburyport's own personification of this struggle. Muldoon, the son of Irish immigrants, publicly ridiculed the staid and conservative decorum of Newburyport's leading Yankee families by associating their cultivated propriety with a display of chamber pots hanging from the windows of his house. Later, he openly defied the city council by cutting down elm trees to open a filling station, the permit for which had been denied. Muldoon's popularity and mayoral election indicate that he was not altogether alone in his resentful challenge. Ethnicity, at any rate, created several strong divisions within the community.

Finally, local religious differences also threatened community unity and solidarity. The Protestant religious community itself was increasingly divided by a proliferation of competing sects, some of which accepted beliefs in direct opposition to the ideology of the larger community. More important, however, was the threat of Roman Catholicism. Imported by European immigrants and drawing its membership overwhelmingly from the lower classes, the Catholic church was soon larger than any local Protestant denomination. As Thernstrom points out, it was not easily accommodated to the older community framework:

> The [Catholic] church was so different, so alien—and
> it appeared to fulfill none of the traditional social
> functions of religious institutions. Its leaders were
> not members of the local elite; they came from out-
> side the city, usually from outside the United States.
> Rather than an instrument of community integra-
> tion, the church seemed an agency of separation;
> instead of reinforcing working class obedience to
> the local system of authority, it extended protec-
> tive isolation from the Protestant elite and directed
> the allegiance of its communicants elsewhere.
> [Thernstrom, 1964, pp. 47-48]

Despite these tendencies toward community dissolution, Warner presumed that since Newburyport had not degenerated into anarchy and anomie, it *must* have certain collectively shared symbols and values capable, on ceremonial occasions, of fostering moral integration and social solidarity. These he located in the Memorial Day parade activities.

Warner defined Memorial Day as "a cult of the dead which organizes and integrates the various faiths and national and class groups into a sacred unity." Organized around community cemeteries, "its principal themes are those of the sacrifice of the soldier dead for the living and the obligation of the living to sacrifice their individual purposes for the good of the group." In essence,

Memorial day ceremonies, and subsidiary rites such
as those of Armistice (or Veterans') Day, are rituals
comprising a sacred symbol system which functions
periodically to integrate the whole community with
its conflicting symbols and its opposing, autonomous
churches and associations. . . . [I]n the Memorial
Day ceremonies the anxieties man has about death
are confronted with a system of sacred beliefs about
death which give the individuals involved and the
collectivity of individuals a feeling of well-being.
Further, the feeling of triumph over death by collective action is made possible in the Memorial Day
parade by recreating the feeling of euphoria and the
sense of group strength and individual strength in the
group power which is felt so intensely in time of
war, when . . . the feeling so necessary for the Memorial Day's symbol system is originally created.
[1959, pp. 248-49]

The ceremonies themselves pass through a series of stages,
the sequence of which leads toward "the progressive integration
and symbolic unification of the group" (1962, p. 18). At first,
the many religious, ethnic, and associational groups conduct
their own separate ceremonies. Through a sequence of events,
the groups converge until they are finally united in the parade
itself. Thereafter, they respond collectively to the symbolic
themes of patriotism, war, and the sacrifice of dead soldiers.
Thus, "just as the totemic symbol system of the Australian
represents the idealized clan, and the African ancestral worship
symbolizes the family and state, so Memorial Day rites sym-
bolize and express the sentiments of the people for the total
community and for the state" (1959, p. 277). Warner concludes that Memorial Day rites "dramatically express the sentiments of unity of all the living among themselves, of all the
living with all the dead, and of all the living and dead as a group
with God. God, as worshipped by Catholic, Protestant, and
Jew, loses sectarian definition, limitations, and foreignness as
between different customs and becomes the common object
of worship for the whole group and the protector of everyone"

(1959, p. 279). A clearer statement of American civil religion could hardly be found.

Considering the profound community divisions he describes, Warner's arguments regarding the parade's functions would appear to exaggerate the extent and nature of community unity. (Indeed, some of Warner's critics, faced with his descriptions of both deepening community divisions and local harmony, have wondered if there are not two Newburyports.[3]) Specifically, largely because of his theoretical heritage, Warner fails even to consider the possibility that some groups are more committed than others to Memorial Day ceremonies, that groups derive very different benefits from them, and that, accordingly, they may participate for very different reasons. These concerns, which are addressed to the *substantive* bases of group participation, offer a much more historically and empirically grounded account of Memorial Day ceremonies and their social effects than could be addressed by Warner's ahistoric functionalist perspective.

Parades, Protestants, and Patriots: Old Middle-Class Participation in Memorial Day Ceremonies

The old Yankee middle classes saw labor unrest, the claims of ethnic groups, and the encroachment of Roman Catholicism as threats to their way of life and local control. Their perception was completely accurate, for as class, ethnic, and religious loyalties congealed, the traditional foundations of their dominance were increasingly undermined. More and more clearly, for these and other reasons, the old middle classes fell into decline.

Protestantism had always provided the validating symbolism for the way of life of the old middle classes generally and for the business community particularly. The stratum's *conscience collective*, to borrow a phrase from Durkheim, was primarily Protestant. With the intrusion of competing ethnic and religious values, however, the efficacy of earlier Protestant validations was inevitably diminished. As a result, the older dominant groups were faced with a need for newer, purely secular symbols of unity and self-legitimation. The symbols that received increasing emphasis because of this need were primarily patriotic and military, and were ritualized in such national celebrations as Memorial Day and the Fourth of July.

It is not surprising that old middle-class businessmen selected national patriotic symbols to supplant Protestantism. Indeed, the national loyalty of the old middle classes had always been based primarily on a strong identification with the values that, due largely to their own efforts, were the dominant principles of American society. At a very early date, the small town business stratum had appropriated and adapted the political symbolism of American democracy. Seizing initially on the political rhetoric of Andrew Jackson, who championed their cause against economic restrictions and monopolistic privileges in the 1820s and 1830s,[4] local entrepreneurs were ultimately able to establish themselves as defenders of freedom and equality, the backbone of American democracy. Of course, to the Main Street businessman or independent farmer equality had less to do with political guarantees of basic civil rights than with equality of opportunity. Their concern was for the freedom to compete and profit, the liberty to "get ahead." Nonetheless, by linking *laissez-faire* and free enterprise with political rights, the small town business stratum was able to fuse its own economic and civic ideologies with national patriotism. From this position, it was only a short step to the honoring of military symbols, especially of those soldiers whose supreme sacrifice secured national democratic principles and in the process saved America for business.

Not all of these symbols, values, and emphases were represented in the earliest Memorial Day ceremonies. The initial observances in the middle-1860s appear to have been rather spontaneous commemorations of the lives lost on both sides during the Civil War. As these observances gained legitimacy and legal status,[5] however, they also fell under the control of locally dominant groups who added new emphases to the proceedings. Increasingly stressed, for instance, were sentiments of patriotism, nationalism, loyalty, and civic-mindedness. Memorial Day rites, then, increasingly reflected the values and symbolism of those groups that had greatest control over their contents: the old middle-class business stratum.

Under these circumstances, the Memorial Day ceremonies—consisting largely of events sponsored by local business associations and veterans' organizations for the purpose of promoting nationalism, military power, and business-oriented civic consciousness—provided the old middle classes with a ritual context for both the collective affirmation of their own values and for a self-celebration of sorts. Throughout the ceremonies, such organizational bastions of old middle-class virtue as the Rotary Club, the Elks, and the American Legion are repeatedly praised, most often by their own members or by one another, for their civic contributions, their "Good Americanism," and patriotism. Given the themes of self-congratulation and self-affirmation implicit and often explicit in many Memorial Day events, the ceremonies appear in large part to be an effort by small town business classes to celebrate and reassure themselves of their own value to the community and nation, a testament to their own success. They undoubtedly derived a strong psychological reward for their own participation: a sense of self-justification, of rightness and righteousness. Thus, at one level for these still-dominant but declining classes, the parade may be viewed as a ritual expression of a now-secular theodicy of fortune; and at another level as a swaggering, yet defensive, show of self-importance by a stratum in decline.

In any case, for the old middle classes, the Memorial Day parade did provide a ritual context for the collective celebration of their own values and ideological principles. Their participation in parade events was motivated primarily by their strong identification with these values. This observation is less true for other groups in Newburyport. Because Warner did not distinguish any substantive grounds on which differing commitments might rest, he at least implicitly assumed that parade ceremonies were a celebration of values and symbols shared at similar levels of commitment by all participating groups. If that assumption may be set aside for a moment, it becomes apparent that not all groups participate in the parade for the same reasons or experience it in the same way. Even those groups that ceremonially affirm the ideological values of the old middle classes may do so for reasons quite unlike those of the middle classes themselves. That is, the participation of different groups may rest on very different substantive grounds. And if ritual involvement and social stability are to be adequately understood, those substantive grounds cannot be ignored by methodological fiat.

Parades and Pragmatists: Subordinate Group Participation in Memorial Day Ceremonies

In Newburyport as in many other American towns, by far the largest group of "others" was composed of immigrants and their descendants. First-generation immigrants typically brought to America an attitude of acceptance, considering even the worst jobs and lowest wages to be an improvement over conditions left behind in the old country. For second- and third-generation immigrants, too, America continued to be a land where dreams could come true. Stories of successful men who had risen from their own heritage were passed around with pride and envy as examples of those who "made it" and as proof that it could still be done. Countless immigrants and their descendants hoped and eagerly strove to duplicate such fabled successes, and were no less grateful for the opportunity when the dream was surrendered daily at the factory gates.

For many, involvement in such ceremonies as the Memorial Day parade may easily be interpreted as a public expression of gratitude for that opportunity. No doubt, many of Newburyport's immigrants largely accepted most of the values and symbols ceremonially expressed during that rite. In pointing to substantive grounds for their involvement, then the suggestion is in no way intended that their participation was simple hypocrisy. Nonetheless, for groups that had not been consistently reared on stars, stripes, and middle-class civic virtue, and that were still subject to considerable discrimination by dominant groups, sentiments of patriotism and civic solidarity did not come naturally. We might, therefore, expect that the ritual expression of such sentiments by these groups entails for them a perception of some more practical value.

Many immigrants ultimately achieved some measure of economic success, thus attaining a private portion of the American dream. Typically, as with the so-called lace curtain Irish, such persons then sought to transform their success into respectability.

Where this attempted transformation followed conventional
paths—and it ordinarily did, Biggy Muldoon notwithstanding—it
meant to accept the standards and values of dominant groups
and to emulate their conduct. In Newburyport and most other
American small towns, a fundamental aspect of this effort was
the acceptance and display of patriotic and civic virtues.

However patriotic and civic-minded an Irishman or Pole
might be, his opportunities for displaying these virtues to dominant groups were strictly limited in everyday encounters, for
he did not usually have access to Yankee, middle-class social
circles. Even the successful immigrant attended a different
church, associated largely with his own fellows, and so forth.
Generally unable to assert his claims for respectability on a
day-to-day basis, he could not afford to let pass any established
occasions for doing so. In this context, for upwardly mobile
and status-conscious immigrants, Memorial Day ceremonies
constituted an ideal opportunity to publicly demonstrate their
acceptance of the values appropriate to dominant middle-class
Americans and to claim middle-class respectability on that
basis. Those who organized parade activities for their own
groups could make more ambitious claims. Accordingly, the
more successful and aspiring members of each immigrant group
undoubtedly appropriated such opportunities. However ambitious the attempt, though, for some groups the Memorial
Day events did provide a ceremonial and highly visible forum
for claiming respectability by ritually displaying acceptance of
dominant values.

In this context, Memorial Day ceremonies may be viewed as
a greatly modified version of the older and now considerably
compromised Protestant requirement of proof before any
claims to respectability could be validated. In the sectarian
framework, the claimant for membership and esteem lived
among his judges. Similarly, after the sect had given way to
business associations, the claimant for credit-worthiness regularly crossed paths with potential and watchful creditors as his
qualifications were being evaluated. In both cases, the claimant's character and respectability were judged by scrutiny of
his everyday conduct. As previously mentioned, however, social distance ordinarily separated the immigrant from the audi-

ence to whom his claims were addressed. Established mechanisms for proving and validating claims to respectability, therefore, had to be adjusted accordingly. Hence, in place of the
requirement that ethical (respectable) virtues be proved through
everyday conduct, immigrant claimants were provided with
several ceremonial opportunities for their display, tantamount
to a public testimonial of their conversion to the American
faith. Since these public rites did not require the rigorous self-
rationalization of earlier proofs, however, and since the proofs
could not be verified by daily contact with the claimant, dominant groups continued to be somewhat suspicious of immigrant
claims to patriotism and civic-mindedness. Accordingly, their
claims for respectability were rarely wholeheartedly validated.[6]

In any case, for the socially ambitious, participation in the
rites had positive value; potentially at least, it could help gain
them acceptance and respect. For other groups in the community, however, claims for prestige probably had little to do with
their involvement in Memorial Day events. Blacks, the lower
classes generally, and less Americanized immigrants were not
typically in a position to make such claims even if they wanted
to. Yet, it should not be assumed that such groups participated
(if they did) only or even primarily out of a sincere identification
with the patriotic and civic-minded values and symbols carried
by old middle-class business groups. To make that assumption
for Newburyport's blacks, for instance, virtually all of whom
lacked real opportunities for political participation and economic
mobility, both neglects the actual historical experience of that
period and suggests an enormous amount of faith in the American dream.

Among immigrant groups, a considerable number either resisted or actively opposed the dominant principles of America,
often regarding its customs as immoral, its institutions bourgeois and oppressive, or its attitudes smug and self-righteous.
While these responses are typically associated with different
immigrant "mentalities,"[7] all share a strenuous resistance to
Americanization while retaining loyalty to a different set of
principles. Parochial schools, nationalistic organizations, mutual
aid and benefit societies, secret societies and other such institutions nurtured this resistance and often sustained it across

several generations. Not having very much to gain, a likely
substantive motive for ritual involvement by such groups might
be to avoid offending dominant groups and thus ensure against
possible losses. Certainly, their personal situations could not
be helped by being branded as unpatriotic, un-American, un-
grateful for opportunities, or even communist—all designations
offensive to dominant groups and that could even provoke
retribution of some sort (for example, sudden loss of job opportunities). Members of these groups who became involved
in Memorial Day rites apparently participated in an attempt to
be inoffensive, to stand pat.

Although Warner gives no indication otherwise, it should
not be assumed that all members of such groups, including
some lower class WASPs, participated at all in Memorial Day
ceremonies. Virtually every town, for instance, included a
group—variously designated as the vicarious leisure class, lum-
penproletariat, shack people, white trash[8] —which was socially
marginal at best. Eschewing any claim to acceptance and respectability by the conventional canons, this group often openly
flouted middle-class standards in its family relations, religious
practices (or lack thereof), consumption styles, treatment of
property, appearance, manner, and lack of civic pride. Having
little to gain or lose, these persons lacked a substantive motive
for participating in Memorial Day rites and, for that matter,
tended to avoid all other community affairs as well.[9] For these
groups, the common values and symbols were not only ineffec-
tive in producing integration, but were not really even common.
In either case, such unconventional persons were of little significance to the larger community.[10]

Clearly implicit in the involvement of those groups that *did*
participate is a measure of deference to the dominant stratum
whose values are celebrated in the parade.[11] Participation is
not only a claim for respect or a show of inoffensiveness, but
also a generally obligatory declaration of fealty to America, its
dominant principles, and the groups that coordinate and determine the contents for collective ceremonies. "Native" Americans
expected immigrants in particular to make such a declaration;
it was something owed in return for American munificence and
the opportunity it afforded. As such, participation in community

rites entailed a promise that dominant values would not be challenged and that older loyalties would not interfere with a new allegiance. In this sense, involvement in Memorial Day events was a demonstration of one's cooptability or cooptation (or assimilation in more common parlance). It was simultaneously a demonstration of one's successful "Americanization," which most immigrants viewed as entailing nothing but gain, and on that basis, a claim for entry into the dominant social order.

Psychologically, the sight of so many potentially threatening aliens publicly professing fealty must have been comforting to the dominant but declining groups. It might even be said that one of the "functions" of deference rites is to reduce the anxieties of those being deferred to. In addition, the same rites of deference and emulation confirmed the values and way of life of the dominant groups, thus contributing to an already strong, if now somewhat defensive, sense of self-justification.

The social benefits accruing to dominant groups from deference and emulative rituals are perhaps even more important than the psychological. Since the ritualized claims for entry made by incoming groups were addressed to dominant group standards, the effect was to confirm the middle classes' control of the status system and their own superior position within it. Moreover, by their participation in Memorial Day events, subordinate groups validated the implicit claims for legitimate domination made by the old middle classes, based on their status as primary carriers of the values being celebrated. In this sense, the Memorial Day rites provided an instrument for the "mobilization of bias"[12] on the part of the old Protestant middle-class stratum. Through this ceremonial device, they were able to sustain their own values and ideology and to affirm their own legitimate domination for a little longer.

Memorial Day Rites and Social Solidarity

None of these comments is intended to suggest that social stability, integration, or even emotional solidarity cannot be produced, renewed, and sustained in collective ceremonies. Certainly, for instance, the old Protestant middle classes derived from the Memorial Day participation a renewed sense of emotional solidarity. Since the public values of the collectivity were primarily their own—made so by their own efforts—their ceremonial affirmation of community and society was at the same time an affirmation of self. How, under these circumstances, could they fail to be imbued with a renewed sense of their own "peoplehood," their shared values, their common if mythologized history?[13] For the many aspiring members of subordinate groups, insofar as they accepted ceremonial values and/or insofar as their ritual claims for acceptance were felt to be successful, they no doubt also experienced a sense of belonging and affirmed their attachment to the community on that basis. Thus, Memorial Day ceremonies unquestionably helped sustain Newburyport's social stability.

The above analysis, however, clearly suggests that social order and moral solidarity are not produced by some social equivalent to spontaneous combustion, with ritualized common values and symbols exercising some apparently mystical and unifying power over the minds and emotions of people.[14] To the contrary, groups and individuals do not experience Memorial Day rites in identical fashion, they are differently motivated to participate at all, and they derive very different benefits from their involvement. Even discounting the larger interests in self-celebration, respectability claims, and the like, which have been mentioned, the parade involvement of some groups and individuals might also be accounted for by much more specific motives and benefits. Thus, for instance, local high school bands may derive a sense of pride from the opportunity to strut in public; the antique car collector is able to show off his vintage cars, highly polished for the occasion; and local businessmen may reap higher than usual profits from holiday merchandising promotions.

Once all of these crucial substantive differences are given their due, Memorial Day rites appear to be not so much a ceremonial context for the collective affirmation of shared values as they are a public arena in which groups struggle for control of and access to the ideal and material values available in society. Social order and stability appear to be but one possible outcome of these struggles,[15] one most likely to prevail, perhaps, when a domination has already been stabilized by other than ritual means. By and large, this appears to have been the case in Newburyport, even though challenges to the established domination were occasionally mounted (for example, the shoe strike and the Biggy Muldoon saga). The point, then, is not that Warner is simply wrong concerning the outcome of Memorial Day rites, but rather that he is largely right for insufficient reasons.

As has been argued, Warner at least implicitly assumed that all groups that participated in the parade events did so for much the same reasons (to celebrate the "cult of the dead" and the values they shared) and experienced it in much the same way (as a renewed sense of collective solidarity). Two methodological premises underlie Warner's argument. First is the familiar functionalist assumption, inherited from Durkheim and Radcliffe-Brown, that there *must* exist some common values and symbols to which everyone responds similarly, or else the society could not endure. Of perhaps greater importance in the present context, however, Warner also relied heavily for information, as anthropologists are prone to do, on a select group of informants. As some of his critics have remarked,[16] especially with reference to his subjective measures of stratification, Warner's primary informants appear to be derived from the same middle- and upper-class business stratum that so strongly identifies with community (business) interests and military symbolism and for whom the parade provided a vehicle of self-celebration. From them, Warner apparently derived an ideological image of the whole community[17] which he then extended to all groups and for which he found ritual expression, as required by the functionalist assumption, in the Memorial Day parade.

By and large, Warner transformed the motivational and ritual experience of a single, albeit dominant, stratum into a societal principle, without considering the alternative situations, motives, and experiences of other groups. Thus viewed, Memorial Day rites and the values they celebrate are not so much ceremonial affirmations of the community's "sacred symbol system" or of a genuinely collective religious dimension. Instead, they are ritual expressions of the secularized civic ideology of the still-dominant old Protestant middle classes. The orthodox position or ideological dominance of this creed was sustained not so much by the "sacredness" or even sharedness of its contents as by the mechanisms through which the old middle classes maintained their social dominance. One of these, as we have attempted to demonstrate, was the Memorial Day parade itself.

And yet, in some ways the Memorial Day parade was a final symbol and instrument of old middle-class dominance, for like the old middle classes themselves, neither the contents nor the consequences of Memorial Day ceremonies could withstand the structural revolution that transformed America. As a new middle-class stratum replaced the old, the management and expression of civic virtue were taken out of the hands of Main Street and taken over by Washington bureaucrats, who have become the national arbiters of civic and patriotic celebrations. In this national context, Memorial Day has become part of an annual holiday system that has been rationalized to fit the needs of the modern industrial system and that is increasingly geared to extending the length of certain weekends into three or four days. These developments allow the newer salaried middle classes more leisure time for sports, tourism, entertainment, and recreational pursuits, thereby instituting more of the Devil's workshop as national policy.

For their part, the remaining old middle classes seem to be satisfied with this arrangement if only because it allows a possibility for merchandise promotions, increased local sales, and an expanded volume of trade in resort and tourist towns. By and large, the traditional values of the older middle classes appear to have dissolved into a commercialism devoid even of secular spirituality. What's good for business has become simply good.

CIVIC MORALS AND SOCIAL STRUCTURE IN THE NEW AMERICAN SOCIETY

Structural Contours of the New American Society

The United States emerged from World War II in enviable shape. Politically and militarily, the nation had become a major world power. In sole possession of the most devastating weapon ever witnessed, the United States stood alone at the pinnacle of world powers. Equally important, it was the only nation whose industrial plant survived the war intact. With Europe and Japan rebuilding, American industry faced virtually no international economic competition. As a result, the postwar years witnessed the fruition of American capitalism. Both politically and economically, the world was America's playground. The Age of American Empire had begun.

The old middle classes, of course, loudly applauded these developments, both out of patriotism and an identification with the success of American business. America, in their eyes, had finally assumed its rightful place in world affairs. Ironically, however, the old middle classes were themselves victims of the very developments they celebrated, for the ultimate effect of postwar circumstances was to vastly accelerate the structural changes that had been undermining their class positions, their way of life, and their characteristic morality for the past hundred years.

The structural developments following World War II continued in much the same direction as those that had been gradually changing the face of America for a century. Yet, so sudden and vast and impressive were the changes of the postwar years that it seemed a much more profound transformation had occurred. And in some ways it had, for by dramatically completing the institutional transformation that had been developing for a hundred years, postwar America was a qualitatively different society than what it had been before. America had entered the war as an industrial nation. Only a short time after the war had ended, as various observers agreed, it had become something more. Post-Industrial Society,[1] New Industrial State,[2] New American Society,[3] mass society,[4] monopoly capitalism[5] — each label represents an intellectual effort to comprehend the dimensions of what America had suddenly become. And while each of these descriptions emphasizes different features, all agree on the basic contours of postwar American society.

First, Big Business has become truly enormous. Antitrust and related legislation notwithstanding, virtually every sector of the postwar economy, including agricultural production, has come to be dominated by corporate Leviathans the size and scope of which might have astonished Carnegie himself. By 1962, to give some indication of their magnitude, only 100 corporations controlled 55 percent of the total assets of all manufacturing industries in America; the 1,000 largest controlled 82 percent. By 1976, only 500 corporations controlled 72 percent of all manufacturing assets. Several of the largest corporations, such as General Motors and Exxon, have for some years now enjoyed annual gross receipts larger than those of all but a handful of the world's nations. Given the enormous economic power of Big Business, small independent businessmen can usually survive only in those areas that are either "small potatoes" or not sufficiently profitable to warrant a takeover. At any rate, small business is marginal to the overall economy.

The growth of the federal government has been no less impressive, as might be expected of a developing welfare state and world empire. Nonmilitary growth, located primarily in the expansion of federal services and regulatory agencies, escalated the public payroll by 25 percent from 1957 to 1965. The Defense Department employs over a million persons. Big Business, by any measure, has an equally obese cousin in Big Government.

An almost natural accompaniment to organizational growth and centralization has been a steady increase in bureaucratic organization. As the inescapable price of survival in a complex society, it has penetrated into virtually every area of institutional life, including not only business and government, but also trade unions, universities, churches, hospitals, the arts, and even, to some extent, the family.[6] Since World War II, bureaucracy has emerged as the dominant, and very nearly the only, mode of organization in American society.

These and other developments, especially the emergence of mass communications industries, have virtually destroyed local autonomy, such as once existed for country towns. Replacing local controls, central bureaucratic institutions now tend to direct and coordinate many everyday activities for the whole society. In this sense at least, America has truly become a "mass society."

These same structural changes have also accelerated the revolution in class structures that had been developing for a century. As a result, the old middle classes and their way of life are now virtually exhausted, surviving only on the margins of society. In their place, as Mills (1951) demonstrated, postwar institutional growth and centralization have brought to fruition a new middle class stratum. The positions of these new middle classes are based not on small property holdings, but on occupation. They are the white collar workers and managers for bureaucratic organizations in business, government, and elsewhere. By 1940, in Mills's estimate, the new middle classes constituted 25 percent of the total labor force. Since the 1950s, they have comprised the largest stratum in American society.

These features of postwar American society are too well known to require further elaboration. What has been said is sufficient to lead us to the point. The old Protestant middle-class civic morality existed within and was sustained by an institutional context that no longer exists except, perhaps, marginally. Moreover, not only does the centralized and bureaucratized order which has replaced its institutional supports *not* uphold the civic morals of the old middle classes, it encourages completely different kinds of ethics and conduct relating to civic concerns. Ultimately, the demise of old middle-class civic morals is perhaps best revealed by pointing to the noncivic moralities that have emerged to displace and compete with them.

Bureaucracy and Civic Morality: Morals for Managers and Upper Level Bureaucrats

Rarely does a week go by without news of some improper, illegal, and distinctly un-civic conduct by our central institutions and those who manage them. The Hooker Chemical Company, for instance, knowingly endangered the life and health of many people by dumping poisonous chemical wastes into the Love Canal at Niagara Falls. Ford Motor Company continued producing the Pinto despite warnings of the explosive potential of its fuel tank. The FBI and CIA have systematically violated the civil rights of citizens and have repeatedly broken some laws to selectively enforce others. Pharmaceutical industries have fabricated test data in order to market unsafe but profitable drugs. Corporate bribery and payoffs have become as commonplace and as publicized as price fixing. And, of course, there is Watergate, the most dramatic and best known case of all.[7] Many other examples could also be cited.[8]

So extensive and numerous and routine are such offenses that they have become "normal" features of American society, in much the same sense as Durkheim regarded crime and suicide rates to be normal for societies. As such, these and similar infractions cannot be explained as the isolated misdeeds of a relatively few individuals, but rather must be considered as part of the structure and performance of American institutions. Specifically, it appears that the kind of behavior described here expresses a morality forged by direct experience in the bureaucratic organizations which have come to dominate postwar American society. Bureaucracy appears to create its own morality and selects its own carriers for what it creates.[9]

At first glance, such activities involve grave risks for their perpetrators. Some of these activities are illegal and if discovered could not only cost a person his or her job (for the good of the company), but could also result in prison sentences. Equally important, some of the activities which managers of organizations undertake may well contradict their own basic values, such as honesty or a belief in the sanctity of human life. If they were fully aware of the import of their decisions and actions, perhaps only the most callous managers would persist in such behavior. This is not the case, however. Bureaucratic organizations, as part of their very structure, establish what might be termed a "moral context" which is conducive to such conduct. Most features of this context tend to separate bureaucrats from the consequences of their decisions and actions and thus allow them to evade responsibility (at both social and psychological levels) for their own behavior.

Bureaucracies consist of offices, each with its own particular duties. Largely as a result of this arrangement, officials are often able to evade legal penalties for possible criminal activities. Simply put, because authority and responsibilities are parcelled out, accountability is difficult to locate within bureaucracies. For example, top level executives who may have ordered illegal acts can claim ignorance as to the activities of zealous underlings. Without unusual access to an organization's internal lines of communication, prosecutors are hard pressed to dispute such claims. Hence, in several cases a corporation has been convicted for illegal acts while all or most of its executives have been acquitted for lack of evidence. It is precisely this problem of accountability which added drama to the unfolding Watergate scandal and which found its clearest articulation in the question, "What did he know and when did he know it?" Despite all manner of circumstantial evidence and the accusing testimony of some underlings, the extent of Nixon's involvement might still not be known had it not been for the chance discovery of the White House tapes. In most cases, of course, such evidence is not ordinarily available.

Not only does specialization of offices enable officials to avoid legal penalties, but also it provides them with a means of assuaging, or even completely evading, whatever guilt might otherwise result from their actions. Office specialization assigns particular tasks to each office and its incumbents, and in doing so also limits the actions for which any single bureaucrat is responsible. The contributions of any particular bureaucrat to organizational policy might therefore be integral, yet confined to a specific task or issue. Accordingly, in cases of organizational malfeasance, the individual bureaucrat can frequently rationalize away his or her own involvement through a form of self-deception made available by the structure of bureaucracy itself—that is, by focusing exclusively on specific official duties and ignoring the larger policy to which those duties contribute. Thus, for instance, when the B. F. Goodrich Company attempted to fabricate test data in order to pass the defective aircraft brakes it had designed for military use, one of the engineers charged with writing the report justified his involvement by claiming that, "After all . . . we're just drawing some curves, and what happens to them after they leave here, well, we're not responsible for that." As his fellow report-writer later admitted: "He was just trying to persuade himself that as long as we were concerned with only one part of the puzzle and didn't see the complete picture, we really weren't doing anything wrong" (Vandivier, 1972, p. 17). Conceivably, the most successful practitioners of such self-deception might even be able to obscure their own complicity to themselves and thereby avoid even the realization that their actions have larger consequences for which they might be responsible.

Another opportunity for self-deception is afforded by the bureaucratic spirit of instrumental rationalism. There appears to be no issue or situation, however grave its effects on human beings, which cannot be converted into a purely pragmatic concern by bureaucratic reasoning.[10] Thus, for instance, when General Motors in the late 1960s received widespread complaints that its schoolbuses were defective and unsafe, it neither reevaluated the quality of its buses nor recalled them for correction. At no point, in fact, did General Motors's management appear to consider the potential dangers of these defects to schoolchildren. Instead, virtually all actions by company functionaries—including withholding records of repairs, lying, and delaying—were addressed to the more practical problems of preventing news of the defects from reaching public notice and presumably of protecting the company's sales and reputation. Only after newspapers reported on the defective buses did the company order a recall.[11] In thus converting moral issues into practical concerns, bureaucracies enable officials to ignore the moral implications of their own actions, thereby making unethical actions somewhat easier to perform.

The impersonal nature of bureaucratic organization provides much the same opportunity. Bureaucracies can offer only standardized solutions to the average needs, interests, and problems of average people, thus rendering it incapable of administering to the idiosyncratic needs and desires of particular individuals. The personal peculiarities of those to whom a bureaucracy and its officials administer are thus blurred, leveled, and reduced to a lowest common denominator: their interest in the product or service which the bureaucracy offers. As a result, in carrying out their official duties bureaucrats often conceive of the public not as particular flesh and blood people, but as an impersonal, amorphous category. Victimization can only be facilitated when the potential victims are depersonalized.[12] The same people who might be revolted by crimes of violence perpetrated by one individual upon another can themselves make policy decisions leading to far more widespread suffering when the potential victims are shrouded by anonymity.[13]

An additional factor is that officials are typically separated from those affected by their decisions. The chances are very good that the actual victims will remain anonymous, for rarely do they directly confront the bureaucratic decision-makers responsible for their suffering. Thus, not having to face the human consequences of their actions (which, sometimes, as in the thalidomide case, can be hideous and grotesque), bureaucrats do not have to fully face their own responsibility and guilt.

Each of these features of bureaucracy contributes to a context in which morality itself is rationalized, sin is impersonalized, and guilt is rendered almost obsolete. The moral milieu thus created is almost ideally suited to behavior like that described in the above examples. By separating bureaucratic decision-makers from the social and psychological consequences of their actions, bureaucracies systematically provide them with opportunities or invitations to indulge in such behavior.

The mere existence of such opportunities, however, does not fully explain how this kind of conduct has become almost intrinsic to American institutions. Bureaucracies must also have some means of encouraging or compelling bureaucratic decision-makers to take advantage of the opportunities with which they are provided. This is accomplished by internal disciplinary procedures that transform these opportunities into esteemed and rewarded conduct and ultimately into moral virtues.

Bureaucratic morals leading to improper behavior are largely the products of organizational disciplinary procedures that operate very much like those of the Protestant sects and of the various fraternal and businessmen's associations to which they gave rise. Indeed, one type of modern organization, the business corporation, appears to be a direct descendant of these earlier organizational forms. Clearly indicating Protestant influence, for example, the earliest American corporations were expected to serve some "ethical as well as public good," and most did in fact take the form of a private beneficial association tending to some public need. Only later did they become concerned with a more exclusively private interest. As Huizinga (1972, p. 59) points out:

> We can observe in a number of points this transition from the beneficial association to the business company. . . . The first fire insurance company in Philadelphia began as a club which met monthly and which fined absentees. The oldest life insurance company in Pennsylvania had the name in 1759 of "The Corporation for the Relief of Poor and Distressed Presbyterian Ministers, and of the poor and distressed widows and children of Presbyterian ministers." The oldest bank, Robert Morris's, developed out of a patriotic enterprise set up during the war to support the shaky credit of the United States. The first business corporation in New Jersey was carefully named the "Society for Establishing Useful Manufactures." The freedom to form corporations

> was still limited to societies with religious, charit-
> able, and literary purposes. . . . North Carolina was
> the first state to establish general freedom to form
> corporations in 1795.[14]

In any case, the disciplinary procedures of modern corporations particularly and of bureaucratic institutions generally
closely resemble those of the earlier sects and associations.
Like the devout Puritan seeking sect membership or the small
town businessman seeking credit, the modern manager is compelled to prove himself or herself to company superiors as a
condition for career advancement (the occupational version
of salvation). Salary and social self-esteem depend primarily
upon office and title, and preferred positions cannot be attained
except by consistently demonstrating the requisite ethical
virtues. In this sense, the modern manager makes himself over
in accordance with organizational and career requirements and
comes ultimately to possess the social character and moral
virtues of the Organization Man.[15]

For the Main Street businessman, both social self-esteem
and business opportunities were inextricably linked to the
possession, or at least display, of civic morals. For the Organization Man, on the other hand, self-interest focused on career
mobility takes a very different path. Civic contributions count
for little or nothing; rather, only that conduct which benefits
the organization is esteemed.

As a result of these organizational mechanisms for instilling
values and character traits, the requisite virtues of the Organization Man include not only the conspicuous conformity and
social adaptability emphasized by Whyte (1956) and Reisman
(1950), but also a moral myopia that sometimes finds expression in actions like those described earlier. Generally, the manager must be willing and able to dispense with any ideology or
standard of judgment apart from that of organizational expediency.[16] To the degree, then, that organizational discipline
is effective, the moral universe of successful managers is nar-
rowed to the normative context of the organizations for which
they work. Organizational and ideological commitments are
made synonymous.[17]

Ethical conduct for managers and aspiring bureaucrats comes to be defined as whatever advances the particularistic interests of one's organization, whatever those interests might be (profits, power, preservation of internal secrecy, punishment of enemies, and so forth), however they are pursued (lies, bribes, payoffs, cheating, stonewalling, fraud), and apparently, at whatever risk to public safety. By the same token, those who "rock the boat" or "blow the whistle" on internal goings-on, or generally take seriously the older notions of civic morality, have become bureaucratic equivalents to the heretics and "knockers" of an earlier age. They are the "moral lepers" of bureaucracy.

Obviously, not all managers share these traits to the same degree. Rather, these traits are ideal typical features of the social character of the Organization Man, showing up more clearly in one manager than another. Nonetheless, these characteristics express a morality that is given sufficient encouragement within America's central bureaucratic institutions to at least produce some approximations to the ideal. And, of course, it is a morality far removed from that of the old middle classes. Civic morality has been sacrificed for organizational expediency.

Bureaucracy and Civic Morality: Typical Responses to Bureaucratic Structure

Those who make decisions in and for bureaucratic organizations, or who aspire to, are scarcely alone in being affected by their moral climate. So pervasive and extensive is the influence of bureaucratic organizations that it is difficult to imagine anyone whose life has not been touched by them. The vast majority of people, however, including lower- and middle-level personnel as well as those not employed by bureaucracies, do not share the situation of the Organization Man. Rather, they have experienced the social power, instrumentalism, and impersonality of bureaucratic organizations primarily from the other side, not as directors but as those being directed and manipulated by them. From this vantage, large segments of the society have come to regard many of America's central institutions with resentment, distrust, and even hostility.

Such resentment is largely the result of the impersonal nature
and operation of bureaucratic organizations. The average American is confronted daily by a host of faceless institutions with
sterile and anonymous-sounding names: Exxon, FBI, CIA, Con
Ed, IBM, ITT, HEW, TRW, CBS, and so on. In regular association with these and other organizations, individuals are treated
as impersonal entities, as numbers, as nonpersons whose sole
worth lies in their possession of money with which to pay taxes
and bills or to make consumer choices. Rarely are individuals
recognized for characterological attributes, such as honesty and
trustworthiness, and seldom are they extended even the basic
courtesies of friendliness and politeness. This is especially the
case when someone registers a complaint or seeks redress for
overcharges, and in the process is required to endure all manner
of discomfort, indignity, and frustration. So well known are
such instances that they have even entered into the folklore of
bureaucratic society, finding expression in popular literature,
jokes, pop music, television sitcoms, and cartoons. All told, so
impersonally do many institutions operate that they have come
to be widely perceived as uncaring, unresponsive to human
needs, and unconcerned for human welfare.

Increasingly, American institutions are also being perceived
as exploitative, a perception aided in no small way by routine
reports of organizational malfeasance like those already discussed. So accustomed have people become—either directly or
vicariously through the news media—to being victimized by
unsafe products and practices, "gouged" by price manipula-
tions, "screwed" by the government, and "ripped off" by corporations that they now take for granted that organizations
operate solely for their own benefit, without concern for the
social consequences of their actions. Thus, for instance, when
the United States experienced an oil shortage in 1978, many
people quickly and automatically assigned blame to oil company conspiracies. Whether such conspiracies were actually
responsible is less important to present concerns than the fact
that so many people were ready to believe they were, even
before any supporting evidence was available.[18] Such suspi-
cion is symptomatic of a general distrust and resentment, the
objects of which are scarcely confined to the oil companies. It

is not to prurient curiosity, for instance, that we must attribute the success of the late 1970s bestseller, *The Screwing of the Average Man* (Hapgood, 1974).

Finally, many people feel generally powerless in the face of America's large and impersonal institutions. Since it is ordinarily as solitary individuals rather than organized groups that they are confronted by the far greater power and resources of these institutions, such a perception is hardly surprising. In any case, "the system" (even this expression indicates its impersonality) is widely thought to be so powerful as to be seldom responsive to pressures from below. Many people consider themselves marionettes dancing to the tugs and pulls of a faceless puppeteer.

These perceptions of the impersonality, exploitativeness, and power of American institutions inevitably influence the ways groups respond to and behave toward and within them. Several of these responses are sufficiently widespread to merit our attention. None is notable for civic content.

Going Through the Motions

In a well-known psychology experiment, caged dogs are administered random electric shocks. After initially trying to avoid the shocks, the dogs finally give in to their ineluctable misfortune and simply lie down to endure it. In the end, having acquired "learned helplessness," the dogs will remain in the cage even when the door is open.

The dogs in this experiment appear to have a great deal in common with large numbers of contemporary Americans, who also apparently feel unable to control their own fates. Feeling themselves subject to and manipulated by powerful, impersonal forces which can be neither controlled nor comfortably endured, they first grow cynical (a response presumably not available to their canine counterparts) and ultimately retreat into an attitude of invincible indifference.[19] Seldom can they be shaken from such apathy, for the energy required to resist is efficiently drained by a stronger sense of futility and cynicism. Even assuming that City Hall or Exxon or Con Ed can be successfully fought, few have the force of will necessary to do so.

An especially important variant of this response might be termed "going through the motions." Those afflicted are themselves often bureaucratic workers—most often those who receive more orders than they dispense or who see no opportunity for advancement within their organizations. They may also be blue collar laborers, service professionals—virtually anyone. They do their jobs, fulfilling all requirements, but like automatons, they work mechanically and matter-of-factly, with a minimum investment of personal commitment. Neither their jobs nor apparently any other of America's rationalized institutions furnish them with adequate fulfillment and meaning.

While feeling generally powerless to improve their own life fate, they are in any case too dependent on a regular salary to throw off their present predicament. The salary sustains that aspect of life to which their energies are most often devoted: a chosen style of life with its attendant standard of consumption.[20] The paycheck provides the basis on which each constructs and sustains his or her own personal system of meaning.[21] To virtually all else, including notions of civic obligation, they tend to be relatively indifferent, and they remain so at least as long as the economic basis for their life-style is unchallenged.

Dropping Out

For many others, even "going through the motions," with its acceptance of a conventional job, entails too great a personal commitment to the rationalized structures of the modern industrial order. Either unable or disinclined to meet the system on its own terms, which might be regarded as "joining the rat race" or "selling out," a considerable number withdraw altogether from active involvement within its institutions. In more common parlance, they "drop out," seeking personal meaning and fulfillment in alcohol and drug subcultures, nonindustrial life-styles (for example, back-to-nature and communal movements), sectarian movements (both religious and political), and so forth. Unlike the situation among earlier Protestant sectarians, for a great many dropouts quests for personal meaning and fulfillment are not connected to any sort of social obligations.[22] Accordingly, from the point of view of major institutions, dropping out can be interpreted only as a willful abdication of civic responsibilities. Indeed, even those dropouts whose rejection of the existing society is coupled with a dedication to change it for the better, as they perceive it (for example, would-be revolutionaries and terrorists) are not usually regarded as civic-minded according to the conventional canons. In any case, it may well be, as some have suggested,[23] that a sizable and distinct, if somewhat disorganized, "counterculture" (many segments of which hold noncivic ideologies) has become an endemic and therefore permanent feature of modern industrial society.

Working the System

Still other groups neither retreat from nor helplessly endure the system of contemporary American society. Rather, their resentment of its rationalized institutions motivates them to resist and even to strike back, either by "bending" the system to the pursuit of personal goals or by defeating it in selected encounters.

The first response is often referred to as "working the system." Sometimes justified by participants as "just looking out for Number One," it generally refers to an effort by individuals to exploit their positions within American institutions to personal advantage. Employee theft is perhaps the simplest and most frequent instance of working the system, but it scarcely exhausts the options of those with sufficient nerve and imagination. Many low-level bureaucrats, for example, are routinely confronted with the possibility of supplementing their incomes by using their limited but strategic authority for purposes of bribery and graft. That the knock of opportunity is frequently answered is attested by recently reported cases in Chicago, where apparently city inspectors routinely accepted bribes as a precondition for granting required licenses to restauranteurs, and in the Immigration Service, where bribes are often accepted in exchange for entry visas. University professors have also been known to work the system, otherwise known as grantsmanship, by utilizing research monies for purposes other than those for which they were intended.

Beating the System

The same exploitative orientation toward social institutions also finds expression among those groups who attempt to "beat the system" in some contest of their own choosing. While the varieties of this response are many, most appear to involve some form of theft. A considerable and apparently increasing number of Americans, for instance, now systematically cheat on their income tax returns. Many others devise methods for stealing services, particularly from the telephone company and electric utilities. Shoplifting, by far the most popular method for beating the system, has reached epidemic proportions, totaling over $5 billion in annual losses.[24] If such figures do not sufficiently indicate the pervasiveness of this attitude toward American institutions, one need only look to popular culture, in which a D. B. Cooper[25] is lionized and movies enjoy great success by pitting a resourceful David against the system's malevolent Goliath.

The same resentful and exploitative response to the rationalized institutions of American society has, in some circles, found expression in even more sublimated and ideological form. Adherents of the "rip-off ethic," which differs only in degree from the more generalized efforts to "beat the system," unabashedly regard the theft of goods and services from most institutions to be meritorious activity. Although not necessarily typical of its practitioners, Abbie Hoffman best articulated the basics of this response in his book, appropriately titled *Steal This Book*. Essentially a manual for putting the ethic into practice, the book details the most recent techniques of "inventory shrinkage" (shoplifting) and, in the words of one reviewer, offers advice on how to furnish oneself with free "food, clothes, housing, transportation, medical care, even money and dope" (Rader, 1971, p. 19).

Efforts to beat or rip-off the system may, of course, be undertaken purely for personal gain. More often than not, however, they seem also to be motivated by adventurism, gamesmanship (the rip-off ethic particularly has many characteristics of sport), and an apparently genuine sense of justice, administered cowboy style. Hence, it is not unusual for participants to justify their conduct on the basis that they are reclaiming what they feel should not have been expropriated in the first place in the form of overcharges, high taxes, and the like.

All of these generalized ideologies, it bears repeating, appear to have emerged as responses to the structural arrangements of postwar American society, especially to the bureaucratic operation of its large-scale institutions. This being so, it can reasonably be expected that those groups most exposed to bureaucratic organization will most frequently adopt these responses. This does, in fact, seem to be the case, as these subcultural ideologies and moralities appear to find most support in urban areas, where population density creates greater demands for efficient organization, and among youth, whose entire life experience has been spent within the institutional structure of postwar society.

To reiterate some themes, the old Protestant middle classes, their way of life, and their characteristic morality were sustained by an institutional framework that no longer exists. Slowly at first, but finally and spectacularly in the years following World War II, a new, qualitatively different institutional order undermined and replaced it. Not only has the new order not given special encouragement to the older civic morals, but it has also fostered subcultural attitudes, ideologies, and moralities that can only be considered noncivic in content. As these noncivic ideologies emerged, including that of the Organization Man, the Protestant-based, old middle-class civic morality was nudged ever closer to obsolescence.

Viewed in terms of a long-term secular and historical trend, these developments indicate that the values of individualism and civic responsibility, which had been sustained in a state of balanced tension first by Puritanism and later by the framework of small town business, were finally split apart as a result of changing institutional structures. That is, individual conduct has been separated from the ideational and institutional contexts that once channeled it into civic directions, so that it now stands alone, largely unregulated by collective controls. The resulting unrestrained individualism is given rampant expression in pursuit of personal gain even as individual identity is leveled and repressed by bureaucratic society. At the same time, the civic morality that once served to guide individual conduct appears today to be virtually exhausted, continuing to exist primarily as public relations images promoted through speeches of public officials and through such national holidays as Memorial Day, the Fourth of July, and, to some extent, Super Bowl Sunday. Thus, only half of the original Puritan dialectic remains operative: an individualism which, without the moral restraints of the other half, is oriented ever more exclusively by nothing more than instrumental rationalism. The covenant, as Bellah suggests, has indeed been broken.

And yet, despite the ever-deepening effects of this secular trend, neither the civic nor the economic components of the old Protestant middle-class morality has faded completely and obligingly into oblivion. Throughout history, during and following the decline of a dominant stratum, some groups continue to embrace its values and attitudes, either in whole or in part. The present case offers no exception. Thus, for instance, as another product of organizational and especially corporate discipline, a self-sacrificing devotion to labor survives among those strata in which "workaholics" and routine overtimers proliferate: the managerial ranks of the upper middle classes. With regard to civic values, various small town and rural communities throughout the country, still dominated by surviving remnants of the old middle classes, have managed to resist to some degree the penetration of larger social changes, accepting cultural backwardness as the price for their tenacity. Fundamentalist and rural communities in the South and Midwest are the most obvious holdouts of this sort. Also continuing to espouse the old Protestant middle-class standards is a large proportion of clergymen, who apparently feel less able to regulate morality in a rationalized, organized society whose interactants are impersonalized (as in situations described above) and where sin is virtually obsolete.

According to Weber, a stratum of intellectuals usually also remains in some way devoted to the values of the displaced past. We are interested in only a small segment of this stratum in America, a segment that has remained committed to the older Protestant civic values and that has sought to reformulate and integrate them into the institutional framework and operating rationale of the new American society. Being academic intellectuals, these thinkers have, of course, recognized the secularization of Puritan values and thus, unlike clergymen and fundamentalists, have not sought biblical supports for their efforts. They have instead found in Durkheim's theory of religion both nonbiblical support for their own Protestant-based civic values and a means to transform those values into a national ideology and operating rationale for the new bureaucratic society. Two major exponents of this new rationale are Talcott Parsons and Robert Bellah, both of whom have attempted the fundamental transvaluation in question.

CIVIC MORALS AND THE SOCIAL SYSTEM: PARSONS, PROTESTANTISM, AND AMERICAN CORE VALUES

"Core Values" of American Society

According to Talcott Parsons, the common or core values of American society have their origins in "fundamental religious roots, above all, in the traditions which Max Weber, in *The Protestant Ethic and the Spirit of Capitalism*, called those of 'ascetic Protestantism'." In virtually eliminating the individual's reliance on an external churchly authority and thereby making the relationship between mortals and God a more personal one, Protestantism strongly emphasized the individual's personal autonomy and "responsibility for positive action." In addition, it established as an ethical injunction that he actively work to construct God's kingdom on earth. Taken together, these emphases form a value system that Parsons terms "instrumental activism" and defines as

> the subordination of the personal needs of the individual to an objective "task" to which he is expected to devote his full energies, and the subjection of the actions of all to universalistic standards of judgment. Associated with this is the importance of universalizing the essential conditions of effective performance through equalization of civil rights and of access to education and health. [1960, p. 311]

Associated with the orientations of ascetic Protestantism, Parsons argues, was the voluntary principle and its implicit toleration of denominational differences. Ultimately, religious tolerance was expressed in "a common matrix of value-commitment which is broadly shared between denominations, and which forms the basis of the sense in which the society as a whole forms a religiously based moral community" (1963, p. 62).[1] While the core of this matrix is clearly derived from Protestantism, Parsons echoes Herberg (1960) in arguing that "the three dominant 'faiths' of American society (Protestantism, Catholicism, and Judaism) have come to be integrated into a single socio-religious system [and that] . . . the basic value pattern common to all three faiths has been at least partially institutionalized at a higher level of generality" (1964, p. lxii).

Although the society has changed considerably since Protestant values were first established in America, Parsons insists that its core values—instrumental activism—"have not been fundamentally changed in the course of our national history" (1960, p. 311). By this, Parsons does not mean, of course, that religion itself has endured three hundred years unmarked. Clearly, the religion of today is not that of our Puritan ancestors. Through the process of secularization, in Parsons's special sense of structural differentiation,[2] organized religion has been affected by a considerable "loss of function." However, he insists, it does not follow "that secularization in *this* sense is synonomous with value change" (1960, p. 12). In fact, the original Protestant values have been extended and institutionalized throughout secular society. Thus, despite the enormous structural revolution that has taken place in American society, and especially its "tremendous process of economic growth," American core values have been largely unaffected. While the structural reorganization of society has, of course, had "very important repercussions on people," Parsons insists that these be regarded as modifications in the more personal role-values and not as changes "in the general value-orientation of the society as a whole on the highest levels" (1960, p. 319).

In short, Parsons concludes, "the Protestant Ethic is far from dead." Structural and institutional developments notwithstanding, "it continues to inform our orientations to a very important sector of life today as it did in the past" (1974, p. 221). And it does so, Parsons would argue, in terms of both the economic and civic values associated with the Protestant Ethic. Contemporary American values continue to center on economic production and development (1969, p. 206) and to stress individual responsibility for positive action within a collective context. It is at least partly on the basis of these surviving value patterns and the shared orientations derived from them that American society is sustained as a morally solidary "collectivity."[3]

Little imagination is required to see that this value-pattern, with its emphasis on individual responsibility, obligation to the collectivity, toleration, and universal standards of judgment, is very nearly the same set of values which Warner described as characteristic of Newburyport and which, as we have argued, were imprinted as fairly typical features of American small towns by its primary carriers, the old Protestant middle and business classes. And yet, by the time Parsons addressed himself to the problem of order in America, these values had already declined to the point that they no longer guided the conduct of many Americans. Therefore, in considering Parsons's work, we shall be most concerned to discern why these particular values continued to occupy a central role in his efforts to understand American social order.

Social Heritage: Parsons and Protestantism

Parsons gives the relationship between core values and social integration both theoretical emphasis and, with reference to American society, substantive content. These features of Parsons's work, however, cannot simply be addressed as if intellectual influences, especially Durkheim, were alone important in their development. If, as many have rightly contended, the most important aspect of Parsons's inheritance from Durkheim was a concern with the fundamental problem of order, it can safely be said that he brought to that problem, in both its theoretical and empirical features, a good deal more than his considerable intellectual talents and scholarly resources. In particular, he brought to it a *Weltanschaaung* that was formed largely by his own personal exposures and experiences, especially by those of his early years. That is, Parsons's ideas on society generally and on America particularly were shaped in a historical and institutional context of which he himself was a part. A key feature of that context was Protestantism.

The influence of Protestantism on early American sociology has been well established. Just as Main Street businessmen who were more interested in business than religion were nonetheless strongly influenced by a fading religious ideology, so social thinkers of the same era were affected in a similar manner. The problems they addressed were undeniably substantive,[4] but the Protestant influences of their own heritage consistently informed their work. Some, after all, had left the ministry to become sociologists. Protestantism constituted much of their personal, intellectual, and moral background; it could not be easily jettisoned by simply exchanging pulpits. Protestant conceptions, though transvalued into secular expression, frequently provided a resource for dealing with their respective substantive concerns. In this sense, Albion Small, Edward Alsworth Ross, William Graham Sumner, Charles Horton Cooley, George Herbert Mead, and others were the academic carriers of secularized Protestant values and conceptions. One might even suggest, without too much exaggeration, that American sociology itself is an outgrowth of Protestant secularization.[5]

It is ordinarily assumed that Parsons, by virtue of his exposure to European thinkers, personified and sealed a break with the Protestant foundations of American sociology. It is often noted, for instance, that his first major work, *The Structure of Social Action* (1968), conspicuously omits any reference to American sociologists as precursors of the theoretical position developed therein. Nonetheless, Parsons did not escape the heritage of Protestantism; its influence is only less obvious in his work. Parsons is more accurately viewed not as representing the first generation of secular sociologists in America, but as a major figure in a continuing line of Protestant-informed sociologists whose primary theoretical themes are derived from Durkheim.

The Protestant ideals, conceptions, and values that decisively influenced Parsons appear to be derived primarily from two sources. First, he grew up in an American small town during the first two decades of the 1900s, a time when, as in Newburyport, the patterns of secularized Protestantism were still strongly characteristic of small town cultures. Second, and far more important, a distinctly Calvinist influence was added by his father, the last representative of a long line of Congregational clergymen. As a result of these youthful exposures, Protestantism figured prominently in Parsons's world view and affected his work to such an extent that, in Diggins's (1979, p. 483) apt phrase, "religion and society merge like an epiphany." It is against this backdrop of Protestant conceptions rather than with reference to the theoretical sources he cites in tracing his own intellectual development (1977) that many of Parsons's ideas are perhaps most meaningful and understandable.

A Protestant-based world view enters into Parsons's work both in his theoretical formulations on the problem of order and in his empirical treatment of that problem with respect to American core values. These shall be examined separately. Before proceeding, however, a word of caution is in order. In placing Parsons's work against the social background that helped shape his ideas, the intention is not to offer an *ad hominem* attack on the content and substance of those ideas, the danger of which Popper (1962) warned all who would work in the sociology of knowledge. Rather, this effort seeks to do full justice to an aspect of Parsons's work that has hitherto been largely neglected. It is no disgrace that one's ideas are informed and given shape by one's social and cultural background. Rather, it is unavoidable. Frequently, in fact, it is the very fount of creativity. Therefore, to fully understand the thinker and his work, we would be remiss if we ignored that background.

Protestantism and the Social System: The Transvaluation of Protestantism into Parsonian Theory

The Protestant influences on Parsons's thought are not clearly visible in his work. Nor should one expect them to be. Protestantism was a subliminal facet of his general world view, not an ideological position the ideas and vocabulary of which are brought consciously into play in his work. The influence is subtle. Protestant "ways of seeing" inform his efforts and ideas; Protestantism provides a generalized context in which certain ideas rather than others "make sense" and are thus acceptable. It is in this general sense that Protestant conceptions and understandings were transvalued into abstract notions of societal operation as Parsons sought to come to terms with his substantive concern with the problem of order.

At the broadest level, this transvaluation of Protestantism into Parsonian theory is reflected in the very nature of Parsons's "system." Commentators on Parsons's work frequently state that the social system constitutes a functional replacement for God in the age of His demise.[6] The analogy has much to recommend it, for even if the social system cannot be regarded as a deity, it can certainly be considered a mechanistic marvel which the Almighty set in motion just before He died. Indeed, as if to suggest divine handiwork, Parsons's system constitutes a near-perfect, virtually complete, and internally self-sufficient moral universe centered about a set of core values which, if no longer considered genuinely divine, are no less functional and integrative for their secularization.

These "divine" characteristics of the social system reflect Parsons's own perception of the world as a fundamental totality, characterized by an essential "oneness" to which all component parts contribute. He did recognize, of course, as all but the most unsympathetic of his critics would agree, that division and segmentation exist in the world, but nonetheless, as Nelson (1965, p. 598) observes: "Parsons never strays from the central fact his work celebrates—the progress of a universalist morality of achievement and performance. He perceives particularistic communities, whether of religion, caste, or kindred, mainly in their negative aspects, as barriers to full institutionalization of the Federal Covenant of all men equally and in all regards."

The specific means through which Parsons sought to overcome particularism and to establish, or reestablish, the fundamental oneness of the world is through the construction of a unified, deductive conceptual framework. Parsons's concepts are not so much ideal types as they are conceptual impositions

onto the empirical world. His major work, *The Social System*
(1951), as he describes it, represents "an attempt to bring together in systematic and generalized form, the main outlines
of a conceptual scheme for the analysis of the structure and
processes of social systems." The "test of significance" for
Parsons's constructs, however, is made not in comparison to
some aspect of empirical reality, as are Weber's ideal types, but
in terms of their "functional relevance" for the conceptual
system as a whole. As a result, Parsons's work is largely restricted
to studying the relationships between reified concepts, from
which features of the empirical world are deduced.

In conceptually unifying what is often empirically divided,
Parsons's categories appear to entail functions not only for his
larger system, but also for Parsons himself. As Alvin Gouldner
(1970, pp. 208-209) has indicated:

> For Parsons . . . the making of conceptual distinc-
> tions is . . . his distinctive way of bringing the world
> *together*. . . . Parsons' categories are . . . self-sufficient
> conceptual extrusions that cover rather than reveal
> the world. They make the world whole by overlaying
> its gaps, tensions, conflicts, incompletenesses with a
> conceptual encrustation. The mountains of categories
> to which Parsons' labors have given birth are the pro-
> duct of an inward search for the world's oneness
> and a projection of his vision of that oneness.
> [Gouldner's emphasis]

As Gouldner suggests, Parsons's work constitutes not only an
intellectual effort to understand the problem of order and unity,
but also a personal effort to achieve it. In this sense, Parsons's
conceptual imposition of order and oneness may be viewed as
a latter-day Calvinist's mastery of the world through his calling.

That Protestantism constituted a subliminal resource for
Parsons is apparent not only in his conceptualization of the
social system, but also in some of the more specific features of
its operation. With regard to his theory of social action, for

instance, several critics have taken Parsons to task for what
they perceive to be an apparent change of emphasis. They contend (usually disparagingly), that the voluntarism described in
The Structure of Social Action (1968) was abandoned for a
functionalist model that regards human action as a mechanistic
response to values and norms internalized into the personality,
institutionalized in society and culture, and manifest in role
behavior. For his own part, Parsons continued to insist that
his work contained no such break and that the two positions
were quite consistent. The intriguing question is not whether
such a break actually does exist in his work, for the change in
emphasis is indisputable, but why for Parsons the two positions
are not contradictory.

Parsons's position is quite understandable when one realizes
that his notion of voluntarism is not based on Enlightenment
notions of individualism, but rather is distinctly Protestant.
Regenerate Puritans, as discussed earlier, were thought free
only to obey spiritual authority and to serve the Holy Commonwealth. By the nature of the internal covenant, spiritual authority was expressed in internal and ethically obligatory norms and
standards so that the individual would not only desire to serve
the collectivity, but also could not desire to do otherwise.
Voluntarism, or individualism, existed only within a moral,
collective context, an emphasis that survived as a secularized
feature of small town culture. In Parsons's work, spiritual
authority has given way to system imperatives and regeneration
to socialization, but the overall effect is strikingly similar.
Properly socialized, and thereby having internalized into the
personality the socially appropriate values, norms, and constraints,
the individual genuinely desires to behave responsibly and to
diligently fulfill his or her own role requirements, in this way
contributing to the collectivity. Action in this sense is a voluntary rather than mechanical response to the internalized social
norms and values. And because social constraints are internal
features of the personality,[7] the individual is ethically and
morally responsible for his or her own behavior.[8] The socialized
individual is thus free but only to serve society and, as among the
early Protestants and later small towns, individualism exists,

but only within a collective, normative context.

Parsons's perception of those who violate that normative context also appears to be a transvaluation of Protestant conceptions. Deviance, as he perceives it, is action that contravenes the norms and values of the social system, thus creating a disturbance in the equilibrium of interaction. To view deviance in this fashion is by no means either obvious or necessary, as a great deal of more recent work on the topic clearly demonstrates.[9] Parsons's understanding of it in this, rather than some other, way at least circumstantially indicates the influence of Protestantism on his thinking, for thus defined, deviance appears quite clearly to be a transvalued version of sin, which also refers to a negative appraisal of action from the perspective of a normative, moral framework.

If Protestantism did provide the resource for Parsons's conception of deviance, as appears to be the case, it likely did so at least partly in its secularized form as the dominant small town ethos. The small town penchant for conformity, especially to the secularized Protestant standards of decency and respectability, has already been mentioned. Nonconformists of various sorts were subject to the disdain and moral condemnation of all decent townsfolk. The village idiot, the town drunk, known atheists, and the vicarious leisure class generally are but a few of the more familiar violators of small town, Protestant-based conventions—secular sinners all. One can readily imagine the operative proscriptive principle for both Protestant small towns and Parsons's social system to be: "Thou shalt not deviate." In any case, as in the Protestant conception, both normal and deviant inhabitants of the social system are defined in terms of their relation to the norms and, ultimately, to the core values of society.

One might take the argument further still. Although conclusive demonstration is not possible, not only evaluations of action in terms of the core values but also the theoretical centrality of core values themselves in Parsons's work may be at least partly a product of his Protestant-based *Weltanschaaung.* It is not necessarily the legacy of more strictly theoretical influences. While, for instance, Parsons claims Durkheim's authority for this argument, Durkheim himself does not appear to have regarded common values as key to social solidarity. Indeed, although his statements on this point are inconsistent, he seems instead to have given greater attention to the strength of a society's integrative force. Thus, for example, the mechanical solidarity of primitive societies does not depend on a value system that holds a low estimation of the individual and high esteem for collective ends. Rather, these values are at least partly derived from an integrative force so strong that individuality is not allowed to develop: "For the individual to occupy so little place in collective life he must be almost completely absorbed in the group and the latter, accordingly, very highly integrated" (Durkheim, 1951, pp. 220-21). The emphasis is not upon the contents of the *conscience collective*, as it is for Parsons, but upon its strength, which again must be connected to an existing framework of structural integration.[10]

Like Parsons's social system, Protestantism stresses a unified, universal, and overarching morality to which all are subject. The morality and its validity are neither connected to nor dependent upon the earthly efforts of particular groups and individuals. Rather, as befits divine constructions, its tenets are timeless, ultimate, and transcendent, directing and evaluating human activity in terms of its own contents. Similarly, in Parsons's work, the core values and attendant morality of a society, though lacking divine connections, are nonetheless made system properties and thus are also unconnected to group structures. On the basis of such similarities, one can reasonably argue that it was Parsons's Protestant heritage that led him to interpret Durkheim's arguments as he did.

American Core Values in Historical and Institutional Context

The centrality of old Protestant middle-class values in Warner's interpretation of American social order, as noted, was derived largely from his reliance on their carriers as his primary informants. Warner generalized the ritual experience of the dominant group to all townsfolk and, by extension, to all Americans. In Parsons's work, by contrast, the intellectual is himself the medium through which these values find expression, for

Parsons is a member of that intellectual priesthood that rationalizes a structure of ideas and makes at least an implicit claim to be their bearers.

Talcott Parsons straddled two Americas. The America he sought to comprehend intellectually was unquestionably that which burst upon the scene following World War II. As already indicated, however, he brought to this effort a world view, including a view of American society, that corresponded to a way of life rapidly receding in the face of postwar structural developments. That is, Parsons applied the conceptions and understandings of the old Protestant small town middle classes—whose value orientations were those of "instrumental activism" and who served as primary carriers of the Protestant Ethic—to the structural contours of a new American society. By and large, Parsons's view of America appears to consist of old Protestant middle- and business class conceptions intellectually sublimated and promoted by an academic stratum.

Parsons's understanding of how power operates in America may be offered as an example. Parsons regards power as relatively neutral and power-holders (including economic as well as political leaders) as exercising authority delegated by the collectivity, as conforming to system "value orientations" (instrumental activism), and as attempting to achieve goals preestablished by the "total system." American power-holders, guided by the civic components of instrumental activism, are regarded as somewhat benevolent, civic-minded leaders diligently doing the work of the society. The fact that power is routinely and systematically utilized in pursuit of personal and group goals even in opposition to societal interests tends to be downplayed. Such a notion of power, to state the obvious, is quite compatible with the ideological self-image of Main Street, which identified its own leadership with the best interests of the community. Indeed, it seems that in Parsons's work the ideological self-justification of small town leaders has been sublimated into theoretical respectability and transposed onto the larger society.

In Parsons's America conflict tends to be deemphasized, to be regarded more as an aberration than as a fundamental feature of the system. This treatment of conflict parallels a similar tendency among both the small town middle classes, for reasons of economy, and earlier, among the Protestant sects, which hoped to shame neither themselves nor God in the eyes of the world. In Parsons's work, the United States continues to be a "city upon a hill," the eyes of the world still upon it in its great experiment. In this sense, Parsons's accounts of America can be said to manifest an academic (and more restrained) form of boosterism expressed in the advertisement of harmony to the rest of the world. It is also expressed in Parsons's later work by the consideration of America as the highest evolutionary stage of modernization and, thus, as the standard by which all other societies are measured.[11]

These comments are not intended to suggest that Parsons shared the values of instrumental activism at an ideological level (though he may have), or that he personally identified with its declining carriers. Rather, in Parsons's work the Protestant-based values, conceptions, and attitudes of the old middle and business classes are generalized out of their institutional settings in American small towns and, through the medium of Parsons's own *Weltanschaaung*, transvalued into operative principles of the American social system. In this sense, Parsons's insistence that the Protestant Ethic continues to orient the conduct of most Americans is more a product of his own world view than it is an accurate description of American social realities.

That it is not the latter should be apparent from our earlier arguments. As we have seen, because of the decline of their primary carriers and their accelerated erosion under the organizational framework of post-industrial society, these values no longer guide the conduct of most Americans but rather are specific to particular groups. At precisely the time of its most rapid decay, then—the decades following World War II—Parsons continued to regard the Protestant Ethic, or instrumental activism, as central to his understanding of American society.

And yet, if due primarily to his personal world view Parsons was mistaken concerning the contents of an American value consensus, he was not altogether wrong in arguing that a consensus of sorts did exist. Postwar America through the early 1960s was characterized by an ideological hegemony so uniform that some analysts even felt justified in proclaiming an "end of

ideology."[12] The consensus of this period was not produced
by a spontaneous, shared commitment to instrumental activism,
however, but by a rather unique set of historical circumstances.[13]

World War II was itself partly responsible for the consensus,
for the war effort was truly a collective undertaking. Many groups
including Southern rednecks and blacks and various ethnic groups
from Northern ghettos, were brought into the mainstream of
American society for the first time by their involvement, even
if they did not remain after the war's end. Even leftist intellectuals, both indigenous and foreign, had no difficulty endorsing
the American war effort against the greater evil of fascism.
Given the enemy, very few groups opposed American involvement; most actively participated.

Following the war, America entered a period of unprecedented
prosperity. As a result of the increasing productivity of industry
and its economic dominance internationally, the United States
enjoyed several decades of almost uninterrupted economic
growth. While economic shares continued to be disproportion-
ately distributed among the various groups in American society,
almost all groups received larger shares than before. The resulting overall gains tended to blunt any serious internal opposition. Virtually all groups were willingly coopted.

Finally, following the war, Americans found another point
of general agreement in their collective hatred and fear of communism. The Cold War, by rallying sentiments against a common
enemy, sustained a widespread sense of common cause and
solidarity. While not all groups shared in that cause, criticism
and dissent were effectively blunted by the fervor and occa-
sional paranoia of Cold War politics. Thus, for instance, especially during McCarthy's inquisition, leftist intellectuals
were either cowed into silence or purged altogether from the
universities. In any case, anti-communism did provide the focus
for a continuing consensus lasting into the 1960s for some
groups and until the beginnings of détente for many others.

Wartime solidarity, general affluence, and Cold War anti-
communism neither prevented nor really even slowed the continuing erosion of old middle-class morals. As a general orientation for action, these morals could not survive the postwar
structural changes that undermined the way of life on which

they were based. By focusing attention on collective needs and interests, however, the ideological hegemony of the postwar period inhibited public recognition both that the older civic morality no longer effectively guided the conduct of most Americans and that, since the changes had been too rapid, no suitable alternatives were yet available for public consumption. In the resulting moral lacunae, the older civic morality continued to receive public acknowledgment from most groups. For some, the remaining small town middle classes, for example, this acknowledgment was sincere. They continued to base their own cooptation and integration primarily on an identification of their own values as the dominant principles of American society. For a good many other groups, however, especially those most involved in postwar institutional developments, the older values increasingly lacked the authenticity of being lived, of finding validation in actual experience. Yet, even obsolete values loosely held are preferable to anomie. Accordingly, the new middle classes continued to publicly espouse the old civic morals even if their espousals smacked ever more frequently of "lip service," hence lacking in genuine commitment. Such, incidentally, is not the substance of solidarity.

As a consequence of the ideological hegemony produced by a unique set of historical circumstances, the old middle-class civic morality—instrumental activism—survived in the public and scholarly imaginations longer than might otherwise have been possible. But for the most part, it survived only in imagination. Again, except for select and increasingly marginal groups, the older values no longer served to guide the conduct of Americans. The hegemony of the postwar period, however, allowed those who viewed America in terms of those values, including those in academic as well as old middle-class circles, to continue doing so for a while longer.

But it could not last. Beginning in the late 1950s and early 1960s, the United States underwent a series of convulsions involving racial conflict, student revolts, and the Vietnam War, and later, oil shortages, Watergate, and corporate scandals. As the shock of these convulsions was absorbed, the architectonic coherence of the postwar ideological orthodoxy began unraveling to reveal a society whose institutional development and

operation had outstripped many of its most fundamental ideological supports. As a result, groups at all social levels began to
experience problems of legitimacy, and a multiplicity of narrow,
specialized interests and ideologies emerged to compete with
one another for social dominance.

The task of formulating new, unified, legitimating ideologies,
or of reconstructing old ones, has always fallen to intellectuals.
In the past two decades in America, this task of ideological
reformulation has become the special problem of a new generation of intellectuals who have been compelled by circumstances
to deal with the decline of the American Empire and with the
dissolution of its orthodoxy. One such thinker is Robert Bellah,
who has both incorporated and updated the earlier efforts of
Durkheim, Warner, and Parsons in his own formulation of
American civil religion.

CIVIC MORALS AND AMERICAN CIVIL RELIGION: ROBERT BELLAH AND THE DECLINE OF ORTHODOXY

Civil Religion in America

According to Robert Bellah's well-known argument, there exist in America

> certain common elements of religious orientation that the great majority of Americans share. These have played a crucial role in the development of America's institutions and still provide a religious dimension for the whole fabric of American life, including the political sphere. This public, religious dimension is expressed in a set of beliefs, symbols and rituals that I am calling the American civil religion. [1970, p. 171]

While the civil religion shares certain common themes with the nation's churches, it exists "alongside and clearly differentiated" from them. It possesses "its own seriousness and integrity and requires the same care in understanding that any other religion does" (1970, p. 171).

Drawing heavily from his Durkheimian heritage, Bellah seeks to study this religion through its ceremonies, and more specifically by examining the content of presidential inaugural addresses and such sacred documents as the Declaration of Independence. He discovers that the nation's founders shaped the

form and tone of American civil religion by establishing a relationship between certain religious notions, including a God,
and the emerging self-conception of the new nation. The God
of American civil religion is described as being somewhat deist,
"rather 'unitarian' (and) also on the austere side, much more
related to order, law, and right than to salvation and love . . .
He is actively interested and involved in history, with a special
concern for America" (1970, p. 175).

During the Civil War, new themes of death, sacrifice, and
rebirth entered the civil religion, symbolized in the life and
death of Abraham Lincoln. Subsequently, the symbolic equation of Lincoln with Jesus and the resulting theme of sacrifice
were expressed ritually in such religious holidays as Memorial
Day[1] and Veterans Day which, along with Thanksgiving, the
Fourth of July, and Washington's Birthday, "provide an annual
ritual calendar for the civil religion" (1970, p. 175).

Thus, as Bellah states, from the earliest days of the republic
there has existed "a collection of beliefs, symbols, and rituals
with respect to sacred things and institutionalized in a collectivity" (1975, p. 175). With the state as its custodian, the civil
religion has been able to develop "powerful symbols of national
solidarity and to mobilize deep levels of personal motivation
for the attainment of national goals" (1970, p. 181). Bellah
thus provides the specific means by which, according to Parsons, religion functions to regulate "the balance of the motivational commitment of the individual to the values of his
society" (Parsons, 1960, p. 302).

Even so, Bellah insists that the American civil religion is not
a narrow form of national self-worship and political chauvinism.
It is at best, he suggests, "a genuine apprehension of universal
and transcendent religious reality as seen in or, one could almost say, as revealed through the experience of the American
people" (1970, p. 179). The nation itself "stands under transcendent judgment and has value only insofar as it realizes, partially and fragmentarily at best, a 'higher law' " (1974, p. 255),
the heart and soul of which consists of "that abstract faith,
those abstract propositions to which we are dedicated" (1976b,
p. 153). Some of the more specific moral norms and values

expressed in that "abstract faith" include, as culled from Bellah's writings on the subject, a commitment to liberty, justice, and charity, a spirit of self-sacrifice for the common good, civic-mindedness fused with an ethical obligation for individual participation, humility, respect for individual rights, a sense of common purpose (chosenness), and dedication to a higher goal. In short, American civil religion expresses an ideal balance between individualism and communal obligation. It is a freedom to serve the community—a conception that is also clearly expressed in the works of Warner and Parsons. Collectively, these common moral and religious understandings expressed in American civil religion "produce both a basic cultural legitimation for a society which is viewed as at least approximately in accord with them and as a standard of judgment for the criticism of a society that is seen as deviating too far from them" (1975, p. ix).

The Crisis "Out There"

In 1967, at the conclusion of his first essay on American civil religion, Bellah spoke forebodingly of an impending time of trial for America. Even so, that essay ends on a note of cautious optimism, tempering concern with confidence in our heritage and ability to learn from it. In subsequent works, however, and particularly in *The Broken Covenant* (1975), Bellah sees darker clouds gathering. America has deviated quite far indeed from its own sacred values, he observes, and is fast approaching a deep moral and spiritual crisis. The American civil religion itself, representing the "highest aspirations" of American society, is today but an "empty and broken shell."

Although Bellah does offer some more specific reasons for the crisis, which we shall discuss presently, the general logic of his argument should not be allowed to pass without comment. Having first assumed, with Durkheim and Parsons, that "all politically organized societies have some sort of civil religion" which provides them with essential functions of guidance and cultural legitimation, and having identified the specific contents of the American civil religion, Bellah recognizes that few traces of it continue to exist within the emergent context of contemporary American society. He has little choice, considering the circumstances, but to declare a crisis. In this sense, Bellah's crisis is in large part the product of prior assumptions.

And yet, in making this point, the suggestion is in no way intended that a crisis does not exist "out there." The crisis is as real, in fact, as the constellation of values, beliefs, and conceptions which Bellah identifies as American civil religion. His discussion of its dimensions, however, is problematic, for having detached the contents of American civil religion from existing social structures and elevated them to a level of transcendence, Bellah must construe any decline of those values to be a crisis for the whole society. A very different—and more accurate—understanding of the crisis is possible if these values are stripped of their imputed transcendence and reconnected to the particular groups that serve as their carriers. Moreover, it is rather apparent that the contents of American civil religion, as Bellah describes them, include a combination of Puritan values and the old Protestant middle-class civic values whose social history has already been traced.

Historically, as has been noted, the primary incentives for old middle-class acquiescence and attribution of legitimacy to American institutions were grounded in the identification of these classes with the values which they made socially dominant and which they perceived to have been embodied in American society. Since the 1960s, however, as these groups have been made painfully aware, these once-dominant values have not been reflected in the operation of American institutions. Concretely, from their perspective, the family has been "weakened"; military dominance (from which they derived feelings of pride and superiority) has "slipped"; the educational system has forsaken the teaching of traditional values and has instead embraced "secular humanism"; Big Business seems corrupt and self-serving; and government, lacking leadership, appears unwilling or unable to do anything about it all. In this sense, insofar as it exists "out there," the crisis of which Bellah speaks is primarily one of legitimacy for the remaining old middle classes and for those groups sympathetic to their values.

One major effect of this development has been to elevate the values of these groups, which were generally taken for granted during the earlier period of orthodoxy, to a level of conscious awareness. The result, as Mannheim certainly would have appreciated,[2] has been a tendency on the part of these groups to embrace political conservatism in an effort to halt and reverse what they perceive to be the immoral direction of American social change. In addition, since the values carried by the old middle classes have been historically connected to religion, one may reasonably speculate that their elevation to the level of self-consciousness has also led to reaffirmations of traditional religiosity, particularly Protestantism. This circumstance might be at least partly responsible for the recent resurgence of traditional religious belief in American society. It might also account for the current fusions of religious energy and indignation with political conservatism in the form of Moral Majority-type movements, anti-abortion and anti-ERA campaigns, and similar efforts to recapture the lost dominance of old middle-class values. These reciprocal connections between religious and political expression would, of course, require more detailed investigation than is possible here, but enough has been said to indicate that the crisis experienced by these groups has by no means been silently endured.

For other groups in American society, on the other hand, particularly for large segments of the new middle classes, the decline of old middle-class civic values is not generally experienced as a problem. These groups appear to have developed entirely different substantive grounds of acquiescence and legitimation. Having emerged at least partly as a result of unprecedented economic growth, they have grown accustomed to a standard of living sufficient to sustain certain life-styles with their attendant standards of consumption. This standard of living—and indeed, the whole foundation for their class positions—is based primarily upon a salary, regular employment, and government subsidies for housing, educational opportunity, pensions, highways, and the like. All of these, in turn, depend upon a certain level of economic performance. Hence, it may well be the case, as some have suggested,[3] that the price of their continued cooptation is the continued expansion and performance of the economy. Accordingly, as this becomes difficult to sustain, due to rising energy costs, inflation, and more intense foreign competition, some portions of the new middle classes may also begin to question the legitimacy of American institutions, as appears to be occurring to some degree at present. Nonetheless, if the old and new middle classes become partners in discontent, or even short-term political allies,[4] the foundations of their respective crises are clearly different, one being primarily ideological, the other economic. The crisis of legitimacy for the old middle classes cannot, in any case, be considered as one for the whole society.

Civil Religion in America: The Faith and Hope of an Intellectual

The legitimacy crisis experienced by the old middle classes is not, of course, the precise one to which Bellah refers in his work, nor can the old middle-class civic ideology be equated with Bellah's conception of American civil religion. As he cautions, American civil religion does not consist of the "American Legion type of ideology that fuses God, country and flag" (1970, p. 182). Accordingly, neither can the crisis be considered in such narrowly political terms. He insists, rather, that the civil religion is "not a form of national self-worship but . . . the subordination of the nation to ethical principles that transcend it and in terms of which it should be judged" (1970, p. 168).

And yet, a kinship does exist between Bellah's American civil religion and the civic morality of the old Protestant small town middle classes. This is no coincidence, for like Parsons, though in a very different way, Bellah is an academic carrier of these values.

Bellah brings to his studies of American society the accumulated influence of a Protestant heritage.[5] In his early years, spent in a Presbyterian remnant of "a once coherent, Southern Protestant culture," Bellah experienced the wholeness and meaning provided by Christian brotherhood and fellowship and acquired an abiding respect for civic and patriotic values. "I grew up," he recalls, "in the 1930s and 1940s in a milieu in which there were few questions about Protestant Christianity or what were taken to be traditional American values." Eventually, however, troubled by the discrepancy between his inherited ideals and "the realities of American life," Bellah raised his own questions and, as thinking persons often do when trapped in a closed system of ideas, escaped by rejecting the whole of his inheritance. The intellectual requirement of meaning and "the religious need, the need for wholeness" could not be so easily abandoned, however. Thus, his brief affair with Marxism in college both provided "a transposition of my Protestantism: idealistic, moral, puritanical" and "fulfilled my needs for personal identity and group belonging." The same functions were furnished later by interests in "the wholeness and integrity" of primitive cultures, "the aesthetic intensity of Japanese culture," and Zen Buddhism. As these turned out to be altogether empty or not permanently diverting, Bellah gradually began to reappropriate fragments of his rejected past. By the late 1950s, according to his own account, he again identified with Christian brotherhood and traditional American values, though not so uncritically as before. "I do not think now," he wrote in 1975, "that the religious and ideological heritage that I was given as a child and as an adolescent was an entirely authentic version of the American tradition, but the subjective sense of continuity with the past is an indelible experience that undoubtedly colors even my present conceptions."

While Bellah shares with Parsons a background of Protestant influence, he brings that heritage to the study of a very different American society. Parsons's major ideas regarding American core values were formed between the 1930s and 1950s in the aftermath of the Depression and World War II. This was a time when, because of unique historical circumstances, it was still possible to contend that the developing order had not abandoned the moral context and contents of the old. For Bellah, on the other hand, as for the old middle classes generally, the dam had broken. Ideology, "ended" in the hegemony of the 1950s, was resurrected with a vengeance in the 1960s. Black

Americans, pressing their own often dramatic claims for shares of the post-industrial pie, rejected the former unity as a shibboleth and as a mask for their continued exclusion. Likewise, the sons and daughters of the rapidly expanding new middle classes, sensing the insincerity of their parents' civic pronouncements and provided with the relative leisure of student life, also noisily rejected all older ideologies of political and civic solidarity, many preferring to "do their own thing" rather than (and often against) that of the system. Finally, for all but the most faithful members of the old middle classes, the moralistic self-image of the nation—also a product of an original Protestant conception—was badly tarnished by its involvement in Vietnam. The decline of the Protestant civic ethos could no longer be ignored.

It was against this background of social upheaval that, in 1967, Bellah published his first account of civil religion in America. The various attacks on then-orthodox morals, values, and understandings had apparently made Bellah self-consciously aware of his own sympathies toward them. Thus conceived, Bellah's initial expression of American civil religion may be regarded as a defensive and personal reaction to attacks on traditional, Protestant, small town civic values, or, as he later reflected, as "a strong endorsement of core American values" (1970, p. xvii). "Civil Religion in America" (1967) represents an affirmation of these values at the precise moment of their general demise.[6]

But American civil religion is more than simply an affirmation of these values; in addition, it represents a distinctly intellectual response to their decline. As he became consciously aware of his own affinity for them, Bellah detached the old middle-class Protestant values from their existence in a historical time and place and from the institutional structures that sustained them and fashioned them into a "higher" and "transcendent" order of value and meaning.[7] These values were then projected onto American society as a whole and given doctrinal expression as American civil religion. In this sense, American civil religion represents an intellectually sublimated and extended version of the small town Protestant civic morality which Bellah shares.

If this interpretation is accepted, it suggests a very important difference in the levels at which Parsons and Bellah, respectively, carry these values. For Parsons, as noted, these values and conceptions were taken-for-granted facets of his larger world view. In his work, sublimated Protestant conceptions were transvalued into abstract principles of societal operation. For Bellah, on the other hand, changes in the structure of American society have resulted in a situation in which these values can only be consciously held. They cannot be taken for granted in a society that constantly discredits their validity. Accordingly, whereas for Parsons the old Protestant values and conceptions were aspects of a larger *Weltanschaaung*, they are central features of Bellah's ideology precisely because they are self-consciously carried.

These differences in the levels at which Parsons and Bellah carry older Protestant civic values largely account for further differences in how they are expressed in their respective works. In terms of these values, Parsons remained a relatively contented moralist. Bellah, faced with the fact of their decline, has become a moral activist, an intellectual prophet delivering analytic jeremiads and prophecies of doom. Nowhere is this better illustrated than in Bellah's subsequent work on the impending crisis of American society.

Bellah's conception of the crisis also clearly illustrates the importance of intellectualism as a dimension of his response to the decline of Protestant civic morals. The crisis of legitimacy for the old middle classes and those still sympathetic to their values is clearly the experience of "men of action," to make use of Radin's term. Showing little concern for the reason or larger meaning of social change, they perceive the social abandonment of their own values as a purely practical problem, one requiring not so much understanding as correcting. Accordingly, their response is a direct effort to recapture the past, by political imposition if necessary.

Bellah's response to the same social changes is, of course, very different. He experiences these changes not so much as a practical problem, though this is also a concern for him, but primarily as a problem of meaning. He seeks, above all, understanding, comprehension, and order.

Responsible for the crisis, Bellah argues, is economic and technological advance and its attendant commercial ethos that has weakened families and neighborhoods, undermined morality, stripped us of tradition, and eliminated brotherliness in favor of mobility, competitiveness, and individual achievement. Technical reason and utilitarianism, though present in American culture almost from the beginning, have been unleashed from the original "common set of religious and moral understandings" which once restrained and provided them with direction. Ours has become a society, Bellah suggests, in possession of virtually unlimited technological means but generally lacking a larger framework of meaning capable of determining ends other than those of individual self-interest. The American civil religion has lost its capacity to provide that larger meaning and no replacement has emerged. Thus, degenerating into egoism and anomie, we have lost our sense of direction. The result is a society in the throes of crisis.

Bellah's crisis is not a purely practical problem calling for a narrow political solution, but an intellectual rationalization, an intellectual's investment of comprehension, meaning, and order into the direction of American social change. It is expressed negatively—that is, as a crisis—because the intellectual shares at an ideological level the values, beliefs, and conceptions, however sublimated, of the displaced past.

Bellah's solutions to the crisis demonstrate at once both the intellectual and Protestant dimensions of his response. To recapture our sense of direction, he argues, will require a "rebirth of imaginative vision." To reharness technical reason, we must reappropriate our sacred traditions. This reappropriation cannot be direct, but must be critical, for unlike "men of action," Bellah does not seek a return to the past. He means only to retain those features of our past which can help sustain us in the future.

Hope for the future may be found, Bellah observes, among those groups that reject the utilitarian and rationalized dimensions of American society and work actively to construct a new vision and new way of life. Consisting primarily of counterculture remnants from the 1960s and of new religious movements, these "core groups" offer us primarily an emphasis on direct experience and a concern for self-actualization within a strong communal context. These emphases are obviously consistent with those of traditional American Protestantism.

Yet, these core groups can only provide, at best, a stimulus to rebirth. Their interests tend to be personal and local, whereas "only a national movement . . . can begin to meet [our] problems." That movement "must be broad enough and deep enough to engage millions of Americans from a variety of cultural backgrounds at the deepest level of the personality." The movement would have "a political, I believe a socialist, side" as well, one connected "with a vision that is moral and religious as well as political." This socialist vision is, of course, distinctly Protestant and distinctly American, owing more to Emerson and the Transcendentalists than to Marx and Engels. Its realization depends not on dialectical conflict but on collective solidarity, and its most important dimension is not economic but cultural, expressed in a hoped-for resurgence of Christian humanism and universal brotherhood, a resurrection of Protestant civic morals. We require, in short, a revival of civil religion, a collective reaffirmation of our "ancient faith," a renewal of the severed ties of brotherhood.[8]

When the longing for community and brotherhood is sublimated out of the religious province and projected onto political and social spheres, the result is to transform religious commitment into an ideology that emphasizes social order and communitarian concerns. Thus viewed, American civil religion is a distinctly intellectual and ideological response to the fragmentation and impersonality of social organization in modern industrial society. Inasmuch as this is true, American civil religion is itself a product of the very rationalization it rebels against.

Intellectuals, Ideology, and the Conflict in American Culture

Parsons and Bellah notwithstanding, the Protestant Ethic is dead. Almost since the end of the Civil War and the beginnings of corporate centralization and mass production, the Protestant

Ethic has been unable to provide the ideological framework for American society. Since that time, American society has experienced a continuous conflict between its institutional operation and ideological rationale.

For a time, *laissez-faire* served as an interim ideology, one especially favored by the old Main Street middle class which carried and sustained it until it was shattered by the Great Depression and smothered by the administrative state. A few years later, World War II filled the ideological void by supplying an external enemy and national cause. Both were sustained in the subsequent Cold War, which offered America a new world destiny of communist containment and free world guardianship, and thus continued to conceal the absence of more stable ideological rationales.

The end of the Cold War, however, has forced the realization that American society lacks a dominant, unified, and coherent ideology. Because this realization has coincided with the decline of Empire and with America having to suffer indignities, insults, and defeats throughout the world, it has been all the more difficult to accept. Not only did America appear to lack a world destiny, but Americans also began fighting with each other both in the streets (student revolts and race riots) and at the highest levels of power (Watergate). The country appeared out of control, in disarray. In many ways America remains a City Upon a Hill, the eyes of the world upon it. And in these eyes as well as its own, America looks bad.

These developments have worried a major segment of American intellectuals as perhaps nothing else ever has. Historically, as Schumpeter (1942, pp. 145-55) observed, though in a more general way, these intellectuals have lived off the criticism of American capitalism, especially of its giant corporations and exploitation of the rest of the world. This was particularly true of the 1930s generation of radical intellectuals and of the next generation—including Bellah—which, though disabused of Stalin, continued to identify with the humanist philosophy of Marx. Today as before, though much of the attack has been taken over by critical thinkers in the rest of the world, American Big Business continues to inspire and sustain an abundant supply of indigenous intellectual critics.

With the United States currently in decline and disarray, apparently for the first time a major segment of American academic intellectuals has shown considerable concern with developing a positive ideology for the society. Bellah is by no means alone in this effort. The recent formulations of "supply side economics," for instance, represent somewhat similar efforts by other thinkers who identify with business but who, in effect, are only seeking to salvage *laissez-faire* under a new label. Bellah has taken on the more formidable ideological problem of locating the deeper and more ancient values of the civilization. In his search, as shown earlier, he has rediscovered, sublimated, and transvalued the older values of Puritanism and the Main Street values of nineteenth-century small towns.

With efforts like Bellah's, it would appear that American intellectuals have come of age, taking on some of the features of classical or traditional intellectual strata in older civilizations. No longer are they but fashionable critics whose illusions remain unstated.[9] Rather, they now respond with fear and concern to an unknown future in which America is no longer the promised land with a world destiny, but an aging country whose internal development can no longer be taken for granted. The future is problematic.

Like all classic intellectual strata, America's academic intellectuals, in Weber's (1946, p. 371) words, "look distrustfully upon the abolition of traditional conditions of the community and upon the annihilation of all the innumerable ethical and aesthetic values which cling to these traditions." As a result, they seek to preserve the values of the past by which their own way of life is defined, stressing the family, morality, the church, and other traditional values and institutions. Hence, they become a major force of conservatism in the society. In this broad context of intellectual reactions to social change, Bellah's work on American civil religion has much in common not only with that of Durkheim, but also with the work of Burke in England and Ranke in Germany, both of whom sought to uphold the older values of tradition against the more rationalized dimensions of an emergent social order.

As once was the case with the ideological constructions of these other classic intellectuals, American civil religion evokes a deep response to an increasingly romanticized version of the nation's past. It is anti-modern in its appeal, rejecting both the values of modernism and the groups that are their bearers. In this sense, the ideology is a product of a larger struggle taking place in the society between the various groups still committed, though often in different ways and with different emphases, to the traditional values and institutions of American civilization, and the disparate groups committed to the newer values and institutions of modernism. In the older civilizations of the world, this struggle has, for the most part, already been decided in favor of modernism, for who now reads Burke or Ranke? While eventually the same result is also likely in the United States, for now, as the very presence of American civil religion and other ideological constructions seems to indicate, the struggle is yet to be resolved. Perhaps a major question of our time is whether the struggle itself will obscure the vision and absorb the energies of a nation which, perhaps now more than ever, needs desperately to cope with its own future.

CONCLUSION

In his original effort to understand the foundations of social order, Durkheim theorized that every relatively stable society will possess a set of shared beliefs, values, and symbols that express the highest aspirations of the collectivity and that are elevated to a level of transcendence, thereby becoming an integrative focus for members of the society and, as Bellah interprets, a standard by which it can be judged. As description and explanation of both the nature of widely shared values and their relationship to social order, the Durkheimian theory is quite limited in that it excludes from consideration a range of empirical materials important to the subject.

To some degree, each of Durkheim's intellectual heirs with whom we have dealt has accepted his theoretical premises as resources in their own empirical studies of particular values and symbols in particular societies. In each case, the theory is treated largely as a matter already decided rather than as a heuristic model to be evaluated with reference to the empirical realities investigated. In other words, Durkheim's heirs have applied the theory to, rather than tested it against, the subjects of their researches. As a result, they have incorporated its limitations into their own work, particularly its neglect of a range of empirical phenomena important to the subject under investigation.

Foremost among the empirical phenomena neglected are the people who make up the society that is the object of study.

Values, even orthodox values, are not transcendent. Durkheimian theory notwithstanding, they do not lead a relatively autonomous existence above and beyond the sphere of everyday
struggles. Rather, they are an integral part of those struggles,
constituting an important means through which specific social
groups express and attempt to further their own ideal and material interests. That is, values always express the needs, aspirations, and ideal and material interests of particular groups of
people existing in particular times, places, and institutional
contexts. At least in a diverse society where, as Durkheim put
it, the "contents of men's minds differ," it is unlikely that the
same set of values and symbols could adequately express the
needs and interests of all social groups. Thus, for instance, the
values and symbols described by Warner, Parsons, and Bellah
do not constitute the "abstract faith" of the American people.
Rather, they represent various lay and intellectual expressions
of the civic ideology of a once-dominant old middle-class stratum at various stages of its decline. An adequate, empirically
grounded understanding of dominant or orthodox values is not
possible apart from the social and historical experience of these
particular social groups.

Neither, for that matter, can the contribution made by dominant values to social order be adequately understood apart
from the experiences of particular social groups. Yet, in generally ignoring the social history of groups and thus treating
orthodox values as in some way transcendent, the Durkheimian analysis excludes from consideration the possibility that
different groups may be differently committed even to orthodox values, and that, therefore, the substantive grounds on
which particular groups respond to those values may also be
very different. If a more empirically adequate understanding of
the relationship between values and social order is to be attained,
one must know not only that certain values and symbols have
attained orthodox stature, or that they have been ceremoni-
alized, but also which groups are most committed to those
values, who controls the rituals, and what, if any, other institutionalized mechanisms for their support exist. One must
also explore the substantive grounds on which particular groups
respond to these values or participate in their ritual celebration.

Unless such questions as these are raised and explored, the substantive foundations of social order cannot be adequately understood.

Primarily because of aspects of its method and approach, the Durkheimian theoretical framework does not raise such questions. This is not to suggest, however, that the general conclusion of Durkheimian analyses—that orthodoxy tends to induce integration and social order—is mistaken. To the contrary, that conclusion is most often correct. Nonetheless, in detaching the social history of dominant values from that of their carrying stratum, and in neglecting the different levels, intensities, and substantive grounds of commitment on the part of responding audiences, the Durkheimian analysis tends to be largely inadequate as an empirical explanation of both the nature of orthodoxy and the foundations of social order.

Our aim, it bears emphasizing, has been less to criticize than to supplement. The social world yields its secrets to diverse perspectives. Not all perspectives, however, are equal in their capacity to uncover or unravel those secrets. The view taken here is that, largely because of theoretical and epistemological presuppositions, the Durkheimian theory of social order is quite limited in that it neglects a range of empirical phenomena important to the subject. It is the limitations of the conclusions reached and not their falsity with which this study has been concerned. And regarding the particular Durkheimian analyses discussed, to the extent that those conclusions have been supplemented with greater empirical depth, to that extent our efforts have been successful.

NOTES

Chapter 1

1. It is on this basis that Durkheim justifies the primacy given the sociology of religion in *L'Annee Sociologique*. Religious phenomena, he argues,

> are the germ from which all the others, or at least almost all the others, are derived. Religion contains in itself, from the beginning, but in a diffused state, all the elements which in dissociating, determining and combining with each other in a thousand ways, have given birth to the diverse manifestations of the collective life. It is from symbols and legends that science and poetry have separated; it is from religious ornamentation and cult ceremonies that the plastic arts have come; law and morality were born from ritual practices. One cannot understand our representation of the world, our philosophic conceptions about the soul, immortality, and life, if one doesn't know the religious beliefs which were their first form. Kinship began by being an essentially religious tie; punishment, contract, the gift, homage are transformations of sacrifice, be it expiatory, contractual, communal, honorary, and so on. At most it will be asked if economic organization is an exemption and derives from another source; although we don't think so, we will allow this question to be reserved. The fact remains nonetheless that a multitude of problems completely change their aspect from

the day we recognize their relation to the sociology of
religion. [Quoted in Bellah, 1965, pp. 166-67]

2. "It is apparent that moral life has not been, and never will be,
able to shed all the characteristics that it holds in common with religion.
When two orders of facts have been so closely linked, when there has
been between them so close a relationship for so long a time, it is impossible for them to be dissociated and become distinct. For this to happen
they would have to undergo a complete transformation and so change
their nature. There must, then, be morality in religion and elements of
the religious in morality" (Durkheim, 1974, p. 48).

3. Compared to religion, Durkheim offers, "the feature of sacredness
(in morality) is less clearcut. Dogmas and myths do not exist here. . . . The
emphasis is upon acts. The difference is nonetheless entirely one of degree" (quoted in Lukes, 1973, p. 414).

4. "Society (of which morality and religion are representations) commands us because it is exterior and superior to us; the moral distance between it and us makes it an authority before which our will defers. But
as, on the other hand, it is within us and *is* us, we love it and desire it,
albeit with a *sui generis* desire since, whatever we do, society can never
be ours in more than a part and dominates us completely" (Durkheim,
1974, p. 57).

5. The relative proportions of obligation and desirability, Durkheim
suggests, will vary both among societies (cf. 1961, p. 100) and, within
the same moral system, among particular moral acts (1974, p. 36).

6. Despite its overwhelming importance to his sociology of religion,
Durkheim made no attempt to demonstrate the validity of this "essential
postulate." Rather, he apparently regarded it as an undeniable assumption
and as true *prima facie*. It is clear, however, that not all thinkers regarded
Durkheim's postulate as either essential or even valid. Marx and his followers at least would certainly have disagreed, and precisely over the
identification of religion, which Marx regarded as but a "fantastic reflection" of the process of material production and as a delusory compensation
for the misery and restricted freedom that people suffer.

7. "Exactly how the combinations occur resulting in the collective
state, what are its constituent elements, how the dominant state is produced are questions too complex to be solved solely by introspection. . . .
We know little as yet how and according to what laws mental states of even
the single individual combine; much less do we know of the mechanism
of the far more complicated combinations produced by group existence.
Our explanations are often mere metaphors" (Durkheim, 1951, p. 130;
1974, p. 27).

8. The concept of "collective representations," beginning with *Suicide*, appears far more frequently in Durkheim's later work. Apparently, as Lukes (1973, p. 6) points out, he found the *conscience collective* too vague and broad, since it refers to a totality of beliefs, to distinguish "between cognitive, moral and religious beliefs, between different beliefs and sentiments, and between the beliefs and sentiments associated with different stages of a society's development." Collective representations account for precisely these distinctions.

9. See Giddens, 1972, for a similar interpretation.

10. The polemical tone and exaggerated substance of this assertion may be attributed to Durkheim's efforts to mark off a field of sociological inquiry over and against that of psychology. In doing so, he apparently indulged in a bit of overkill. See Durkheim, 1938, pp. 111-12.

11. History shows, Durkheim observes, that such diverse "inclinations" as "religious sentiment . . . sexual jealousy, filial piety, paternal love, etc. . . . far from being inherent in human nature, are often totally lacking. Or they may present such variations in different societies that the residue obtained after eliminating all these differences—which alone can be considered of psychological origin—is reduced to something vague and rudimentary and far removed from the facts that need explanation. These sentiments, then, *result* from the collective organization and are not its basis" (Durkheim, 1938, p. 107; Durkheim's emphasis).

12. See Bellah, 1973, for an elaboration of this interpretation.

13. Ritual reintegration, incidentally, is of considerable benefit to the individual as well as to society. Since, as Durkheim contends, it is from society that the individual receives all that is best in himself, he is necessarily exalted by his ritual rebirth. In collective effervescence, "the individual soul is regenerated . . . by being dipped again in the source from which its life comes; consequently, it feels itself stronger, more fully master of itself, less dependent on physical necessities" (Durkheim, 1965, pp. 390-91).

14. It is to collective effervescence, for instance, that Durkheim gives credit for movements as great and varied as the Scholasticism of the twelfth and thirteenth centuries in Paris, the Reformation and Renaissance, the Crusades, the French Revolution, and the socialist upheavals of the nineteenth century. See Durkheim, 1974, pp. 91-92; 1965, pp. 241-42.

Chapter 2

1. Similarly, the ideas on which a class struggle may be based are not necessarily derived from the unpropertied classes.

2. It should be noted that Weber does not consider what he terms "intellectualism as such" to constitute an ideal interest. It refers instead to what he regarded as a metaphysical need of the human mind.

3. Weber makes this point with reference to the world religions which were the primary objects of his study: "All the great religions are historical individualities of a highly complex nature; taken all together, they exhaust only a few of the possible combinations that could conceivably be formed from the very numerous individual factors to be considered in such historical combinations" (Weber, 1946, p. 292).

4. The term "elective affinity" has unfortunately become something of a catch phrase with regard to Weber's sociology of knowledge, occasionally exalted as a unique theoretical contribution. Its meaning, however, is quite simple, referring to a generalized propensity of groups to adopt ideas compatible with their own world images, sense of status, ideal and material interests, and, in the case of religious ideas, religious needs. The term suggests a social phenomenon that is, in fact, largely self-evident.

5. It is perhaps important to note, in order to avoid confusion, that the links postulated by Weber between the social character of a stratum and the unique characteristics of its adopted religion are empirical generalizations rather than causal connections. Moreover, he is quick to qualify them even as generalizations: "Of course, the religions of all strata are certainly far from unambiguously dependent upon the character of the stratum we have presented as having special affinities with them" (1946, p. 284). And again: "Such an unambiguous social determination has not in any way existed" (1946, p. 285). As always with Weber, understanding in a given case requires empirical investigation rather than inference from sociological "laws."

6. For a more detailed interpretation of Weber's theory of secularization, see Hughey, 1979.

7. Taoism, Mithraism, and Zoroastrianism are but a few examples, And obviously, countless others not mentioned by Weber share the same fate.

8. Interested readers should consult R. Stephen Warner's (1972) analysis of Weber's treatment of these connections. Warner's work both contributed to and confirmed my own reading of Weber's work on these issues, and I am indebted.

9. Weber's point is actually somewhat broader. He asserts that, unless rational prophecy intervenes, peoples living close to nature and the land tend to have affinities for magic. The example of peasantry noted earlier is Weber's example. See Weber, 1968, pp. 468-72.

10. Those of Weber's ideas that have been discussed are not restricted to the sociology of religion. The origins and diffusion of religious ideas

are aspects of his more comprehensive sociology of knowledge. The creation and functions of orthodoxy, as we have labeled them, are clearly analogous to the means by which political legitimacy is claimed and sustained, thus belonging also to his sociology of domination.

11. Whitney Pope's (1973) interpretation that Durkheim invests society with despotic authority, though perhaps somewhat overstated because of his polemical intent, seems to be generally consistent with Durkheim's many statements on this issue. To be sure, Durkheim's work displays many ambiguities regarding individual autonomy, and Pope's interpretation touched off a running debate. See Pope, et al., 1975; Pope, 1976.

12. Radin, of course, does not use this terminology, and the issue of legitimacy and social order is not really a concern for him at all. Nonetheless, a basic similarity to Weber's ideas on these subjects is strongly implied in his work.

13. A noteworthy comparison between Weber and Durkheim on these issues has been made by Pope, et al., 1975. I gratefully acknowledge the usefulness of their discussion for this section.

14. The Chinese emperor, for instance, to whom, until recently, "charismatic vestiges" were still attached,

> had to prove his magical charisma through military success or at least he had to avoid striking failures. Above all he had to secure good weather for harvest and guarantee the peaceful internal order of the realm. . . . If he failed he simply lacked charisma. Thus, if the rivers broke the dikes, or if rain did not fall despite the sacrifices made, it was evident . . . that the emperor did not have the charismatic qualities demanded by Heaven. In such cases the emperor did public penitence for his sins. . . . If this was of no avail, the emperor probably had to expect abdication; in the past it probably meant self-sacrifice. [Weber, 1951, p. 31]

15. Radin cites the following example concerning the Yokuts of south-central California:

> . . . if a man, especially a rich one, did not join in a dance, the chief and his doctors would plan to make this man or some member of his family sick. . . . The doctor then sees to it that he is called in to make the cure. He makes several successive attempts to cure his victim, each time being paid for his services. He withholds his cure until he has financially broken the man and got him into debt. If he then cures the

patient, he sucks the shot out and shows it to the bystanders, saying that the nigot (spirit) has made him ill. On the other hand, he may let the person die, in which case the family must perforce join in the mourning ceremony. The money which the shaman has collected as fees in the case, he divides with the chief. Should the victim's relatives seek vengeance, for which they must obtain the chief's permission, the chief refuses his sanction on the ground of insufficient evidence. Has not the doctor shown that the nigot has caused the illness? [Radin, 1957a, pp. 42-43]

16. The account that follows is meant to be synoptic rather than comprehensive. A more complete analysis of the points made in this section may be found in Bendix, 1971.

17. See, for instance, Gouldner, 1970, and Lockwood, 1964.

18. This criticism, to be sure, is by no means original. Durkheim has often been charged with arguing by *petitio principii.* See Needham, 1963, for a detailed critique of Durkheim's tendency in this regard.

Chapter 3

1. See, for example, Radcliffe-Brown's article, "The Present Position of Anthropological Studies," in Radcliffe-Brown, 1958.

2. Radin reports that the native interpretation of similar ceremonies among the Arunta lends support to his own: "The native interpretation is a model of realism. Their purpose is to insure the authority and wealth of the older men" (Radin, 1957, p. 91).

Chapter 4

1. Parsons's original interpretation of Durkheim's work is to be found, of course, in *The Structure of Social Action* (1937). For critical accounts of that interpretation similar to the one here advanced, see Giddens, 1972, and Pope, 1973.

2. In Durkheim's words, rational autonomy accordant with moral individualism emerges as follows:

All development of individualism has the effect of opening moral consciousness to new ideas and rendering it more demanding. Since every advance that it makes results in a higher conception, a more delicate sense of the dignity of man, individualism cannot be developed without making apparent

to us as contrary to human dignity, as unjust, social relations
that at one time did not seem unjust at all. Conversely, as a
matter of fact, rationalistic faith reacts on individualistic
sentiment and stimulates it. For injustice is unreasonable and
absurd, and consequently, we are the more sensitive to it as
we are more sensitive to the rights of reason. Consequently,
a given advance in moral education in the direction of greater
rationality cannot occur without also bringing to light new
moral tendencies, without inducing a greater thirst for justice,
without stirring the public conscience by latent aspirations.
[Quoted in Bellah, 1973, p. xl]

Chapter 5

1. The form of their church association was, in Hooker's words, to be
that of a *"Visible Covenant* agreement or consent whereby they give up
themselves unto the Lord, to the observing of the ordinances of Christ
together in the same society, which is usually called the Church-Covenant;
For we see not otherwise how members can have Church-power one over
another mutually" (quoted from Schneider, 1958, p. 19).

2. As the Reverend John Eliot put it, just as the Elect had inwardly
covenanted with the Lord, who

caused them inwardly by faith, to give up themselves, unto
him, to be forever his, to love, serve, and obey him, in all his
Word and Commandments; so now, do they outwardly, and
solemnly with the rest of God's people joyn together so to
do in their Civil Polity, receiving from the Lord both the
platform of their Civil Government, as it is set down (in the
essentials of it) in the holy Scriptures; and also their Laws,
which they resolve through his grace, to fetch out of the
Word of God making that their only Magna Charta; and
accounting no law, Statute or Judgement valid, farther than
it appeareth to arise and flow from the Word of God. [quoted
from Schneider, 1958, p. 25]

3. It was authoritarian, of course, to those who were not members
of the church.

4. Ward's caveat, in his own words, is as follows:

I dare take upon me, to be the Herauld of New-England so
farre, as to proclaime to the world, in the name of our Colony,

that all Familists, Antinomians, Anabaptists, and other En-
thusiasts, shall have free Liberty to keep away from us, and
such as will come to be gone as fast as they can, the sooner
the better. Secondly, I dare averre, that God doth no where
in his word tolerate Christian States, to give Tolerations to
such adversaries of his Truth, if they have power in their
hands to suppress them. [For this and other details of Ward's
strictures on the virtues of intolerance, see his *The Simple
Cobbler of Aggawam,* portions of which are reprinted in
Miller and Johnson, 1938, pp. 226-36]

5. Native American Indians, of course, did not count.

6. In terms of historical significance, the sectarian pattern shared by
these Protestant groups is probably more important than the many theological issues over which they disagreed. These differences are also of less
importance than the general theology they held in common. In the present discussion, therefore, Puritanism should be considered as a fairly
typical case of Protestant sectarianism, not as an exceptional example.

7. It is perhaps important before proceeding further to make explicit
a point only assumed in the foregoing presentation. Those only super-
ficially acquainted with Weber's work on the Protestant Ethic have sometimes tended to connect New England Puritanism with his ideal-typical
accounts of Calvinist theology. Clearly, however, Calvinism underwent
an important casuistic transformation in Puritan hands. Original Calvinism
held that human knowledge of salvation was forever uncertain. God had
already made His choices, and exertions by mortals to penetrate His
inscrutability were not only futile but also blasphemous. But while such
uncertainty was logically acceptable, it was psychologically unbearable
in a world dominated by religious concerns, where the attainment of
salvation was the principal goal of an individual's life. Inevitably, the
inner need for certainty began gradually to displace the less acceptable
aspects of predestination so that, by the time the *Arabella* set sail, Puritan
divines were already convinced that grace is made manifest. This conviction was even stronger among other Protestant sects.

8. See Perry Miller, 1954, pp. 49-63. Much of the present discussion
owes a great debt to Miller's work, which I gratefully acknowledge.

9. Although Weber almost certainly provided the inspiration, the
term *self-rationalization* is Mannheim's. See Mannheim, 1940, pp. 55-57.

10. Cotton finds biblical support for this view: "Seek not every man
his owne things, but every man the good of his brothers."

11. The failure to consider Weber's arguments on this matter, especially

the failure to consider his essay, "The Protestant Sects and the Spirit of Capitalism" (1946, pp. 302-22), along with his more famous *The Protestant Ethic and the Spirit of Capitalism* (1958), is primarily responsible for the misunderstanding of Weber as an idealist. What matters most, he maintained, "is not the ethical doctrine of a religion, but that form of ethical conduct upon which premiums are placed" (1946, p. 321). Weber himself, it should be noted, defended himself with precisely this line of reasoning against those critics who objected to his "idealism" (1978).

12. While Veblen did not connect the "test of country town fitness" to secularized patterns of sectarian discipline, his essay, "The Country Town" (1923, pp. 142-65) and his "Supplementary Notes" to Chapter VI of *Imperial Germany and the Industrial Revolution* (1915) may be profitably read as an extension of Weber's own analysis of "The Protestant Sects and the Spirit of Capitalism" (1946, pp. 302-22). Such a reading takes Weber's argument considerably further, both historically and analytically, than Weber himself found it necessary to go for his own purposes. Despite considerable differences in the qualities premiumed, that sectarian discipline and the "test of country town fitness" are structurally identical is unmistakable from Veblen's discussion.

> The successful man under [the test of country town fitness] succeeds because he is by native gift or by training suited to this situation of petty intrigue and nugatory subtleties. To survive, in the business sense of the word, he must *prove himself* a serviceable member of this gild of municipal diplomats who patiently wait on the chance of getting something for nothing; and he can enter this gild of waiters on the still-born increase, only through such *apprenticeship as will prove his fitness.* To be acceptable he must be reliable, conciliatory, conservative, secretive, patient and prehensile. The capacities that make the outcome and that characterise this gild of self-made businessmen are cupidity, prudence, and chicane. . . .
>
> The ways and means of the making of the self-made man in American business are of this character, and the product is of such quality as these ways and means may be expected to yield, acting as they do with great uniformity both by *training* and *selection.* [Veblen, 1915, pp. 336-37; my emphasis]

13. These public virtues (for example, selflessness), of course, often stood in stark contrast to the businessman's private motives (for example, greed). The ultimate lampoon of the small town businessman's image of

respectability, especially honesty, was delivered by Mark Twain in his wonderful short story "The Man That Corrupted Hadleyburg" (1976). A less humorous but equally worthy account can be found in Sinclair Lewis's better known *Babbitt* (1922).

14. Community service was not, of course, the only means by which a businessman could claim prestige. Apparently, the most important means of acquiring prestige was to be successful in one's business. "Solvency," observed Veblen, "is always a meritorious work, however it may be achieved or maintained" (1923, p. 158). But even the prestige conferred by personal success was not entirely unrelated to the older Protestant requirement of community service. In that context, production of goods and commodities was the mainstay of group welfare. He who produced most contributed most. This conception was carried over from an era of commodity production to that of financial production. As the most productive member of the community—as measured in money—the successful businessman also ranks among the most esteemed. Nothing, it seems, succeeds like success.

15. In Veblen's satiric view, "the salesmanlike interest in the 'prestige value' " of visible philanthropy is responsible for "many deeds of Christian charity and Christian faith." Indeed, he observes, "one hesitates to imagine what would be the fate of the foreign missions, e.g., in the absence of this salesmanlike solicitude for the main chance in country towns" (Veblen, 1923, p. 162).

16. Even as late as the 1940s in Elmtown, a rather typical midwestern small town, the middle-class businessmen continued to be "hyperactive" in civic associations and community service, even after real community leadership had been usurped by old upper class families. Although Hollingshead does not link such activities to their historical background, he does make clear that they continue to be performed in an ambitious quest for prestige. See Hollingshead, 1975, pp. 62-67.

17. Along with the booster policy of local patriotism, shopping locally rather than in neighboring towns or through mail-order houses was held to be an admirable demonstration of civic fealty. To heed the slogan "Shop in Middletown," for instance, was a matter of civic pride. See Lynd, 1929, p. 487.

18. See Lynd, 1937, p. 451.

19. As Lynd (1937, p. 73) reports, these points were the crux of an appeal to General Motors that it place a plant in Middletown, as revealed in the mayor's overture to that company: "I, as mayor . . . invited General Motors to locate here with a promise of cooperation and freedom from labor disturbance. . . . Permit me again to invite you to locate General Motors units here for mutual benefit, a profitable operation of plant with

employment for our people, and a continuation of good will and cooperation from a community that appreciates industry."

20. See Lyman, 1978, for a discussion of this tendency under the more general rubric of "envy." See also Warner and Srole, 1945.

21. In some cases, and often in towns dominated by paternalistic textile mills, rental housing was routinely made available to employees. Although rents were generally quite reasonable, even cheap, employer ownership of housing offered an obvious means of controlling labor. See Liston Pope, 1942, and Wallace, 1978, pp. 171-72.

22. This requirement seems to have been especially pronounced in the early to middle 1800s. Textile employees in Rockdale, for instance, were routinely dismissed or otherwise punished (for example, docking wages, blacklisting, suspension) for such transgressions as fighting, swearing, drinking alcohol, "undue familiarity between the sexes," and tardiness. See Wallace, 1978, pp. 177-80.

23. Quite a large number of Protestant charities were in fact administered by the wives of well-to-do businessmen, who had more time for such pursuits. Taking seriously their Protestant obligation to upgrade the less fortunate morally as well as materially, organizations of female volunteer Christian soldiers emerged as the descendants of Mather's Societies To Do Good. Their tactic, as Veblen sardonically observed, was to present themselves and their own leisure-class ethos as models of emulation, often with deleterious results for those they sought to improve:

> These good people who go out to humanize the poor are
> commonly, and advisedly, extremely scrupulous and silently
> insistent in matters of decorum and the decencies of life.
> They are commonly persons of an exemplary life and gifted
> with a tenacious insistence on ceremonial cleanness in the
> various items of their daily consumption. The cultural or
> civilizing efficacy of this inculcation of correct habits of
> thought with respect to the consumption of time and com-
> modities is scarcely to be overrated; nor is its economic value
> to the individual who acquires these higher and more reput-
> able ideals inconsiderable. Under the circumstances of the
> existing pecuniary culture, the reputability, and consequently
> the success, of the individual is in great measure dependent
> on his proficiency in demeanor and methods of consumption
> that argue habitual waste of time and goods. But as regards
> the ulterior economic bearing of this training in worthier
> methods of life, . . . the effect wrought is in large part a sub-
> stitution of costlier or less efficient methods of accomplish-

ing the same material results. . . . The propaganda of culture
is in great part an inculcation of new tastes, or rather of a
new schedule of proprieties, which have been adapted to the
upper-class scheme of life under the guidance of the leisure
class formulation of the principles of status and pecuniary
decency. This new schedule of proprieties is intruded into
the lower class scheme of life from the code elaborated by
an element of the population whose life lies outside the
industrial process; and this intrusive schedule can scarcely
be expected to fit the exigencies of life for these lower classes
more adequately than the schedule already in vogue among
them, and especially not more adequately than the schedule
which they are themselves working out under the stress of
modern industrial life. [Veblen, 1953, pp. 223-24]

24. Lynd observed rather matter of factly that philanthropy constituted an important aspect of the *X* Family's control of Middletown. For
a good discussion of philanthropic institutions as agencies of cooptation
in modern America, see Bensman and Vidich, 1971, pp. 213-35. A similar
argument has been made regarding the operation of contemporary federal
welfare distribution—that it operates not only as state benevolence, but
also as a means of social control and a mechanism for the cooptation of
the welfare classes. See Piven and Cloward, 1971.

25. The civic contributions made by businessmen on the one hand and
labor unions on the other were sometimes pointedly compared to high-
light the selfishness and moral bankruptcy of the latter against the natural
and beneficial leadership of the former. In 1841, for instance, Alonzo
Potter, bishop of Pennsylvania, declared that little social benefit could
result from trade associations: "Trades Unions . . . convene their members
to hear of 'equal rights,' 'rapacious capitalists,' 'grinding employers.' But
we are informed of no libraries that they have established; of no lectures
that they have instituted; nor, indeed, of any measures for the diffusion
of useful knowledge, which were not already prevalent and of easy access"
(quoted in Wallace, 1978, pp. 336-37).

26. The strategies of cooptation and ideological diffusion mentioned
are fairly typical of the Main Street efforts to sustain its own local control. An analysis of the structure of domination in any particular small
town would, of course, require a more detailed empirical investigation.

27. The best and most systematic statements of this small town ideological self-image can be found in "The Middletown Spirit" (Lynd and
Lynd, 1937) and "Springdale's Image of Itself" (Vidich and Bensman,
1968). Although neither the Lynds nor Vidich and Bensman trace this

small town ethos directly to the older Protestant virtues, both imply that the ethos is at least partly sustained by the backing of local Protestant churches, which have maintained traditionally close ties with the small town businessmen who are the carriers of the ethos. See also L. Pope, 1942.

28. These figures are taken from Nevins, 1927, and Tarbell, 1936.

29. See Tarbell, 1936; Josephson, 1962; and Nevins, 1927.

30. See Mills, 1951, for a more detailed treatment of the old middle-class decline.

31. For references, see Ewen, 1976; Potter, 1954; Rorty, 1934; and Veblen, 1923.

32. The significance of installment buying is also recognized by Daniel Bell (1976, pp. 54-84) in his perceptive analysis of the decline of the Protestant Ethic as a general cultural orientation.

33. Veblen was in many ways the last of the Puritans. Not only *The Theory of the Leisure Class* but also the whole of his work may be regarded as a sustained jeremiad on the decay of the Protestant virtues of productivity and frugality, and as a satiric condemnation of their passing.

34. The classic work on the penetration of American small towns by the agencies of the emergent order is Vidich and Bensman's *Small Town in Mass Society* (1968).

35. The challenge of immigrants will be considered in some detail when the work of Lloyd Warner is examined. For the moment, we wish to concentrate primarily on the structural transformations of the American economy and society and their effects.

36. As a focus for the old middle-class reaction to their own decline, the Temperance Movement had much to recommend it. Not only did it assert a Protestant value (sobriety) against emergent corrupting influences, but it could also be specifically directed at certain immigrant groups not properly versed in Protestant virtues. (The Irish, for instance, were an especially overworked target.) In his excellent work *Symbolic Crusade* (1963), Joseph Gusfield explicitly links the Temperance Movement to the declining old middle classes.

37. In a later effort to improve local business, some would ultimately even sacrifice the older morals altogether by accepting pornographic bookstores and theatres, hippies and rock concerts, "head shops," and the like.

Chapter 6

1. The mythical dimensions of this craft age are exposed by Stephen Thernstrom (1964), whose historical studies of Newburyport furnished

far more reliable information about the town's past than could be provided by Warner's ahistoric functionalism and reliance on myth. Thernstrom makes clear, for instance, that despite Warner's acceptance of the community's consensus that the strike "could not have happened earlier," in fact "strikes had taken place in Newburyport—in 1858, in 1875, and a good many times since. The strike of 1933 was distinctive only in that it was more successful than previous strikes, and not much more successful at that." See Thernstrom, 1964, p. 212.

2. Indeed, humming an almost Marxist refrain, Warner suggests that

> our industrial system is molding a new category of class relations. If those members of the three lower classes who work with the machines of industry act and feel alike in their social relations, we may be forced to recognize that a new social pattern of behavior is being created which will cut across, or considerably modify, our social classes . . . [this] seems to be related to the fact that they are all engaged in a type of work in which they are thrown into a far closer relational pattern than are others of similar social status in the total community. [Warner, 1948, pp. 159-60]

3. See especially Thernstrom, 1964, p. 211.

4. "Originally a fight against political privilege," Hofstadter (1948, p. 67) writes,

> the Jacksonian movement had broadened into a fight against economic privilege, rallying to its support a host of "rural capitalists and village entrepreneurs." When Jackson left office he was the hero of the lower and middling elements of American society who believed in expanding opportunity through equal rights, and by the time of his death in 1845 the "excitement" Webster had noticed had left a deep and lasting mark upon the nation. "This," exulted Calvin Colton, "is a country of self-made men, than which there can be no better in any state of society."

5. Memorial Day was first declared a legal holiday in New York in 1873.

6. It was at least partly in response to immigrant claims for prestige on the traditionally accepted grounds of business success and ethical virtue that old middle- and upper-class groups turned to new and less encroach-

able grounds for making their own claims to status superiority. Some of these included the myth of blood superiority (for example, the Boston Brahmins), date of kin arrival (the *Mayflower* syndrome), and family heroism (Daughters of the American Revolution).

7. W. I. Thomas (1921) describes several immigrant types.

8. Not all of these terms, of course, make specific reference to the unconventional residents of American small towns. One of the better portraits of this group in its local setting may be found in Vidich and Bensman's (1968, pp. 69-71) description of the "shack people" of Springdale.

9. See Vidich and Bensman, 1968, p. 70.

10. Vidich and Bensman suggest that they do have one effect within the community: they help to sustain the more conventional standards of success and decency by setting an example with which the more "respectable" persons could favorably compare themselves and feel justified in their own way of life (1968, pp. 70-71).

11. For a much broader discussion of deference rituals, though at an interpersonal level, see Goffman, 1967, pp. 47-95 and Collins, 1975, pp. 161-224.

12. Lukes (1977) makes this point in his own analysis of collective rites in Durkheimian sociology.

13. For a mythical reconstruction of Newburyport history primarily from the point of view of these old middle classes, see the section on the Tercentenary celebrations in Warner, 1959.

14. One is left with this impression of "mystical power" because the substantive bases of ritual participation are never investigated. Instead, it is presumed that virtually all persons are similarly oriented to the values and symbols themselves, especially where they are ritually expressed. This presumption, as we have attempted to demonstrate, is mistaken.

15. Functionalists have been justly accused of selectively studying only those public ceremonies that do fulfill this possible outcome of sustaining social order, and of then generalizing their findings to all collective ceremonies. Since they tend to ignore the substantive bases of ritual participation, all that remains which can serve as an integrative force is the participation itself. This allows no possibility for differentiating between integrative and nonintegrative rites since, by definition, all collective rites must be integrative. For a similar argument, see Lukes, 1977.

16. For a discussion of some of Warner's critics on this matter, see Kornhauser, 1953, pp. 248-50.

17. For a classic demonstration of how inaccurate a small town ideological self-image can be, see Vidich and Bensman, 1968.

Chapter 7

1. Bell, 1973.
2. Galbraith, 1978.
3. Bensman and Vidich, 1976.
4. See, for instance, the essays in Olson, 1963.
5. Baran and Sweezy, 1966.
6. See, for instance, Moore, 1958; Miller and Swanson, 1963.
7. For a penetrating analysis of the Watergate affair which focuses on problems of legitimacy in a bureaucratic society, see Vidich, 1975.

8. See, for example, the essays in Geis and Meier, 1977; Douglas and Johnson, 1977; Johnson and Douglas, 1978; Ermann and Lundman, 1978; and Heilbroner, et al., 1972.

9. Behavior and decisions like those mentioned in the above examples receive attention in current sociological literature primarily under two headings: "white collar crime" and "official deviance." Neither tends to be adequate either as classification or explanation. Various of the behaviors and decisions dealt with, while ethically questionable, are nonetheless within the confines of the law. Moreover, many cannot be said to constitute deviance because practitioners are frequently powerful enough to escape that social designation. A more comprehensive understanding of the phenomena here under investigation requires a resurrection of a neglected category in recent sociology: the sociology of morals. What follows is a preliminary effort in that direction.

Robert Jackall's (1980 and 1980a) recent work is among the more insightful analyses of the structural underpinnings of bureaucratic morals. Jackall's work both confirmed and contributed to my own thoughts on the subject.

10. As Scott and Hart (1979, p. 39) indicate, "The rational requirements of technology, the coordination requirements of job specialization, and the productivity expectations of society require that managers direct their energies and talents to finding solutions to the immediate, practical, and material problems that confront them. So the pressures for solving these problems have overridden any propensities for thinking about values." See also Jackall, 1980.

11. An account of this case is offered in McCarthy, 1972. For other examples of how bureaucracies reduce grave moral concerns to practical problems, see Ungar (1972) on how the William S. Merrill Company sought to repress news of the dangerous side-effects of MER/29, an anti-cholesterol drug whose virtues had been fabricated in the first place; and Vandivier (1972) on the already mentioned efforts of B. F. Goodrich to gain contracts for its defective aircraft brakes.

12. According to John DeLorean, a former high-level executive at

General Motors, "Business in America . . . is impersonal. . . . The ultimate measure of success and failure of these businesses is not their effect on people but rather their earnings per share of stock. . . . The first question to meet any business proposal is how will it affect profits? People do not enter the equation of a business decision except to the extent that the effect on them will hurt or enhance earnings per share. In such a completely impersonal context, business decisions of questionable personal morality are easily justified" (quoted in Wright, 1979, p. 62). De Lorean's recent arrest on charges of drug smuggling (allegedly undertaken to finance his struggling automobile company) would appear to provide ironic confirmation of his earlier comments.

13. Edward Alsworth Ross, in his neglected classic, *Sin and Society* (1973), referred to this as the "impersonalization of sin," which he attributed to growing social interdependence and "the mutualism of our time."

14. See Davis, 1917, for similar connections between Protestantism, associations, and corporations.

15. "Organization Man" is not used here with the derogatory connotations the term has acquired. It refers only to the social character bred by the organizational processes under discussion. As such, of course, its applicability is not restricted by considerations of gender.

16. Joseph Bensman (1967) has suggested that the successful repression of independent standards is linked to the degree of bureaucratic organization.

17. See the illuminating discussion by Galbraith (1978) on the conditions that have favored this congruence of organizational and personal goals in the modern corporation. Most particularly, "identification"—"the voluntary exchange of one's goals for the preferable ones of the organization"—has become a motivation of the Organization Man due to the removal of compulsion and to the generous pecuniary compensation. See also the classic work of Whyte (1956) and the recent efforts of Scott and Hart (1979).

18. The Departments of Justice and Energy later refuted charges of conspiracy in this case.

19. Such indifference is symptomatic of the sort of despotism of which de Tocqueville (1966) warned, although it is scarcely restricted to the political order. He argued that centralized direction of society, even within a democratic political context, "covers the whole of social life with a network of petty, complicated rules that are both minute and uniform. . . . It does not break men's will, but softens, bends, and guides it . . . it is not at all tyrannical, but it hinders, restrains, enervates, stifles, and stultifies so much that in the end each nation is no more than a flock of timid and hardworking animals. . . . It never drives men to despair, but

continually thwarts them and leads them to give up using their free will. It slowly stifles their spirits and enervates their souls." (1966, pp. 692, 694).

20. See Bensman and Vidich (1971) for a discussion of middle-class life-styles and their economic foundations.

21. See Luckmann, 1967, and Berger and Luckmann, 1966.

22. This is a major reason why the past decade has been called narcissistic and the "me generation." Of course, quests for personal meaning and fulfillment have certainly not been restricted to the past couple of decades. But for the first time on a large scale, such quests are no longer connected to collective obligations. Without such a connection, they can only be recognized as self-serving.

23. See, for instance, Bensman and Vidich, 1976.

24. It is worth noting that the great size of contemporary institutions—one of their most characteristic features—is often called upon to rationalize offenses against them, as when the shoplifter declares, "They're so big they won't miss it."

25. D. B. Cooper is the name used by a hijacker who, with apparent success, parachuted from a Northwest Orient Airlines plane in 1971 with $2 million in ransom. Cooper subsequently became, though *in absentia*, a pop celebrity of sorts, as T-shirts advertising his name became hot-selling items. A movie dramatizing his exploits has also recently appeared.

Chapter 8

1. Parsons refers to the institutional manifestation of this common matrix as "denominational pluralism." See Parsons, 1960 and 1963.

2. See Parsons, 1960, 1963, and 1974.

3. As Parsons defines it, to the extent that there exists "a solidarity among those mutually oriented to the common values . . . the actors concerned will be said to constitute, within the area of relevance for these values, a collectivity" (Parsons, 1951, p. 41).

4. That their concerns were substantive is a crucial point, for to ignore it either relegates their work to the status of "valueless and quaint antiques" having little or no relevance for contemporary sociological concerns—a charge that is patently untrue—or invites the sort of simplistic and shallow treatment of their work to be found in the recent *Sociologists of the Chair* (Schwendinger and Schwendinger, 1974). The centrality of substantive concerns is stressed by Lyman and Vidich (1980, pp. 99-112), who combine an accurate if trenchant critique of contemporary American sociology with a worthy manifesto for its practitioners.

5. A perceptive analysis of the relationship between religion and the

treatment of authority in American sociology can be found in Diggins, 1979. Diggins views with unusual clarity the significance of Protestantism in Parsons's work on the subject.

6. See, for example, Gouldner, 1970, and Diggins, 1979.

7. Both internal controls and individual responsibility imply a Protestant as opposed to Catholic emphasis.

8. Presumably, since social constraints are internalized as features of the personality, violation of these constraints would produce anxiety in the actor. Such anxiety would appear rather similar to the Christian notion of the conscience.

9. To note just a few examples, see Lemert, 1951; Becker, 1963; Douglas, 1970; and Collins, 1975.

10. The difference of emphasis between Parsons and Durkheim on this point can be illustrated with reference to the suicide rates found among Protestants and Catholics, the Protestants tending to do themselves in with greater frequency. According to Parsons, the explanation "lies in the different *content* of the different value systems" (1968, p. 333). To Durkheim, on the other hand, the difference results from a discrepancy of integrative force:

> If Protestantism concedes a greater freedom to individual
> thought than Catholicism it is because it has fewer common
> beliefs and practices. Now a religious society cannot exist
> without a collective *credo* and the more extensive the *credo*
> the more unified and strong is the society. . . . Inversely, the
> greater concessions a confessional group makes to individual
> judgment, the less it dominates lives, the less its cohesion
> and vitality. We thus reach the conclusion that the superior-
> ity of Protestantism with respect to suicide results from its
> being a *less strongly integrated* church than the Catholic
> church [Durkheim, 1951, p. 159]

For an extension of these arguments concerning the differences between Parsons and Durkheim in this regard, see W. Pope, 1973, and Johnson, 1965.

11. For a view of Parsons's ideas on modernization as a kind of missionary work, see Casanova, 1979.

12. See Bell, 1962, and Lipset, 1959. The most significant portions of the debate regarding the end of ideology thesis can be found in Waxman, 1969.

13. Parsons is often maligned for his emphasis on order and consensus. Considered as general sociological theory, much of the criticism directed at his work is warranted, for he transformed a unique historical situation

into a general system characteristic. Considered in terms of the social
settings that gave shape to his work, however, Parsons's emphases are quite
understandable and generally accurate. For a period of years, during which
Parsons came to intellectual maturity, America was characterized by a
remarkable consensus; order was generally secure and social change was
largely controlled.

Chapter 9

1. The reference to Memorial Day connects Bellah's analysis to the
earlier study done by Warner, whom Bellah cites with approval.

2. In one of the most seminal essays in the sociology of knowledge,
Mannheim (1971) argued that conservatism is but tradition made self-
conscious. The recent experience of the old Protestant middle classes in
America would appear to support his thesis.

3. See, for instance, Bensman and Vidich (1976).

4. Such an alliance is not only possible, but to some degree has already been established. As the new middle classes experience economic
losses, they tend to become status and class defensive, one expression of
which is an apparent willingness to offset these losses by backing income and
property tax cuts, even though these mean a decline in social services (the
brunt of which is usually borne by the lower classes). The broad appeal
of "tax revolt fever," as the media labeled it, would seem to illustrate the
point, as would the success of Proposition 13 in California and the recent
election of Ronald Reagan, who appealed to both the old middle-class
dissatisfaction and new middle-class economic insecurities. And, of course,
since fiscal austerity is a time-honored tenet of old middle-class political
and economic thinking, old and new middle classes, especially during a
sustained economic decline, will frequently find themselves on the same
side on issues concerning economic policy.

5. The account that follows is derived from Bellah's autobiographical
comments in the "Introduction" to *Beyond Belief* (1970) and in the
Preface to *The Broken Covenant* (1975).

6. These circumstances might also help to explain the enormous
amount of attention that essay attracted. As Bellah himself acknowledges,
the idea of a "public religious dimension" in American life is by no means
new. Well before the appearance of his celebrated essay, phenomena now
regarded as aspects of the American civil religion had received a good
deal of attention from sociologists, religious historians, and students of
American culture. (See, for instance, Boorstin, 1953; Herberg, 1960;
Mead, 1963; and Arieli, 1964, among others.) But if Bellah's essay was
not wholly original, its effect was nonetheless electric, for his argument

resonated deeply in academic and clerical circles. None of the earlier efforts at conceptualization came near to arousing the interest stimulated by Bellah's essay. Bellah's own lucid prose and Durkheimian framework should not be underestimated in attracting attention to the essay. As Jones and Richey (1974, p. 4) rightly point out, the subject had lacked "a commonly accepted concept in terms of which description, analysis, and interpretation could proceed. Adequate scholarly attention awaited a concept" that Bellah certainly provided. The bewitching power of the concept, however, attracting scholars like moths to the flame, is not an entirely convincing explanation of the popularity of Bellah's work. Something more seems to be involved. I would suggest that many others reacted to the social changes discussed in much the same way as Bellah, that their own values were brought to a level of conscious awareness. Bellah evidently managed to articulate concisely what many felt vaguely.

7. To some extent, this had been done earlier by Robin Williams, another of Parsons's students. In his text *American Society: A Sociological Interpretation* (1960), Williams enumerates certain "value-orientations" as American, thus detached from any specific groups that might serve as the carriers of these values.

8. Bellah's formulation of American civil religion and his call for its revival struck an apparent affinity with President Carter, himself a Southern Baptist with intellectual inclinations. Bellah was one of many people invited to Camp David in July 1979 to consult with the president on the general condition of American society and on the direction of American policy, especially energy policy. If the language and tone of Carter's subsequent address *(New York Times, July 16, 1979)* to the nation may be taken as an indication, Bellah was apparently one of the more influential Camp David consultants. In his speech, Carter spoke of "a crisis of confidence . . . that strikes at the very heart and soul and spirit of our national will" and that is manifest "in the growing doubt about the meaning of our own lives and in the loss of unity and purpose for our nation." In order to recapture our original confidence and spirit, Carter continued, "we simply must have faith in each other" and in the nation's future. And especially, we must forsake the path of self-interestedness and take up "the path of common purpose and the restoration of American values," for only this latter path can lead to "true freedom for our nation and ourselves." Clearly, Carter sought not only to propagate Bellah's construction as an ideological framework for the new American society, but also, from his own powerful pulpit, to initiate our collective rebirth in the American civil religion.

9. According to Hans Gerth, fashionable cultural criticism (he mentions Sinclair Lewis and H. L. Mencken specifically):

belongs to a society undergoing ceaseless cultural change
and it is part of the fashion process. Ideas are consumed and
then rejected the moment they become fashionable outside
of their originating advanced cultural circles. It is part of the
same illusionist parade of ever-changing styles of house facades
and automobile models with nickel snouts and their array of
gadgets. . . . Americans search forever for new things, and new
illusions to live by. And America's cultural criticism, partly
because it makes this its subject matter, reflects this same
tendency. Moreover, the lack of older, secure cultural traditions makes the criticism of novelty itself an endless search
for novelty. [See "Reflections on the American Intelligentsia"
in Gerth, 1982]

REFERENCES

Ahlstrom, Sydney E.
    1972   *A Religious History of the American People.* New Haven,
            Conn.: Yale University Press.

Alpert, Harry
    1941   Emile Durkheim and the Theory of Social Integration.
            Journal of Social Philosophy 6, No. 2 (January): 172-84.
    1961   *Emile Durkheim and His Sociology.* New York: Russell
            and Russell.
    1965   Durkheim's Functional Theory of Ritual. In Robert Nisbet,
            ed., *Emile Durkheim.* Englewood Cliffs, N. J.: Prentice-Hall.

Anthony, Dick, and Thomas Robbins
    1975   From Symbolic Realism to Structuralism, Review Sym-
            posium on the Sociology of Religion of Robert N. Bellah.
            Journal for the Scientific Study of Religion 14, No. 4:
            403-13.

Apter, David, ed.
    1964   *Ideology and Discontent.* Glencoe, Ill.: Free Press.

Arieli, Yehoshua
    1964   *Individualism and Nationalism in American Ideology.*
            Cambridge, Mass.: Harvard University Press.

Arnold, Thurman Wesley
    1937   *The Folklore of Capitalism.* New Haven, Conn.: Yale
            University Press.
    1962   *The Symbols of Government.* New York: Harcourt, Brace
            & World, Inc. (First published in 1935.)

Atherton, Lewis
   1954   *Main Street on the Middle Border.* New York: Quadrangle.
Baltzell, E. Digby
   1964   *The Protestant Establishment.* New York: Random House.
Baran, Paul A., and Paul M. Sweezy
   1966   *Monopoly Capital: An Essay on the American Economic and Social Order.* New York: Modern Reader.
Becker, Howard
   1963   *The Outsiders.* New York: Free Press.
Bell, Daniel
   1962   *The End of Ideology.* Revised Edition. New York: Free Press.
   1973   *The Coming of the Post-Industrial Society.* New York: Basic Books.
   1976   *The Cultural Contradictions of Capitalism.* New York: Basic Books.
Bellah, Robert N.
   1965   Durkheim and History. In Robert Nisbet, ed., *Emile Durkheim.* Englewood Cliffs, N. J.: Prentice-Hall.
   1966   Words for Paul Tillich, *Harvard Divinity Bulletin* 30 (January): 15-16.
   1968   Response to Commentaries on Civil Religion in America. In Donald R. Cutler, ed., *The Religious Situation: 1968.* Boston: Beacon Press.
   1970   *Beyond Belief: Essays on Religion in a Post-Traditional World.* New York: Harper & Row.
   1973   Introduction to Robert N. Bellah, ed., *Emile Durkheim on Morality and Society.* Chicago: University of Chicago Press.
   1974   American Civil Religion in the 1970s. In Russell E. Richey and Donald G. Jones, eds., *American Civil Religion.* New York: Harper & Row.
   1975   *The Broken Covenant: American Civil Religion in Time of Trial.* New York: Seabury Press.
   1976   New Religious Consciousness and the Crisis in Modernity. In Charles Y. Glock and Robert N. Bellah, eds, *The New Religious Consciousness.* Berkeley, Calif.: University of California Press.
   1976a   Comment on "Bellah and the New Orthodoxy." *Sociological Analysis* 37 No. 2: 167-68.
   1976b   Response to the Panel on Civil Religion. *Sociological Analysis* 37, No. 2: 153-59.

1980   *Varieties of Civil Religion.* San Francisco: Harper & Row.
Bend, Emil, and Martin Vogelfanger
1970   A New Look at Mills' Critique. In James E. Curtis and
        John W. Petras, eds., *The Sociology of Knowledge: A
        Reader.* New York: Praeger Publications.
Bendix, Reinhard
1971   Two Sociological Traditions. In Reinhard Bendix and
        Gunther Roth, *Scholarship and Partisanship: Essays on
        Max Weber.* Berkeley, Calif.: University of California Press.
Bensman, Joseph
1967   *Dollars and Sense: Ideology, Ethics, and the Meaning of
        Work in Profit and Nonprofit Organizations.* New York:
        Macmillan.
1979   Max Weber's Concept of Legitimacy: An Evaluation. In
        Arthur J. Vidich and Ronald M. Glassman, eds., *Conflict
        and Control: Challenge to Legitimacy of Modern Govern-
        ments.* Beverly Hills, Calif.: Sage.
Bensman, Joseph, and Robert Lilienfeld
1973   *Craft and Consciousness: Occupational Technique and the
        Development of World Images.* New York: John Wiley.
Bensman, Joseph, and Arthur J. Vidich
1971   *The New American Society: The Revolution of the Middle
        Class.* New York: Quadrangle.
1976   The Crisis of Contemporary Capitalism and the Failure of
        Nerve. *Sociological Inquiry* 46, No. 3-4: 207-17.
Berger, Peter L.
1967   *The Sacred Canopy: Elements of a Sociological Theory
        of Religion.* Garden City, N. Y.: Doubleday.
Berger, Peter L., and Thomas Luckmann
1966   *The Social Construction of Reality.* Garden City, N. Y.:
        Doubleday.
Birnbaum, Norman
1955   Monarchs and Sociologists: A Reply to Professor Shils
        and Mr. Young. *Sociological Review* 3-4: 5-23.
Black, Max
1961   Some Questions About Parsons' Theories. In Max Black,
        ed., *The Social Theories of Talcott Parsons.* Englewood
        Cliffs, N. J.: Prentice-Hall.
Boorstin, Daniel
1953   *The Genius of American Politics.* Chicago: University of
        Chicago Press.

Bremner, Robert H.
    1960   *American Philanthropy.* Chicago: University of Chicago
            Press.
Brogan, D. W.
    1944   *The American Character.* New York: Alfred A. Knopf.
Brooks, Van Wyck
    1958   *America's Coming-of-Age.* Garden City, N. Y.: Doubleday.
Bunzel, J. H.
    1955   The General Ideology of American Small Business. *Political
            Science Quarterly* 70 (March): 87-102.
Campbell, Joseph
    1960   Primitive Man as Metaphysician. In Stanley Diamond, ed.,
            Primitive Views of the World. New York: Columbia Uni-
            versity Press.
Carnegie, Andrew
    1886   *Triumphant Democracy; or Fifty Years March of the
            Republic.* New York: Scribner's.
    1962   *The Gospel of Wealth.* Cambridge, Mass.: Belknap Press
            of Harvard University Press. (First published in 1889.)
Casanova, Jose
    1979   Legitimacy and the Sociology of Modernization. In Arthur
            J. Vidich and Ronald M. Glassman, eds., *Conflict and
            Control.* Beverly Hills, Calif.: Sage.
Christenson, James A., and Ronald C. Wimberley
    1978   Who Is Civil Religious? *Sociological Analysis* 39, No. 1
            (Spring).
Clebsch, William A.
    1968   *From Sacred to Profane America: The Role of Religion
            in American History.* New York: Harper & Row.
Cochran, Thomas C.
    1972   *Business in American Life: A History.* New York: Harper
            & Row.
Cochran, Thomas C., and William Miller
    1961   *The Age of Enterprise.* Revised Edition. New York: Harper
            & Row.
Cohen, A. A.
    1956   Religion as a Secular Ideology. *Partisan Review* 23 (Fall):
            495-505.
Cohen, Jere; Lawrence E. Hazelrigg; and Whitney Pope
    1975   De-Parsonizing Weber: A Critique of Parsons' Interpretation
            of Weber's Sociology. *American Sociological Review* 40:
            229-41.

Cole, William A., and Phillip E. Hammond
1974   Religious Pluralism, Legal Development, and Societal
       Complexity: Rudimentary Forms of Civil Religion. *Journal
       for the Scientific Study of Religion* 13: 177-89.
Collins, Randall
1968   A Comparative Approach to Political Sociology. In Rein-
       hard Bendix, ed., *State and Society*, Berkeley, Calif.: Uni-
       versity of California Press.
1975   *Conflict Sociology: Toward an Explanatory Science*. New
       York: Academic Press.
Creelan, Paul G.
1978   Social Theory as Confession: Parsonian Sociology and the
       Symbolism of Evil. In Richard Harvey Brown and Stanford
       M. Lyman, eds., *Structure, Consciousness, and History*.
       London: Cambridge University Press.
Cuddihy, John Murray
1978   *No Offense: Civil Religion and Protestant Taste*. New
       York: Seabury Press.
Curti, Merle
1946   *The Roots of American Loyalty*. New York: Columbia
       University Press.
Cutler, Donald A., ed.,
1968   *The Religious Situation*. Boston: Beacon Press.
Dahrendorf, Ralf
1968   *Essays in the Theory of Society*. Stanford, Calif.: Stanford
       University Press.
Davis, Joseph Stancliffe
1917   *Essays in the Earlier History of American Corporations*.
       2 vols. New York: Russell and Russell, Inc.
de Tocqueville, Alexis
1966   *Democracy in America*. Edited by J. P. Mayer; translated
       by George Lawrence. Garden City, N. Y.: Doubleday.
Diamond, Stanley, ed.
1960   *Primitive Views of the World*. New York: Columbia Uni-
       versity Press.
Diggins, John P.
1978   *The Bard of Savagery: Thorstein Veblen and Modern
       Social Theory*. New York: Seabury Press.
1979   The Socialization of Authority and the Dilemmas of
       American Liberalism. *Social Research* 46, No. 3.
Dorfman, Joseph
1946   *The Economic Mind in American Civilization*. Vols. 1

and 2. 1606-1865. New York: Viking Press.

1947   *The Economic Mind in American Civilization.* Vol. 3, 1865-1918. New York: Viking Press.

Douglas, Jack D., ed.

1970   *Deviance and Respectability: The Social Construction of Moral Meanings.* New York: Basic Books.

Douglas, Jack D., and John M. Johnson, eds.

1977   *Official Deviance: Readings in Malfeasance, Misfeasance, and Other Forms of Corruption.* New York: J. B. Lippincott.

Drucker, Peter F.

1968   *The Age of Discontinuity: Guidelines to Our Changing Society.* New York: Harper & Row.

Durkheim, Emile

1933   *The Division of Labor in Society.* New York: Free Press.

1938   *The Rules of the Sociological Method.* New York: Free Press.

1951   *Suicide.* New York: Free Press.

1956   *Education and Sociology.* Glencoe, Ill.: Free Press.

1958   *Professional Ethics and Civic Morals.* Glencoe, Ill.: Free Press.

1961   *Moral Education.* New York: Free Press.

1965   *The Elementary Forms of the Religious Life.* New York: Free Press. (First published in 1915.)

1972   *Selected Writings.* Edited with an Introduction by Anthony Giddens. London: Cambridge University Press.

1973   *Emile Durkheim: On Morality and Society.* Edited with an Introduction by Robert N. Bellah. Chicago: University of Chicago Press.

1974   *Sociology and Philosophy.* New York: Free Press.

Durkheim, Emile, and Marcel Mauss

1963   *Primitive Classification.* Translated with an Introduction by Rodney Needham, Chicago: University of Chicago Press.

Edelman, Murray

1964   *The Symbolic Uses of Politics.* Urbana, Ill.: University of Illinois Press.

1971   *Politics as Symbolic Action: Mass Arousal and Quiescence.* New York: Academic Press.

Ermann, M. David, and Richard J. Lundman, eds.

1978   *Corporate and Governmental Deviance.* New York: Oxford University Press.

Evans-Pritchard, E. E.

1965   *Theories of Primitive Religion.* London: Oxford University Press.

Ewen, Stuart
  1976   *Captains of Consciousness: Advertising and the Social
          Roots of the Consumer Culture.* New York: McGraw-Hill.
Faris, Ellsworth
  1934   Emile Durkheim on the Division of Labor in Society.
          American Journal of Sociology 40: 376-77.
Fenn, Richard K.
  1972   Toward a New Sociology of Religion. *Journal for the
          Scientific Study of Religion* 11, No. 1 (March): 16-32.
  1974   Religion and the Legitimation of Social Systems. In Alan
          Eister, ed., *Changing Perspectives in the Scientific Study
          of Religion.* New York: John Wiley.
  1976   Bellah and the New Orthodoxy. *Sociological Analysis* 37,
          No. 2: 160-66.
  1978   *Toward a Theory of Secularization.* Monograph Series,
          Number 1. Storrs, Conn.: Society for the Scientific Study
          of Religion.
Foss, Daniel
  1963   The World View of Talcott Parsons. In Maurice Stein and
          Arthur J. Vidich, eds., *Sociology on Trial.* Englewood
          Cliffs, N. J.: Prentice-Hall.
Franklin, Benjamin
  1966   *Autobiography.* Boston: Houghton Mifflin. (First pub-
          lished in 1868.)
Galbraith, John Kenneth
  1978   *The New Industrial State.* 3rd Edition, Revised, Boston:
          Houghton Mifflin. (First published in 1967.)
Gaustad, Edwin Scott
  1968   *The Great Awakening in New England.* Chicago: Quadrangle.
Geertz, Clifford
  1973   *The Interpretation of Cultures.* New York: Basic Books.
Gehlke, C. E.
  1968   *Emile Durkheim's Contributions to Sociological Theory.*
          New York: AMS Press.
Geis, Gilbert
  1978   White Collar Crime: The Heavy Electrical Equipment
          Anti-trust Cases of 1961. In M. David Ermann and Richard
          J. Lundman, eds., *Corporate and Governmental Deviance.*
          New York: Oxford University Press.
Geis, Gilbert, and Robert F. Meier, eds.
  1977   *White-Collar Crime: Offenses in Business, Politics, and the
          Professions.* Revised Edition. New York: Free Press.

Gerth, Hans H.
    1982   Politics, Character, and Culture: Perspectives from Hans Gerth.
            Edited by Joseph Bensman, Arthur J. Vidich, and Nobuko
            Gerth. Westport, Conn.: Greenwood Press.
Gerth, Hans H., and C. Wright Mills
    1953   Character and Social Structure. New York: Harcourt,
            Brace & World, Inc.
Giddens, Anthony
    1971   The "Individual" in the Writings of Durkheim. European
            Journal of Sociology 12: 210-28.
    1971a   Capitalism and Modern Social Theory. London: Cambridge
            University Press.
    1972   Introduction. In Emile Durkheim: Selected Writings. Edited
            by Anthony Giddens. London: Cambridge University Press.
    1976   Functionalism Apres la lutte. Social Research 42, No. 2
            (Summer): 325-66.
Goddard, David
    1972   Anthropology: The Limits of Functionalism. In Robin
            Blackburn, ed., Ideology in Social Science. New York:
            Vintage.
Goffman, Erving
    1976   Interaction Ritual. New York: Doubleday.
Goldenweiser, A. A.
    1933   History, Psychology and Culture. New York: Alfred A.
            Knopf.
    1975   Review of Emile Durkheim, Les Formes elementares de
            la vie religieuse. In W. S. F. Pickering, ed., Durkheim on
            Religion. London: Routledge and Kegan Paul.
Goldman, Eric F.
    1960   The Crucial Decade and After: America, 1945-1960. New
            York: Random House.
Goldstein, Kurt
    1960   Concerning the Concept of "Primitivity." In Stanley Dia-
            mond, ed., Primitive Views of the World. New York:
            Columbia University Press.
Goode, William J.
    1951   Religion Among the Primitives. New York: Free Press.
Goody, J.
    1961   Religion and Ritual: The Definitional Problem. British
            Journal of Sociology 12: 142-64.
Gouldner, Alvin W.
    1970   The Coming Crisis of Western Sociology. New York: Avon
            Books.

Gracey, Harry L.
1977   Morality in the Organized Society. In Dennis H. Wrong
        and Larry L. Gracy, eds., *Readings in Introductory Socio-
        logy.* 3rd Edition. New York: Macmillan.
Greeley, Andrew M.
1972   *The Denominational Society: A Sociological Approach
        to Religion in America.* Glenview, Ill.: Scott, Foresman.
Griffin, Clifford S.
1960   *Their Brothers' Keepers: Moral Stewardship in the United
        States, 1800-1865.* New Brunswick, N. J.: Rutgers Univer-
        sity Press.
Gusfield, Joseph R.
1963   *Symbolic Crusade: Status Politics and the American Tem-
        perance Movement.* Urbana, Ill.: University of Illinois Press.
Hadden, Jeffrey K.
1975   Review Symposium on the Sociology of Robert N. Bellah.
        Journal for the Scientific Study of Religion 14, No. 4:
        385-89.
Halbwachs, Maurice
1938   Individual Psychology and Collective Psychology. *American
        Sociological Review* 3: 615-23.
Hammond, Phillip E., and Benton Johnson
1970   *American Mosaic.* New York: Random House.
Hapgood, David
1974   *The Screwing of the Average Man.* New York: Doubleday.
Heilbroner, Robert L., et al.
1972   *In the Name of Profit.* Garden City, N. Y.: Doubleday.
Heimert, Alan
1966   *Religion and the American Mind.* Cambridge, Mass.:
        Harvard University Press.
Herberg, Will
1960   *Protestant, Catholic, Jew.* Revised Edition. Garden City,
        N. Y.: Doubleday.
Hertz, Karl H.
1962   Max Weber and American Puritanism. *Journal for the
        Scientific Study of Religion* 1, No. 2 (April).
Hodgson, Godfrey
1976   *America in Our Time: From World War II to Nixon:
        What Happened and Why,* New York: Random House.
Hofstadter, Richard
1948   *The American Political Tradition.* New York: Random
        House.
1955   *The Age of Reform.* New York: Random House.

Hollingshead, A. B.
    1975   *Elmtown's Youth and Elmtown Revisited.* New York:
            John Wiley.
Hudson, Winthrop S.
    1949   Puritanism and the Spirit of Capitalism. *Church History*
            18: 3-17.
    1970   *Nationalism and Religion in America.* New York: Harper
            & Row.
Hughes, H. Stuart
    1958   *Consciousness and Society.* New York: Vintage.
Hughey, Michael W.
    1979   The Idea of Secularization in the Works of Max Weber: A
            Theoretical Outline. *Qualitative Sociology* 2, No. 1 (May):
            85-111.
Huizinga, Johan
    1972   *America.* New York: Harper & Row.
Jackall, Robert
    1980   Crime in the Suites, *Review Essay in Contemporary Socio-
            logy* 9 (May): 354-58.
    1980a   Structural Invitations to Deceit: Some Reflections on
            Bureaucracy and Morality. *Berkshire Review* 15: 49-61.
Johnson, Barclay D.
    1965   Durkheim's One Cause of Suicide. *American Sociological
            Review* 30 (December): 875-86.
Johnson, Benton
    1976   Comments on "A Symposium on Civil Religion." *Socio-
            logical Analysis* 37, No. 2: 150-52.
Johnson, E.A.J.
    1961   *American Economic Thought in the Seventeenth Century.*
            New York: Russell and Russell.
Johnson, John M., and Jack D. Douglas, eds.
    1978   *Crime at the Top.* Philadelphia: J. B. Lippincott.
Jones, Donald G., and Russell E. Richey
    1974   The Civil Religion Debate. In Donald G. Jones and Russell
            E. Richey, eds., *American Civil Religion.* New York:
            Harper & Row.
Josephson, Matthew
    1962   *The Robber Barons.* New York: Harcourt, Brace & World.
Kanter, Rosabeth Moss, and Barry A. Stein, eds.
    1979   *Life in Organizations: Workplaces as People Experience
            Them.* New York: Basic Books.
Kolb, William
    1953   Values, Positivism and the Functional Theory of Religion:

The Growth of a Moral Dilemma. *Social Forces* 31 (May): 305-11.

1961   Images of Man and the Sociology of Religion. *Journal for the Scientific Study of Religion* 1 (October): 5-22.

Kornhauser, Ruth Hosner

1953   The Warner Approach to Social Stratification. In Reinhard Bendix and S. M. Lipset, eds., *Class, Status and Power*. Glencoe, Ill.: Free Press.

Kornhauser, William

1959   *The Politics of Mass Society*. New York: Free Press.

Lane, Robert E.

1953   Why Businessmen Violate the Law. *Journal of Criminal Law, Criminology, and Political Science* 44: 151-65.

Lemert, Edwin M.

1951   *Social Pathology*. New York: McGraw-Hill.

Lenski, Gerhart

1962   The Sociology of Religion in the United States. *Social Compass* 9: 307-37.

Lewis, Sinclair

1920   *Main Street*. New York: Harcourt, Brace & World.

1922   *Babbitt*. New York: Harcourt, Brace & World.

Lipset, Seymour Martin

1959   *Political Man: The Social Bases of Politics*. Garden City, N. Y.: Doubleday.

Lipsitz, Lewis

1968   If, As Verba Says, The State Functions as Religion, What Are We to Do Then to Save Our Souls? *American Political Science Review* 62: 527-35.

Lockwood, David

1964   Social Integration and System Integration. In G. K. Zollschan and W. Hirsch, eds., *Explorations in Social Change*. Boston: Houghton Mifflin.

Long, Charles H.

1974   Civil Rights—Civil Religion: Visible People and Invisible Religion. In Donald G. Jones and Russell E. Richey, eds., *American Civil Religion*. New York: Harper & Row.

Lowie, Robert H.

1952   *Primitive Religion*. New York: Liveright. (First published in 1924.)

1966   *Culture and Ethnology*. New York: Basic Books. (First published in 1917.)

Luckmann, Thomas

1967   *The Invisible Religion*. New York: Macmillan.

Lukes, Steven
  1973   *Emile Durkheim, His Life and Work: A Historical and
           Critical Study.* Baltimore: Penguin.
  1977   Political Ritual and Social Integration. In Lukes, *Essays in
           Social Theory.* New York: Columbia University Press.
Lyman, Stanford M.
  1978   *The Seven Deadly Sins: Society and Evil.* New York: St.
           Martin's Press.
Lyman, Stanford M., and Arthur J. Vidich
  1980   Prodigious Fathers, Prodigal Sons—Review of "A History
           of Sociological Analysis" by Thomas Bottomore and
           Robert Nisbet, eds. *Qualitative Sociology* 2, No. 3 (Janu-
           ary): 99-112.
Lynd, Robert, and Helen Lynd
  1929   *Middletown.* New York: Harcourt, Brace & World.
  1937   *Middletown in Transition.* New York: Harcourt, Brace
           & World.
MacIntyre, Alastair
  1965   Weber at His Weakest. *Encounter* 25.
Malinowski, Bronislaw
  1961   *Argonauts of the West Pacific.* New York: E. P. Dutton.
  1972   *Crime and Custom in Savage Society.* Totowa, N. J.: Little-
           field, Adams & Co.
Mann, Michael
  1970   The Social Cohesion of a Liberal Democracy. *American
           Sociological Review* 35: 423-39.
Mannheim, Karl
  1940   *Man and Society in an Age of Reconstruction.* New York:
           Harcourt, Brace & World.
  1943   *Diagnosis of Our Time.* London: Routledge and Kegan Paul.
  1971   Conservative Thought. In Kurt Wolff, ed., *From Karl
           Mannheim.* New York: Oxford University Press.
Marty, Martin
  1970   *Righteous Empire: The Protestant Experience in America.*
           New York: Harper & Row.
  1974   Two Kinds of Civil Religion. In Donald G. Jones and
           Russell E. Richey, eds., *American Civil Religion.* New
           York: Harper & Row.
Marx, Karl, and Friedrich Engels
  1964   *Marx and Engels on Religion.* Edited by Reinhold Niebuhr.
           New York: Schocken.
Mason, Edward S., ed.
  1959   *The Corporation in Modern Society.* Cambridge, Mass.:
           Harvard University Press.

Mather, Cotton,
1966   *Bonifacius, An Essay Upon the Good.* Edited with an
        Introduction by David Levin. Cambridge, Mass.: Belknap
        Press. (First published in 1710.)
May, Henry F.
1949   *The Protestant Churches and Industrial America.* New
        York: Harper & Row.
McCarthy, Coleman
1972   Deciding to Cheapen the Product. In Robert L. Heilbroner,
        et. al., *In the Name of Profit.* Garden City, N.Y.: Double-
        day.
McCloskey, Herbert
1964   Consensus and Ideology in American Politics. *American
        Political Review* 58: 361-82.
McLoughlin, William G.
1969   Changing Patterns of Protestant Philanthropy, 1607-1969.
        In Donald R. Cutler, ed., *The Religious Situation 1969.*
        Boston: Beacon Press.
McNamara, Patrick H.
1972   Comment on Fenn's "Toward a New Sociology of Religion.
        Journal for the Scientific Study of Religion 12, No. 2:
        237-39.
McWilliams, Wilson Carey
1973   *The Idea of Fraternity in America.* Berkeley, Calif.: Uni-
        versity of California Press.
Mead, Sidney
1963   *The Lively Experiment.* New York: Harper & Row.
Merk, Frederick
1963   *Manifest Destiny and Mission in American History.* New
        York: Alfred A. Knopf.
Miller, Daniel, and Guy Swanson
1963   The Family and Bureaucracy. In Philip Olson, ed., *America
        as a Mass Society.* New York: Free Press.
Miller, Perry
1953   *The New England Mind: From Colony to Province.* Cam-
        bridge, Mass.: Harvard University Press.
1954   *The New England Mind: The Seventeenth Century.* Cam-
        bridge, Mass.: Harvard University Press.
1970   *Orthodoxy in Massachusetts, 1630-1650.* New York:
        Harper & Row. (First published in 1933.)
Miller, Perry, and Thomas H. Johnson, eds.
1938   *The Puritans: A Sourcebook of Their Writings.* New York:
        Harper & Row.

Miller, William L.
1965   *Piety Along the Potomac: Notes on Politics and Morals
in the Fifties.* Boston: Houghton Mifflin.
Mills, C. Wright
1951   *White Collar.* New York: Oxford University Press.
1963   The Professional Ideology of Social Pathologists. In Irving
Louis Horowitz, ed., *Power, Politics and People.* New York:
Oxford University Press. (First published in 1943.)
1963a   The Social Life of a Modern Community. In Irving Louis
Horowitz, ed., *Power, Politics and People.* New York:
Oxford University Press. (First published in 1942.)
Mintz, Morton
1972   A Colonial Heritage. In Robert L. Heilbroner, et al., *In the
Name of Profit.* Garden City, N. Y.: Doubleday.
Moore, Barrington, Jr.
1958   Thoughts on the Future of the Family. In Moore, *Political
Power and Social Theory.* Cambridge, Mass.: Harvard
University Press.
Nagle, Paul C.
1971   *This Sacred Trust: American Nationality, 1798-1898.* New
York: Oxford University Press.
Needham, Rodney
1963   Introduction to Emile Durkheim and Marcel Mauss, *Prim-
itive Classification.* Chicago: University of Chicago Press.
Nelson, Benjamin
1965   Review of Max Weber, The Sociology of Religion. *American Sociological Review* 30, No. 4 (August).
Neuhaus, H. Richard
1970   The War, the Churches, and Civil Religion. *Annals of the
American Academy of Political and Social Science* 387:
128-40.
Nevins, Allan
1927   *The Emergence of Modern America, 1865-1878.* New York:
Macmillan.
Nisbet, Robert A.
1943   The French Revolution and the Rise of Sociology in
France. *American Journal of Sociology* 49: 156-64.
1952   Conservatism and Sociology. *American Journal of Sociology* 58: 167-75.
1965   *Emile Durkheim.* Englewood Cliffs, N. J.: Prentice-Hall.
1966   *The Sociological Tradition.* New York: Basic Books.
1969   *Social Change and History.* New York: Oxford University
Press.

Nye, Russel Blaine
    1967   *This Almost Chosen People*. East Lansing, Mich.: Michigan State University Press.
    1974   *Society and Culture in America, 1830-1860*. New York: Harper & Row.

Olson, Philip, ed.
    1963   *America as a Mass Society*. New York: Free Press.

Parkes, Henry Bamford
    1955   *The American Experience: An Interpretation of the History and Civilization of the American People*. New York: Alfred A. Knopf.

Parsons, Talcott
    1949   *Essays in Sociological Theory Pure and Applied*. Glencoe, Ill.: Free Press.
    1951   *The Social System*. New York: Free Press.
    1954   *Essays in Sociological Theory*. New York: Free Press.
    1956   Foreword to Emile Durkheim, *Education and Sociology*. Glencoe, Ill.: Free Press.
    1960   Some Comments on the Pattern of Religious Organization in the United States. In Parsons, *Structure and Process in Modern Societies*. Glencoe, Ill.: Free Press, pp. 295-321.
    1960a   Authority, Legitimation and Political Process. In Parsons, *Structure and Process in Modern Societies*. Glencoe, Ill.: Free Press.
    1961   Comment on William Kolb "Images of Man and the Sociology of Religion. *Journal for the Scientific Study of Religion* 1 (October): 22-29.
    1963   Christianity and Modern Industrial Society. In Edward A. Tiryakian, ed., *Sociological Theory, Values, and Socioculture Change*. New York: Harper & Row.
    1964   Introduction to Max Weber, *The Sociology of Religion*. Boston: Beacon Press.
    1966   Religion in a Modern Pluralistic Society. *Review of Religious Research* 7 (Spring): 125-46.
    1967   Durkheim's Contribution to the Theory of Integration of Social Systems. In Parsons, *Sociological Theory and Modern Society*. New York: Free Press. (First published in 1960.)
    1968   *The Structure of Social Action*. 2 vols. New York: Free Press. (First published in 1937.)
    1968a   On the Concept of Value-Commitments. *Sociological Inquiry* 3 (Spring).

1969   "Voting" and the Equilibrium of the American Political
        System. In Parsons, *Politics and Social Structure*. New
        York: Free Press.
1971   *The System of Modern Societies*. Englewood Cliffs, N. J.:
        Prentice-Hall.
1973   Durkheim on Religion Revisited: Another Look at the
        Elementary Forms of the Religious Life. In Charles C.
        Glock and Phillip E. Hammond, eds., *Beyond the Classics?:*
        Essays in the Scientific Study of Religion. New York:
        Harper & Row.
1974   Religion in Post-Industrial America: The Problem of
        Secularization. *Social Research* 41, No. 2 (Summer):
        193-225.
1974a   Comment on "Current Folklore in the Criticisms of Par-
        sonian Action Theory." *Sociological Inquiry* 44, No. 1:
        55-58.
1974b   The Life and Work of Emile Durkheim. In *Emile Durkheim,*
        Sociology and Philosophy. New York: Free Press.
1977   On Building Social System Theory: A Personal History.
        In Parsons, *Social Systems and the Evolution of Action*
        Theory. New York: Free Press.

Pierce, Albert
1960   Durkheim and Functionalism. In Kurt H. Wolff, ed., *Essays*
        on Sociology and Philosophy. New York: Harper & Row.

Piven, Frances Fox, and Richard A. Cloward
1971   *Regulating the Poor: The Functions of Public Welfare*.
        New York: Random House.

Poggi, G.
1971   The Place of Religion in Durkheim's Theory of Institutions.
        European Journal of Sociology 12, No. 2: 229-60.
1972   *Images of Society: Essays on the Sociological Theories of*
        Tocqueville, Marx and Durkheim. Stanford, Calif.: Stanford
        University Press.

Pope, Liston
1942   *Millhands and Preachers*. New Haven, Conn.: Yale Univer-
        sity Press.

Pope, Whitney
1973   Classic on Classic: Parsons' Interpretation of Durkheim.
        American Journal of Sociology 38, No. 4: 399-415.
1976   *Durkheim's Suicide: A Classic Analyzed*. Chicago: Univer-
        sity of Chicago Press.

Pope, Whitney; Jere Cohen; and Lawrence E. Hazelrigg
1975   On the Divergence of Weber and Durkheim: A Critique of

Parsons' Convergence Thesis. *American Journal of Sociology* 40, No. 4: 417-27.

Popper, Karl
1962   *The Open Society and Its Enemies.* Princeton, N. J.: Princeton University Press.

Potter, David M.
1954   *People of Plenty: Economic Abundance and the American Character.* Chicago: University of Chicago Press.

Radcliffe-Brown, A. R.
1952   *Structure and Function in Primitive Society.* New York: Free Press.
1958   *Method in Social Anthropology.* Edited by M. N. Srinivas. Chicago: University of Chicago Press.
1964   *The Andaman Islanders.* Glencoe, Ill.: Free Press (First published in 1922.)
1977   *The Social Anthropology of Radcliffe-Brown.* Edited by Adam Kuper. London: Routledge and Kegan Paul.

Rader, Dotson
1971   Review of Abbie Hoffman, *Steal This Book. New York Times Book Review,* July 18, 1971.

Radin, Paul
1932   *Social Anthropology.* New York: McGraw-Hill.
1957   *Primitive Religion.* New York: Dover Press. (First published in 1937.)
1957a *Primitive Man as a Philosopher.* New York: Dover. (First published in 1927.)
1966   *The Method and Theory of Ethnology: An Essay in Criticism.* New York: Basic Books. (First published in 1933.)
1971   *The World of Primitive Man.* New York: Dutton. (First published in 1953.)

Rasmussen, Knud
1908   *The People of the Polar North: A Record.* Philadelphia: J. B. Lippincott.
1969   *Across Arctic America.* New York: Greenwood Press. (First published in 1927.)

Redfield, Robert
1960   Thinker and Intellectual in Primitive Society. In Stanley Diamond, ed., *Primitive Views of the World.* New York: Columbia University Press.

Richard, Gaston
1975   Dogmatic Atheism in the Sociology of Religion. In W. S. F. Pickering, ed., *Durkheim on Religion.* London: Routledge and Kegan Paul.

Richey, Russell E., and Donald G. Jones, eds.
1974 *American Civil Religion.* New York: Harper & Row.

Richtner, Melvin
1960 Durkheim's Politics and Political Theory. In Kurt H. Wolff, ed., *Essays on Sociology and Philosophy.* New York: Harper & Row.

Riesman, David, et al.
1950 *The Lonely Crowd.* New Haven, Conn.: Yale University Press.

Robertson, Roland
1970 *The Sociological Interpretation of Religion.* New York: Schocken.

Rocher, Guy
1975 *Talcott Parsons and American Sociology.* New York: Barnes & Noble.

Rogow, Arnold A.
1975 *The Dying of the Light: A Searching Look at America Today.* New York: Putnam.

Rorty, James
1934 *Our Master's Voice: Advertising.* New York: John Day Co.

Ross, Edward Alsworth
1973 *Sin and Society: An Analysis of Latter-Day Iniquity.* New York: Harper & Row. (First published in 1907.)

Runciman, W. G.
1969 The Sociological Explanation of "Religious" Beliefs. *European Journal of Sociology* 10: 149-91.

Schneider, Herbert W.
1958 *The Puritan Mind.* Ann Arbor, Mich.: University of Michigan Press.

Schnore, Leo F.
1958 Social Morphology and Human Ecology. *American Journal of Sociology* 63 (May): 620-34.

Schumpeter, Joseph A.
1942 *Capitalism, Socialism and Democracy.* New York: Harper & Row.

Schwendinger, Herman, and Julia R. Schwendinger
1974 *The Sociologists of the Chair: A Radical Analysis of the Formative Years of North American Sociology (1883-1922).* New York: Basic Books.

Scott, William G., and David K. Hart
1979 *Organizational America: Can Individual Freedom Survive Within the Security It Promises?* Boston: Houghton Mifflin.

Seger, Imogen
   1957   *Durkheim and His Critics on the Sociology of Religion.*
           Monograph Series. Bureau of Applied Research, Columbia
           University.
Shepherd, William C.
   1975   Robert Bellah's Sociology of Religion: The Sociological
           Elements, Review Symposium on the Sociology of Religion
           of Robert N. Bellah. *Journal for the Scientific Study of
           Religion,* 14, No. 4: 395-402.
Shils, Edward, and Michael Young
   1953   The Meaning of the Coronation. *Sociological Review* 1-2:
           63-81.
Smith, Elwyn A., ed.
   1971   *The Religion of the Republic.* Philadelphia: Fortress Press.
Spiro, Melford E.
   1966   Religion: Problems of Definition and Explanation. In M.
           Banton, ed., *Anthropological Approaches to the Study of
           Religion.* London: Tavistock.
Stanner, W. E. H.
   1967   Reflections on Durkheim and Aboriginal Religion. In M.
           Freedman, ed., *Social Organization: Essays Presented to
           Raymond Firth.* Chicago: Aldine Publishing Co.
Stauffer, Robert E.
   1973   Civil Religion, Technocracy, and the Private Sphere: Further
           Comments on Cultural Integration in Advanced Societies.
           Journal for the Scientific Study of Religion 12: 415-25.

   1975   Bellah's Civil Religion, Review Symposium on the Socio-
           logy of Religion of Robert N. Bellah. *Journal for the
           Scientific Study of Religion* 14, No. 4: 390-94.
Stone, Christopher D.
   1975   *Where the Law Ends: The Social Control of Corporate
           Behavior.* New York: Harper & Row.
Sutton, F. X., et al.
   1956   *The American Business Creed.* Cambridge, Mass.: Harvard
           University Press.
Tarbell, Ida M.
   1936   *The Nationalizing of Business, 1878-1898.* Chicago: Quad-
           rangle.
Tarkington, Booth
   1918   *The Magnificent Ambersons.* Garden City, N.Y.: Double-
           day, Page & Co.

Thernstrom, Stephan
   1964   *Poverty and Progress: Social Mobility in a Nineteenth Century City.* Cambridge, Mass.: Harvard University Press.
Thomas, Michael C., and Charles C. Flippen
   1972   American Civil Religion: An Empirical Study. *Social Forces* 51: 218-25.
Thomas, W. I.
   1921   *Old World Traits Transplanted.* Montclair, N. J.: Patterson Smith.
Tiryakian, Edward A.
   1962   *Sociologism and Existentialism: Two Perspectives on the Individual and Society.* Englewood Cliffs, N. J.: Prentice-Hall.
Tolles, Frederick B.
   1963   *Meeting House and Counting House: The Quaker Merchants of Colonial Philadelphia, 1682-1763.* New York: Norton.
Tuveson, Ernest C.
   1968   *Redeemer Nation: The Idea of America's Millennial Role.* Chicago: University of Chicago Press.
Twain, Mark
   1976   The Man That Corrupted Hadleyburg. In the *Unabridged Mark Twain.* Edited by Kurt Vonnegut. Philadelphia: Running Press.
Ungar, Sanford J.
   1972   Get Away With What You Can. In Robert L. Heilbroner, et al., *In the Name of Profit.* Garden City, N.Y.: Doubleday.
Vandivier, Kermit
   1972   Why Should My Conscience Bother Me? In Robert L. Heilbroner, et al., *In The Name of Profit.* Garden City, N. Y.: Doubleday.
Veblen, Thorstein
   1915   *Imperial Germany and the Industrial Revolution.* New York: Viking Press.
   1923   *Absentee Ownership.* New York: Viking Press.
   1953   *The Theory of the Leisure Class.* New York: New American Library. (First published in 1889.)
Verba, Sidney
   1968   If, As Lipsitz Thinks, Political Science Is to Save Our Souls, God Help Us! *American Political Science Review* 62:576-77.
Vidich, Arthur J.
   1975   Political Legitimacy in Bureaucratic Society: An Analysis of Watergate. *Social Research* 42 (Winter): 778-811.

Vidich, Arthur J., and Joseph Bensman
　1968　*Small Town in Mass Society.* Revised Edition. Princeton, N. J.: Princeton University Press.
Vidich, Arthur J., and Ronald M. Glassman, eds.
　1979　*Conflict and Control: Challenge to Legitimacy of Modern Governments.* Beverly Hills, Calif.: Sage.
Wallace, Anthony F. C.
　1966　*Religion: An Anthropological View.* New York: Random House.
　1978　*Rockdale: The Growth of an American Village in the Early Industrial Revolution.* New York: Alfred A. Knopf.
Wallwork, Ernest
　1972　*Durkheim: Morality and Milieu.* Cambridge, Mass.: Harvard University Press.
Warner, Robert Stephen
　1972　The Methodology of Max Weber's Comparative Studies. Doctoral Dissertation, University of California, Berkeley.
Warner, W. Lloyd
　1958　*A Black Civilization: A Social Study of an Australian Tribe.* New York: Harper & Row. (First published in 1937.)
　1959　*The Living and the Dead: A Study of the Symbolic Life of Americans.* New Haven, Conn.: Yale University Press.
　1962　*American Life: Dream and Reality.* Revised Edition. Chicago: University of Chicago Press.
Warner, W. Lloyd, and J. O. Low
　1947　*The Social System of the Modern Factory.* New Haven, Conn.: Yale University Press.
Warner, W. Lloyd, and Paul S. Lunt
　1941　*The Social Life of a Modern Community.* New Haven, Conn.: Yale University Press.
　1942　*The Status System of a Modern Community.* New Haven, Conn.: Yale University Press.
Warner, W. Lloyd, and Leo Srole
　1945　*The Social Systems of American Ethnic Groups.* New Haven, Conn.: Yale University Press.
Waxman, Chaim, ed.
　1969　*The End of Ideology Debate.* New York: Simon & Schuster.
Weber, Max
　1946　*From Max Weber: Essays in Sociology.* Edited by Hans Gerth and C. Wright Mills. New York: Oxford University Press.
　1949　*The Methodology of the Social Sciences.* New York: Free Press.

1951   *The Religion of China.* New York: Free Press.
1952   *Ancient Judaism.* New York: Free Press.
1958   *The Protestant Ethic and the Spirit of Capitalism.* New
         York: Charles Scribner's Sons.
1958a   *The Religion of India.* New York: Free Press.
1963   *The Sociology of Religion.* Boston: Beacon Press.
1968   *Economy and Society.* 3 vols. New York: Bedminister
         Press.
1978   Anti-Critical Last Word on "The Spirit of Capitalism."
         Translated by Wallace Davis. *American Journal of Socio-
         logy* 83, No. 5 (March).
Whyte, William H., Jr.
1956   *The Organization Man.* New York: Simon & Schuster.
Williams, Robin M.
1960   *American Society: A Sociological Interpretation.* New
         York: Alfred A. Knopf.
Wilson, Bryan
1979   The Return of the Sacred. *Journal for the Scientific Study
         of Religion* 18, No. 3 (September).
Wolff, Kurt H., ed.
1960   *Emile Durkheim (1858-1917).* Columbus, Ohio: Ohio
         University Press.
Wright, D. M.
1953   Democracy and Economics in American Ideology. *Con-
         fluence* 2 (March): 55-56.
Wright, J. Patrick
1979   *On a Clear Day You Can See General Motors: John De-
         Lorean's Look Inside the Automotive Giant.* New York:
         Avon Books.

INDEX

About the Author

MICHAEL HUGHEY received his Ph.D. from the Graduate Faculty of the New School for Social Research, and is currently Assistant Professor of Sociology at Moorhead State University in Minnesota. His articles have appeared in *Qualitative Sociology*, the *Journal of Ethnic Studies*, and *Social Research*.